THE FUTURE OF POLICE REFORM

The Future of Police Reform

The U.S. Justice Department and the
Promise of Lawful Policing

Samuel Walker

NEW YORK UNIVERSITY PRESS

New York

NEW YORK UNIVERSITY PRESS
New York
www.nyupress.org

Library of Congress Cataloging-in-Publication Data
Names: Walker, Samuel, author.
Title: The future of police reform : the U.S. Justice Department
and the promise of lawful policing / Samuel Walker.
Description: New York : New York University Press, 2024. |
Includes bibliographical references and index.
Identifiers: LCCN 2023022568 | ISBN 9781479826025 (hardback) | ISBN 9781479826049
(ebook) | ISBN 9781479826056 (ebook other)
Subjects: LCSH: Police—United States. | Police administration—United States. | Police
regulations—United States. | Consent decrees—United States. | Law enforcement—United
States. | Law reform—United States. | United States. Department of Justice.
Classification: LCC KF5399 .W35 2024 | DDC 363.20973—dc23/eng/20231010
LC record available at https://lccn.loc.gov/2023022568

This book is dedicated to Mary Ann Lamanna,
partner and friend for over forty years.

CONTENTS

PREFACE

American society suffers from a deep and continuing policing crisis, which is interwoven in the nation's racial crisis, which has a longer history than the country's police crisis. To be sure, there have been considerable improvements in policing over the past fifty years, and these gains should not be dismissed. In the mid-1970s, meaningful controls over police use of deadly force were just beginning to appear in a few police departments. As a result of the feminist movement, police departments were just beginning to develop the first policies related to the handling of domestic disturbance and violence cases. Training of officers has improved significantly, with field training officers for new recruits and annual in-service training programs for all officers. Despite these and other important advancements, however, our society is still plagued by serious crime and poor relations between police departments and African American communities.

Important reforms are nonetheless occurring across the country. This book examines the most important federal effort in this regard. The U.S. Justice Department's pattern or practice program, created by Congress in 1994, is authorized to investigate police departments with patterns of unconstitutional police practices, bring civil suits against individual departments, and obtain judicially enforced consent decrees that mandate sweeping reform. Chapters in this book examine the specific reforms mandated by those consent decrees, the issues surrounding implementation of reforms, and the progress that various departments have made and are making in improving the quality of police services. There have been a number of difficult challenges and problems, but overall, the program has been a success.

The Justice Department's pattern or practice program, however, is only one part of the larger picture of police reform. While discussing the program, this book also examines the surrounding social, political, and legal contexts that deeply affect the Justice Department's reform efforts.

This includes political opposition to police reform from two presidential administrations and three police departments; the power of the traditional police subculture, which has blocked many reforms for over half a century; the enormous power of police unions to limit and sometimes block needed reforms; and finally, the failure of local political leaders to fully support not just the Department of Justice reforms but other needed reforms proposed by other sources. We cannot fully understand the Justice Department's program without also examining the various efforts to block those reforms, which this book does.

Perhaps the most important contribution of the Justice Department's pattern or practice program has been its influence in stimulating a variety of police reforms by activists and organizations across the country. The final chapter of this book examines the important reform efforts that have developed over the past fifteen years and the contributions they are making. The combined work of these other reform efforts, which this author believes are almost certain to continue, is cause for optimism. The future of police reform in this country will not be the result of just a few organizations but a large national network of local and state centers of activity.

1

Our National Police and Race Crisis

The Death of George Floyd: Another Crisis Erupts

Almost immediately after the brutal murder of George Floyd, an African American, by Minneapolis police officer Derek Chauvin on May 25, 2020, a wave of protests swept across the country. The protests were even broader in scope than those following the death of Michael Brown at the hands of a Ferguson, Missouri, police officer in August 2014.[1] The Ferguson protests prompted then president Barack Obama to appoint a President's Task Force on 21st Century Policing, the first-ever presidential commission or task force in American history devoted exclusively to the police. The task force issued a sweeping report on the problems of American policing in 2015, including a lack of legitimacy in the eyes of the public and a failure to engage community members in decisions over police policies and strategies.[2] In response to the Floyd murder, the *New York Times* in July 2020 counted over 4,700 separate protests against police misconduct across the country, in both large cities and small towns. A Kaiser Family Foundation survey estimated that twenty-six million people participated in demonstrations during one week in June, while the Pew Center estimated fifteen million.[3]

The massive outpouring of people demanding police reforms clearly indicated a seismic shift in public concern and activism over police misconduct and the need for major changes, particularly on police officers' use of force and racially discriminatory police actions. The television and print media coverage of the demonstrations also revealed that even in small towns in Nebraska and Iowa, a majority of protesters were white. The combined impact of the Michael Brown death in 2014 and George Floyd's horrifying death in 2020, which was captured on a cell phone video, produced a significant shift in Americans' thinking about race and police misconduct. A 2020 Gallup poll found that the percentage of Americans who believed that "civil rights for black adults have improved in their lifetimes" fell from 89 percent in 2011 to only 59 percent in 2020.[4]

To Americans familiar with this country's history of police misconduct, officer violence and racial discrimination were already known, although few fully understood the scope and severity of police abuses. Among African Americans, fatal shootings and brutality in their communities reinforced a community folk memory of the long history of discriminatory, brutal, and illegal police actions. Criminologist David Kennedy, in a fascinating discussion of the racial divide in American society, argues that in street encounters both young African American men and police officers bring their own "narratives" about the other side. Both narratives involve negative stereotypes of each other, based on personal experience in some cases but primarily on what they had heard from friends, neighbors, and acquaintances. Police officers stereotype young African American men as crime-prone with no respect for the police, while young African Americans see police officers as racist and brutal.[5]

We Can't Continue Like This

We cannot continue like this. As a society we cannot continue the endless cycle of police shootings and beatings of African Americans, followed by protests and then piecemeal reforms that do not address the deeper problems of policing and race. We must address the pervasive problems that exist in virtually every law enforcement agency in this country, while at the same time bridging the racial divide at the neighborhood level that David Kennedy identified.

The Scope of This Book

The Justice Department's pattern or practice program is the centerpiece of this book. Created by federal law in 1994, the program is authorized to investigate local and state law enforcement agencies, and where it finds a pattern of unconstitutional police practices to obtain consent decrees mandating sweeping reforms.[6] Race and ethnicity are integral parts of unconstitutional policing. The primary victims of police use of excessive force and unconstitutional traffic and pedestrian stops are members of the African American and Latino communities.

The pattern or practice program, however, is only one part of the larger story of the pattern or practice program's current police reform effort. That effort has been influenced in many ways by important external factors, which this book weaves into the narrative. One external factor is the historical legacy of previous reform efforts, reaching back to 1900. While the police professionalism movement made some important contributions, it was largely a piecemeal effort that failed to address the uncontrolled conduct of police officers on the street. A major part of that misconduct was directed toward the growing African American communities in America's cities outside the Southeast. The reforms that emerged in the 1960s in response to the urban riots were also piecemeal efforts and largely inadequate.

Perhaps even more important, the efforts of the pattern or practice program were profoundly affected by important external developments, all of which cannot be ignored when we try to take a broad overview of police reform in recent decades. To take one important example, the pattern or practice program made a significant contribution in limiting police officer use of force through restrictive written policies. But police officer use of force was also affected by the development of, for example, de-escalation, a strategy and tactic designed to settle difficult police-citizen encounters without the use of force. Written police department policies clearly state that officers have a "duty to intervene" when they see other officers violating department policy and/or the law. Academic research on procedural justice, meanwhile, has entered policing as both a strategy and a tool for making officers more respectful of the people they encounter, and numerous police departments have embraced it as a means of reducing the tensions and conflicts that pervade our urban communities.

The pattern or practice program also embraced the principle of community engagement not only as a means of developing better relations with the communities the police serve, but also as a way of giving community members a formal voice over police department policies. Community engagement programs, when they work properly, help to build the legitimacy of the police in the eyes of the public, particularly among communities of color. The idea of community engagement developed

out of a small but growing effort to ensure greater democratic participation in the development of police policies and strategies. Some of
the pattern or practice program efforts have also attempted to abandon
traditional aggressive policies and strategies in favor of collaborative
problem-oriented policing approaches to the problems of democracy.
Research as far back as the 1960s found that aggressive policing not only
fails to reduce crime but also has an extremely negative impact on communities of color. Problem-oriented policing grew out of creative academic thinking about how to improve the quality of police services to
the community and was adopted by many police departments.

Police reform, in short, does not exist in a vacuum, but is influenced
by many factors that were initially external to policing. Only a few have
been discussed here, but they and others are important factors in virtually all of the chapters that follow in this book.

Chapter 2 provides an overview of the history of police reform, start-
ing with the professionalization movement that began around 1900 and
continued into the 1970s. It was the first real reform movement in American policing.[7] It was joined by the controversial police-related decisions
of the Supreme Court in the 1960s on searches and custodial interrogations, which brought the first constitutional standards to policing.[8] The
civil rights movement in the 1960s and the urban riots from 1964 to
1968 created a national crisis and spurred a new round of police reform
efforts.[9] While some of these reforms made useful contributions to policing, they were piecemeal in nature and were inadequate for the fundamental problems facing American policing. The reforms related to race
discrimination, in particular, failed to address the national trauma of
the riots, and did not touch on fundamental issues of policing, particularly the failure of police departments to control police officer discretion,
which allowed pervasive misconduct to continue. Chapter 2 also covers the advent of administrative rulemaking, the process of controlling
police officer conduct through written rules. Based on the 1946 federal
Administrative Procedure Act, it was finally embraced by the police in
the mid-1970s and soon developed into the cornerstone of modern police management today.[10]

Chapter 3 covers the political context that led to the enactment of
Section 14141 of the 1994 Violent Crime Control and Law Enforcement
Act, which created the pattern or practice program.[11] It discusses in de-

tail how the program was created from scratch, and how the Civil Rights Division of the Justice Department created procedures for identifying police departments where patterns of unconstitutional policing existed and then bringing consent decrees to mandate major reforms. Harvard Law School professor William Stuntz in 2006 argued that the 1994 pattern or practice program was "the most important legal initiative of the past twenty years in the sphere of police regulation."[12] This book agrees with that judgment.

It is impossible to fully understand policing and police reform without taking into account the social, legal, and political contexts in which the police work. Chapter 4 covers the operational heart and soul of the pattern or practice program, examining the implementation of the program and the consent decrees it mandates. The chapter focuses on seven consent decree reforms and the key elements of each one, including their impact on police conduct, police departments as organizations, and the communities they serve. Five of these reforms involve a common set of substantive reforms: establishing a set of rules and procedures designed to control officer conduct. Two reforms, however, involve establishing greater engagement between police departments and the communities they serve and also reorienting police programs related to addressing crime and disorder.[13]

Chapter 5 examines six important collateral issues surrounding the pattern or practice program: resistance to federal intervention at both the national and local levels and the success or failure of those efforts; police unions and their capacity to impede police reforms, along with how the pattern or practice program circumvented police union power to achieve reforms; the controversies over the financial costs of consent decrees, along with the largely neglected positive benefit of the substantial cost savings resulting from reduced officer misconduct and fewer payouts from lawsuits against police departments; the published evaluations of consent decrees; the positive collateral impact of consent decree reforms on the police officer subculture, a subject that has not received sufficient study; and finally, the challenge of sustaining consent decree reforms after decrees are ended.

Chapter 6 concludes the book with a discussion of the future of police reform, focusing on the growing range of police reform efforts that today supplement the Justice Department's pattern or practice program.

The chapter argues that, despite many news media stories reporting an alleged failure of police reform, these efforts provide a solid foundation for future police reform. The chapter and the book end on an optimistic note, arguing how the current police reform efforts can be further strengthened and expanded through local grassroots community engagement on police reform.

Major Themes in the Pattern or Practice Program

Three major themes are developed in the chapters in this book. The first is the extent to which the pattern or practice program investigations have exposed the depths of police misconduct in departments subject to consent decrees. The abuses are not only serious in nature but are tolerated by police departments and not fully revealed to the general public. The second theme involves the web of accountability, which was not planned, but developed as part of several consent decree reforms. Several consent decree requirements establish close relations among officers at different ranks and generate a mutual commitment to accountability. In this respect, the web has been a positive achievement of consent decree reforms. The third theme has been the pattern or practice program's commitment to the organizational transformation of police departments and the relationship between that development and the success or failure of police reform efforts. Both the web of accountability and organizational transformation are discussed in detail below.

Exposing the Hidden Depths of Police Misconduct

One of the major accomplishments of the pattern or practice program has been its detailed exposure of the hidden depths of officer misconduct and managerial dysfunction in troubled police departments. Even to people reasonably well-informed about policing, the Justice Department findings letters (which are written after the initial DOJ investigations and are the bases for negotiating a consent decree) are truly shocking in terms of the extent of police abuse, the pervasive lack of accountability for both officers and their departments, and the dysfunctional management that exists in many departments.[14] Professor Christy Lopez, former deputy director of the Special Litigation Section, argues that through the findings letters the program has "a unique ability to reveal and explain how policing harms individuals and communities," including not only the "nature and breadth" of police misconduct "but also its causes."[15] The findings letters are conveniently available on the website of the Special Litigation Section (SLS), the Civil Rights Division unit tasked with implementing the pattern or practice program.[16] A few examples indicate the depth, seriousness, and in some cases horrific nature of the misconduct in police departments investigated by the Justice Department.

- In Cleveland, Justice Department investigators found that officers "shoot at people who do not pose an imminent threat of serious bodily harm or death to the officers or others"; "hit people in the head with their guns in situations where the use of deadly force is not justified"; and "use less lethal force that is disproportionate to the resistance or threat encountered."[17]
- The Seattle findings letter reported that officers regularly used force against persons who "talk back" to them (a phenomenon the police label "contempt of cop").[18] Particularly shocking was the finding that in "multiple cases" officers "failed to report the use of force at all," often using instead euphemisms such as "guiding" a person to the ground to cover their actual use of force. Equally disturbing, department policy did not require supervisors to respond to all force incidents, a near-universal requirement in most departments. Officers were required to respond only to incidents involving "three or more TASER applications and/or circumstances requiring an on-scene medical evaluation."[19]
- The New Orleans findings letter found that the department had "Inadequate policies and procedures, deficiencies in training, and extraordinary lapses in supervision [which] contributed to a systemic breakdown in NOPD handling of sexual assault investigations." Many cases were "misclassified," and as a result were never properly investigated. Officers had "poor victim interviewing skills" and often failed to search for witnesses to the incident. Similar problems affected the department's response to domestic violence calls.[20]
- The investigation of the Newark police department found that "there is reasonable cause to believe that NPD officers have engaged in a pattern or practice of theft from civilians, and that the NPD has taken inadequate measures to prevent, investigate, and remediate incidents and allegations

of such theft." The investigation also found a serious problem of "theft from arrestees [which] has been more than an aberration limited to a few officers or incidents within NPD."[21]

- In Portland, Oregon, where the DOJ investigation focused on the police department's response to people with mental illnesses, encounters between "officers and persons with mental illness too frequently result in a use of force when force is unnecessary or in the use of a higher level of force than necessary or appropriate, up to and including deadly force." Additionally, there was "a pattern of dangerous uses of force against persons who posed little or no threat and who could not because of their mental illness comply with officers' commands."[22]

- In Washington, DC, the findings letter reported that the "deployment of canine units resulted in bites [of citizens] nearly 70 percent of the time," compared with "only about 10 percent of deployments" in well-managed departments. The problem of excessive canine bites resulted from a "find and bite" policy, allowing dogs to bite the subject "upon locating him or her," rather than the accepted best practice of a "find and bark" policy.[23]

- The investigation of the Baltimore police department identified the many forms that the rank-and-file officer subculture took in violations of the law, department policy, and basic human dignity. Officers were regularly not punished for citizen complaints filed against them; 43 percent of policy violations resulted in no action because officers simply failed "to appear in court." The department also failed to take action against "officers known to engage in repeated misconduct," thereby creating a culture of immunity among rank-and-file officers. These officers were reportedly "well known" to department officials, who took no further action. Some officers were reluctant to "report misconduct by their fellow officers," and some officers told Justice Department investigators that fellow officers had been retaliated against for reporting improper actions by other officers. Some officers coerced sexual activity from women in exchange for immunity from arrest. All of these improper and illegal activities continued, the Baltimore findings letter explained, because of "systemic deficiencies" in the department's "policies, training, supervision, and accountability" procedures.[24]

The "Accountability Deficiency"

The examples cited above are only a small sample of the range of misconduct and illegality that pervade police departments across the country.
The Portland, Oregon, investigation and consent decree focused on
police handling of people experiencing mental health crises, but it is
almost certain that similar practices exist in other police departments.[25]
It is also likely that many other departments engage in gender discrimination similar to the New Orleans finding described above, although not
to the same extent. Taken as a group, the findings letters provide the first
well-documented national picture of the patterns of officer misconduct
and management-level indifference in American police departments.
It is unfortunate that police scholars have almost completely ignored
the wealth of information about policing contained in the pattern or
practice program's findings letters. The examples cited here are not the
result of the proverbial small number of "rotten apples" in policing. Far
from it. Instead, the examples cited here are a part of the systematic
failure of police departments to effectively control their officers. As
three criminologists put it a few years earlier, they represent a serious
"accountability deficiency" in policing, in which many officers are not
subject to meaningful rules and regulations and ignore the few that do
exist.[26] The Justice Department's pattern or practice program is designed
to end this unacceptable problem and create genuinely accountable
police departments. Police scholars have ignored this invaluable body
of detailed information about a critically important feature of routine
policing in this country.

Building a Web of Accountability

A subtle but very important impact of the pattern or practice program's
consent decrees has been the creation of a "web of accountability."[27] This
web includes the close working relationships among officers of different ranks and/or in different units of a police department. The case of
an officer's use of force illustrates the phenomenon. A consent decree
requires officers in a police department to file a detailed and honest
report on each use of force. The sergeants who supervise officers are
required to critically review force reports and either approve, demand

more detail, or send the report to internal affairs for investigation and possible discipline. Use of force reports also go to the use of force review board (UFRB), which reviews all force reports and is mandated to identify any departmental problems in policy, training, supervision, or other aspects of department operations. After identifying a problem, the UFRB is mandated to make formal recommendations for improvement to the police chief or commanders of the affected units. Finally, force reports are sent to the department's early intervention system, which maintains a computerized database of selected officer activity that makes it possible to identify officers with significant performance problems.

A single use of force report, therefore, creates interactions among people of different ranks and in different units of a police department. These interactions serve to develop new working relationships and understandings about the proper standards for police work, particularly with respect to accountability. Other police activities requiring reports follow the same scenario. The overall effect is the gradual development of a mutual commitment to accountability throughout the department, one that did not previously exist. Over time, these commitments result in the growth of a culture of accountability.

Transforming Police Organizations

Another theme discussed in this book is the commitment of the pattern or practice program to organizational transformation, in which formerly troubled police departments slowly develop an organization-wide commitment to lawfulness, professionalism, and respect for the public.[28] The Civil Rights Division mentions organizational transformation several times in its 2017 report on over twenty years of police reform work, but does not label it an official goal of the program. The report uses several different terms, such as "institutional reforms" or "systemic institutional failures," in describing it, but never provides a detailed description of what it involves. As will be discussed in chapter 3, the concept developed in the late 1970s as an approach to reforming complex organizations, such as medicine, the airline and nuclear power industries, and others.[29]

Because organizational transformation is such an important framework for understanding the Justice Department's pattern or practice program, it is important to give it a clear definition. Organizational transformation in policing can best be defined as *the sum total of a set of reforms and their impact on a particular organization*. Organizational transformation is not the same as organizational *change*, which may involve changes in one or more policies or procedures, but does not result in any systemic change in an organization. *In a police department, organizational transformation involves changes in the most important policies and procedures, which, interacting with each other, result in a new organizational culture, which includes the values, commitments, and working norms of employees throughout an organization.*

The Changing Political, Social, and Organizational Contexts of Police Reform

Police departments and police reform do not exist in a vacuum. They are subject to the constantly changing currents of politics, changes in patterns of crime and disorder, and changes in the organizational context of police departments. In various ways, and interacting with each other in complex ways, many factors have shaped the development of the pattern or practice program.

The social and political context of policing from 1900 through the 1990s had a profound impact on police reform. The police professionalization movement that began around 1900 was the first meaningful police reform effort in this country. It succeeded in achieving a number of long overdue reforms, including advancing the fundamental principle that policing is a profession, attempting to eliminate the political influence that had dominated local police departments from the beginning, and creating the first formal standards for police recruits and the first police training programs. These reforms, however, left much undone. No attempt was made to either reduce police officer abuse or improve police relations with racial and ethnic minority communities.

The tumultuous decade of the 1960s introduced new and very serious problems for the police. The U.S. Supreme Court in a series of landmark decisions imposed for the first time constitutional standards on police searches and seizures and interrogations of criminal suspects. The dramatic escalation of the civil rights movement in the early 1960s and the urban riots of 1964 to 1968 created a national racial crisis. Although the riots prompted some reforms, there were no meaningful efforts to address the serious police-community relations crisis. The most significant development regarding police officer conduct arose in the mid-1970s with the adoption of administrative rulemaking to control officer discretion. The rulemaking process caught on, and by the late 1980s had emerged as the basic management tool for running a police department.

The growth of the civil rights movement, especially the election of more African Americans to political office, including Congress, created the first significant black political power. One direct result was the 1994 Violent Crime Control and Law Enforcement Act, which through Section 14141 gave the U.S. Justice Department authority to investigate and then bring civil suits against local police departments where a pattern or practice of unconstitutional policing existed. The Justice Department undertook the first-ever attempt at comprehensive reform of police departments, and the resulting reforms are the primary story of this book.

The Positive Collateral Effects of Consent Decree Reforms

One of the important changes resulting from consent decrees has been the positive collateral effects of reforms on the traditional police officer subculture.[30] This effect has had very important consequences for police reform because police experts have long seen the officer subculture as one of the greatest obstacles to establishing lawful, professional, and respectful policing.[31] At the heart of that subculture are an "us versus them" attitude toward the public; a hostility to rules and regulations designed to curb officer misconduct; and a code of secrecy (sometimes called the "blue wall" of secrecy) designed to keep officers from reporting misconduct of other officers.[32] As discussed later in chapters 4 and 5, evaluations of the consent decrees in both the Pittsburgh and the Los Angeles police departments found that officers complained bitterly about consent decree requirements, for example, the required detailed reports on their actions, and talked openly about reducing their law enforcement efforts (a response labelled "de-policing"). In both departments, however, the official data found no reduction in enforcement activity, and in Los Angeles the quality of arrests rose. Officers, in other words, accommodated themselves to the new consent decree requirements and began working in a more professional manner. If officers did not make contact with certain people or drivers, as they had in the past, it was probably because they understood that they lacked the proper legal justification to stop people. As a result, they had more time to concentrate on serious crimes.[33]

The positive impact of consent decree reforms in New Orleans, meanwhile, is evident from a January 2019 court-appointed monitor's report. It found positive changes in several critical areas of policing, including reductions in police officer shootings, canine deployments, and canine bites of community members. These significant improvements were particularly striking given the fact that in 2013, when the consent decree began, the New Orleans police department was widely regarded as one of the worst and most dysfunctional departments in the country, a point that was confirmed by the Justice Department's 2011 findings letter on the department. The improvements reported in the 2019 report could only have happened if officers had begun complying with consent decree reforms.[34]

A Challenging Issue of Crime Control

One fundamental question hangs over the Justice Department's pattern or practice program. The program is unique in its ambitions regarding a comprehensive approach to reforming police departments. No police reform effort in the previous hundred years had attempted to achieve such a large number of specific reforms in police departments. This raises a challenging question: *Can federal intervention bring lasting improvement to local policing?*[35] The question is the title of the earliest evaluation of a consent decree (Pittsburgh) and raises the difficult question of whether the pattern or practice program should also have crime control as one of its basic goals.

Many police experts will undoubtedly argue that the question is not relevant to a discussion of a reform program authorized by law to end unconstitutional policing but not to reduce crime. In practice, however, the issue is extremely complex. The evidence from monitors' reports on police conduct under a consent decree indicates that substantially reducing unconstitutional policing can and does reduce crime.

The evaluation of the Los Angeles consent decree by a team from Harvard University uncovered some unexpected findings. In interviews and focus groups, rank-and-file LAPD officers complained loudly about consent decree requirements that they claimed hindered their law enforcement work on the street, required too much paperwork, and exposed them to unnecessary discipline. Yet the evaluation by the Harvard group found that officer law enforcement activity actually *rose* when the consent decree was in effect and that crime went *down*. How did this happen?[36]

The interviews and focus groups in Los Angeles were an opportunity for officers to vent their displeasure with the city, the LAPD's leadership, and the consent decree. Such "griping" sessions are common among almost all work groups and the expressed complaints should not necessarily be taken seriously. Second and most important, the rise in enforcement activity (stops and arrests) indicated that officers were in fact working harder and more professionally than before the consent decree. The LAPD's data indicated that a higher percentage of arrests resulted in felony charges than had been the case before the consent decree. Guided by new rules and training, officers were making better decisions in stops and arrests and included better evidence in their arrest reports. In addition, the new rules meant that officers were making fewer stops and arrests of people against whom they had no reasonable suspicion or probable cause, giving them more time to focus on criminal activity where they did have proper legal justification. In short, adhering to constitutional principles in their police work contributed to more effective crime control. We will examine this phenomenon in more detail in chapters 4 and 5.

It's Not Just the Police: America's Race Problem

Building an American policing that is lawful, professional, and respectful requires far more than just "reforming" a police department. The police are but one social institution that affects the daily lives of people. Schools, employers, neighborhoods, and so many other parts of our society are also pervaded by racial issues with long and deeply embedded histories. The 1968 Kerner Commission report on the 1960s riots devoted exactly one out of seventeen chapters to the police. We cannot talk intelligently about American policing, much less try to reform it, without also confronting this country's national race crisis. With justification, some historians and commentators have described racism as this country's "original sin."[37] Call it what you will, that problem has pervaded American policing since the first modern-style police departments were created in the 1830s and 1840s.[38] Within the world of policing there is no issue today that does not involve issues of race and/ or ethnicity: police shootings, use of excessive force, pedestrian stops, arrests, citizen complaints, the hiring, training and promotion of officers, community relations, and more. To discuss these problems without acknowledging the racial dimensions is simply irresponsible.

Recent research on the police has confirmed the existence of a deep racial divide in terms of people's experiences and attitudes toward the police. A small but increasing number of police scholars and experts on race and policing have noted a deeper aspect of the problem, arguing that African Americans and the white majority live in "two worlds" on the issues of crime, the police, and the criminal justice system. The 1968 Kerner Commission report boldly but quite naively and irresponsibly began with the alarming warning that "our nation is moving toward two societies, one black, one white—separate and unequal."[39] In fact, the country was *already* deeply divided on race: in housing, employment, education, opportunities for advancement, houses of worship, music, clothing, and everyday language. It is true that we have made considerable progress toward a more racially integrated society in the decades since 1968. We elected the first African American president in 2008 and appointed many African Americans as police chiefs and university presidents across the country. But the racial divide persists and has gotten worse because of the steadily growing economic inequality in our society, building higher barriers that prevent low-income people from moving up economically. We should not berate the police for not fixing the problem of inequality in American society, which is far beyond their direct control. But as people with an interest in the police, we should critically examine what they *can* do with regard to race on the issues that are within their capacity to effect.

Criminologist David Kennedy, as already mentioned, noted the separate "narratives" that young African American men and police officers each bring to encounters on the street.[40] A study of traffic enforcement in the Kansas City metropolitan area by political scientist Charles Epp and colleagues found that whites and African Americans experience traffic stops in profoundly different ways. Among whites, traffic stops are largely traffic enforcement events related to driving habits or the condition of their vehicles. Among African Americans, on the other hand, traffic stops are disproportionately "investigative" stops, motivated by police officers' suspicions about the driver, passengers, or both. The cloud of suspicion is perceived as profoundly alienating. Epp and colleagues argue that the message delivered is that you—the suspect—are not a full member of this community or even of this country.[41] Political scientists Mark Peffley and Jon Hurwitz, in a national survey (conducted between October 2000 and March 2001) of attitudes about the criminal justice system and the police, concluded that whites and African Americans live in "different realities," "differentially interpreting actual events in the justice system." Importantly, they have different interpretations of "fairness" in the system, with African Americans believing that they were not receiving the same degree of fairness as whites. Like other scholars, the authors found a deep "racial divide" between whites and African Americans in America. They ask, "Just how enduring is the racial divide in the justice domain?" and conclude that "there are no easy answers" to that question.[42] In the end, both Epp and colleagues and Peffley and Hurwitz see a deeply embedded racial divide in the United States, particularly in the justice system—a divide that will not be easily overcome.

Building a Lawful, Professional, and Respectful Policing

The argument of this book is that American policing should be lawful, professional, and respectful. To that end, police reform must be comprehensive, addressing all major police operations, and not piecemeal as was the case with earlier reform efforts. It is simply not sufficient to install a state-of-the-art use of force policy. If the policy is to work as intended, it is also necessary to ensure that all training programs— police academy, annual in-service training, and field training for new recruits—reflect current best practices on officer use of force. Public complaint procedures need to be open and accessible, and complaint investigations need to be free of any bias. Departments need to develop mid-management units to systematically review officer use of force reports through a use of force review board. Officers with recurring performance problems need to be identified and subject to corrective action by an early intervention system. The recruitment, training, assignment, and promotion of officers need to consider applicants' work histories and current officers' records on use of force, public complaints, and other performance matters. The issues discussed here are just the start of a broader process that leads to a fully lawful, professional, and respectful police department.[43]

Lawful Policing

Lawful policing means that police departments comply with the U.S. Constitution and the many court decisions based on its principles; relevant federal laws, such as equal employment opportunity laws; relevant state and municipal laws; and police department policies and procedures. But there is much more to it than that. The police are regulated by a broad range of rules and regulations based on other sources. This includes state and local civil service laws; collective bargaining agreement provisions (in those departments with police unions); and police oversight agencies, including complaint review boards, police auditors, and inspectors general.[44] Law professor Rachel Harmon argues that police scholars focus on the constitutional law of policing and "rarely write about the rest of the 'law of the police.'" Because of the narrow focus on constitutional law issues, she continues, we know precious little about these other rules and regulations and how they shape American policing, for better or worse.[45] This is a serious void in our understanding about the complete world of American policing.

It is important to note here that, as chapter 4 explains, many of the goals of the Justice Department's pattern or practice program are not constitutionally mandated. These include, for example, improved public complaint procedures, increased community engagement, and requirements that police departments engage in problem-oriented policing. Nonetheless, the pattern or practice staff began incorporating these reforms into consent decrees, recognizing that they are essential as supports of the larger goal of ending unconstitutional policing.

Professional Policing

Professional policing means that police departments are current with recognized national best practices in their policies and procedures, managerial practices, relationships with the community, and technological infrastructure. There is no official list of best practices, which this author views as a strength.[46] An official list would require lengthy processes of proposing, debating, and approving new policies, and later amending existing policies as new ideas and perspectives emerge. Such a list would only stagnate the policy development process. It is far better for individual police departments to develop their own new policies (e.g., on dealing with homeless people or people experiencing a mental health crisis) and to have other departments slowly borrow them, with either minor or major changes. Adoption of a policy by other departments represents the success of a new policy in the "marketplace of ideas." Policies and practices are continually evolving, and that is a sign of a healthy professional atmosphere in policing.

An excellent source of new ideas and reports on critical issues is the reports published by the Police Executive Research Forum (PERF), a professional association of forward-thinking police chiefs and top commanders. The reports are conveniently available on the PERF website, notably the pathbreaking 2016 report *Guiding Principles on Use of Force*, which brings together key parts of earlier PERF reports.[47] William A. Geller and Michael S. Scott's 1992 study *Deadly Force: What We Know* traces the enormous changes in police deadly force policy in just the twenty years since the pioneering New York City police department policy in 1972. They refer to the process of change as a "long march." Additional changes have occurred in the years since their book was published. A similar "long march" has occurred on important policies related to domestic violence, responding to people experiencing mental health crises, and many others. The long march continues, and that is a healthy sign of a continuing commitment to professionalism.[48]

Respectful Policing

Respectful policing means that as a matter of both official policy and day-to-day practice, police departments treat all people with respect.

Respectful treatment has two dimensions. The first involves encounters between police officers and people on the street. The second involves police departments engaging both individuals and community stakeholder groups in formal procedures for discussions of and the development of police department strategies for addressing crime and disorder, policies on use of force and other areas of police work, a department's employment practices, and many other issues.

In the context of street-level encounters, respect involves officers treating people equally regardless of race, ethnicity, gender, sexual orientation, social class, or other characteristics. This goes far beyond simply adhering to the letter of federal, state, or local laws on equal protection. Respectful policing is a matter of *how* police officers treat people in all encounters. The New Orleans police department's bias-free policing policy, mandated by the consent decree, instructs officers on procedural justice tactics in encounters with members of the public. Officers are required to "provide a self-introduction and explain to the subject the reason for the contact"; "answer any questions the person contacted may have"; "provide name and badge number when requested"; and if a stop was made in error, "explain why the error was made and apologize for any inconvenience." The language of the policy comes directly from the academic literature on procedural justice. These requirements are not mandated by constitutional law or any court decision, but they are official policy of the police department and officers can be disciplined for ignoring or violating them. They represent respectful policing in the broadest sense and are important in terms of helping to gain the trust and confidence of members of the public.[49] While the application of procedural justice in certain areas of policing may well make positive gains, it does not overcome the deep racial divisions that exist in the full range of other police interactions with the public.

Treating individuals and groups with respect in discussions of police department policies and strategies to address crime and disorder involves creating formal structures where members of the public can provide input on these important matters. For too long in their history, police departments as institutions isolated themselves from the public, claiming to be the real experts on crime and disorder. The police professionalization movement in the twentieth century became extremely aggressive in *rejecting* public input on important matters such as crime, arguing that ordinary citizens are simply not experts on policing. This argument became firmly entrenched and was not seriously challenged until the police crises of the twenty-first century. The 2015 report of the President's Task Force on 21st Century Policing broke new ground with a set of recommendations for directly involving the public in important matters. Action Item 1.5.1, for example, recommended that "in order to achieve external legitimacy, law enforcement agencies should involve the community in the process of developing and evaluating policies and procedures."[50] Only a few departments have fully embraced this recommendation.

Conclusion: The Challenge We Face

The goals of lawful, professional, and respectful policing represent an enormous challenge for American police departments. The plain truth is that we really have no choice. As explained earlier, we simply cannot continue with the terrible number of people shot and killed by the police every year, patterns of police brutality, and discriminatory policing against African Americans, Latinos, women, and LGBT people. In 2022 the police shot and killed 1,176 people, a new record high and an average of three people a day. The total is also about twice the number reported annually by the FBI, largely because its system is voluntary and many police departments do not report shooting data to the Bureau.[51]

We cannot continue with this terrible pattern of injustice, just as we cannot continue with the current rates of unacceptable use of excessive physical force, unlawful pedestrian and vehicle stops, and other forms of police misconduct. The murders of Michael Brown in 2014 and George Floyd in 2020 brought forth waves of public protests. Those protests represent what the late civil rights leader and member of Congress John Lewis called "good trouble," trouble that exposes serious social problems, forces public debates on these problems, and hopefully leads to meaningful solutions. Lewis caused quite a bit of good trouble in his lifetime, and we honor him today for that.[52]

The "good trouble" that protesters have caused since the deaths of Michael Brown in 2014 and George Floyd in 2020 generated a burst of police reform. As will be discussed in the final chapter of this book, important and overdue police reform activity is already well established by the U.S. Justice Department, several state attorneys general, state legislatures, city councils, reform-minded police chiefs, and a number of nonprofit groups. These efforts provide a solid foundation for the future. In an invaluable 2021 article on achieving accountability in policing, Michael White, Henry F. Fradella, and Michaela Flippin conclude, "We think it is clear that the push for reform has reached a tipping point. . . . The momentum for police reform is unprecedented."[53] The author of this book agrees, and the chapters that follow argue the case for the possibilities of creating better policing for this country. With all of these reform activities in place, the future of a lawful, professional, and respectful police is no dream, it is a very real possibility.

The challenge we face involves reforming the eighteen thousand local and state law enforcement agencies in this country, many of which have serious problems of unlawful and unprofessional conduct.[54] Of course we cannot undertake to reform all of those departments. But we can take on the large and medium-sized departments with serious problems of unlawful and unprofessional conduct in their policing practices. There will be opposition and resistance from many sources: resistance from local political leaders who do not think they have a problem and do not want to bear the costs of reform; opposition from many local residents who also think that their police departments have no serious problems; covert resistance from officers at different ranks who are wedded to their traditional habits; resistance from police unions where they exist; and the considerable costs of developing new policies, revising the training related to them, training supervisors, and on and on. These are very real challenges that must be faced and cannot be wished away.

A major force for the future of police reform involves mobilizing and strengthening the community resources that currently exist. Mobilizing resources in those communities where they are not already organized is a special challenge. The community resources include community activists who have already been hard at work, who can mobilize powerful community-focused lobbying efforts; members and leaders in the faith community who can bring their voices and constituents to the effort; local civil rights, civil liberties, and human rights organizations who have special capacities; the business community and civic leaders who do not want their community to be torn by continued police misconduct and racial strife; local foundations and some corporations who, if presented with a coherent reform plan, would be willing to provide financial support to a reform effort.

Mobilizing community resources where they do not already exist is a major challenge, but it is one that we cannot avoid. The final chapter in this book examines the various police reform efforts that have emerged only in recent years. That development provides grounds for optimism. We can't go on like this.

2

A History of Police Reforms

The Justice Department's pattern or practice program did not come out of nowhere. It was built on the work of earlier police reformers that began around 1900 and continued through the 1970s. This chapter examines both the positive contributions and the shortcomings of these earlier efforts. Beginning around 1900, the police professionalization movement initiated the first real reforms in the history of the American police, achieving a number of important and overdue changes. The movement, however, failed to address the issue of uncontrolled police officer discretion and the resulting officer misconduct and also the serious problem of racial bias in policing. The tumultuous decade of the 1960s included the rising demands of African Americans for justice from the police; these expectations finally exploded in a series of violent riots between 1964 and 1968. The landmark Supreme Court decisions on police procedures in the 1960s took major steps forward by imposing constitutional standards on local and state law enforcement agencies. The court's decisions, however, were piecemeal changes, addressing only the issues before the court, leaving most police work untouched by constitutional standards. The advent of administrative rulemaking in the mid-1970s was the first serious effort to control officer discretion and reduce police officer misconduct. By the late 1980s it had become a basic tool of American police management.

The Beginnings of Police Reform: The Professionalization Movement, 1900–1960s

Professionalization: Important Gains, Major Shortcomings

The police professionalization movement began roughly around 1900 and faced a far greater challenge than later reform efforts for the simple reason that American police departments at the time were completely unprofessional by modern standards. The first modern police departments in the 1830s and 1840s immediately became mired in a swamp of political influence, and each department was essentially an "adjunct" of the local political machine.[1] There were literally no formal standards governing anything in police departments. Officers got their jobs through their political connections. They patrolled their beats on foot and found it easy to sleep on the job or to drink in neighborhood saloons. Famously, future president Theodore Roosevelt, who served as one of the commissioners of the New York City police from 1895 to 1897, went out one night to see what police officers were doing. He had difficulty even finding officers, except for a few who were sleeping in public.[2] Officers easily sabotaged the primitive call boxes that were the means of communication between officers and their superiors. Patrolling on foot, they were no deterrent to crime. Public disrespect for police officers was pervasive and officers readily retaliated with physical force.

The real business of urban policing was not crime fighting or serving the public but corruption: providing jobs for political allies, taking payoffs from saloons, whorehouses, and gambling dens, and harassing establishments owned by rival political factions. There were no officer recruitment standards and, except for some occasional attempts, no pre-service training programs. And particularly important, there was no sense of professionalism and duty to serve the public.[3]

The London Metropolitan Police, created by Robert Peel (who bequeathed us the term "bobbies") in 1829, by contrast, was centrally controlled by the Home Office and governed by strict rules and regulations. As Professor Samuel Walker put it, the problem with the American police was not "a lack of democratic control," but rather a "well-functioning process of democratic governance *in the pursuit of the wrong values*," serving the majority at the minority's expense (italics in original).[4]

The leaders of the professionalization movement set out to do something entirely new. There had been political battles over local police departments for decades, but they were not "reform" efforts in the modern sense. These were contests between two political groups for *control* of police departments, not attempts to reform them. Changing them, in terms of leadership, personnel standards, training, and new police units, was what the leaders of the professionalization movement envisioned.

They were also fairly clear on what their specific reforms would be. Most important, reform involved ending the pervasive corruption, inefficiency, and lack of professionalism in American policing. The reform agenda included ending political influence over police departments and appointing strong leaders as chiefs, often recruiting them from existing professions. Command and control became somewhat more centralized in the chief's office in some but not all departments. Reformers introduced the first formal recruitment standards and created the first permanent recruit training programs. They also created the first specialized units, notably juvenile delinquency prevention units, which were led by the first women officers in American policing. These officers, however, had second-class status, not allowed to carry weapons and not authorized to make arrests. Most important, the professionalization movement introduced the principle that policing was a *profession*, with the mission of serving the public rather than political bosses, and serving all groups equally. For most police departments around the country, however, the goal of professionalization remained a fanciful idea and was not embraced.[5]

The Philadelphia police department between 1911 and 1915 dramatized the achievements and failures of professionalization. The famed muckraking journalist Lincoln Steffens had labeled Philadelphia "the worst governed city in the country," although there were undoubtedly many rivals for this dubious distinction. The reform-minded "good government" forces in the city captured control of city government in 1911 and immediately appointed James Robinson superintendent of the police. He introduced a military ethos into the department, with rigorous military drills. (The military ethos proved to be an unfortunate legacy of the professionalization movement.) He also published a new edition of the patrol officers' manual, which had not been updated since 1897, and created a school of instruction with four weeks of classes. Patrol operations were reorganized with a new system of patrol shifts. Robinson's "Ten Suggestions to Police Officers" began by telling officers, "You are a paid public servant of the public." Few of Robinson's reforms lasted very long, however. The old political machine returned to power in 1915 and quickly abolished or simply ignored most of his reforms.[6] The pattern of reform followed by reversion to the old ways occurred in many departments during the six decades of the professionalization era.

The Shortcomings of Professionalization

By the late 1950s, American policing had made much progress after several decades of professionalization. Many departments were better led and better organized, and delivered police services to the public more professionally than ever before. Police chief William Parker of the Los Angeles police department in the 1950s cultivated a national reputation of professionalism and tough anti-crime policing. His public relations master stroke was to develop a working relationship with what became the popular television show *Dragnet*, which projected a national image of the department as the most professional in the country. As later events would reveal, however, its crime-fighting practices were aggressive and deeply racist. Chief Parker dismissed all criticisms and suggestions for reform from the NAACP, the ACLU, and other groups as unworthy of consideration and possibly communist-inspired. When the California Supreme Court in 1955 imposed the exclusionary rule on state law enforcement agencies, Parker worked with *Dragnet* producer Jack Webb on an episode that denounced the court's decision.[7]

Despite the reforms in many departments, by the end of the 1950s, most departments lacked the basic standards of professionalism. A 1958 report titled *New Jersey Municipal Police Survey* concluded that "only a small minority" of officers in the state had been "exposed to even a minimum program of adequate recruit training," while in-service training programs had "been neglected." Few departments fully realized the potential of well-organized patrol operations, with the result that "morale and efficiency of the patrol officer is low." Supervision of patrol officers "especially on late tours [was] virtually nonexistent." Finally, the report's somber list of police problems began with "politics in policing and policing in politics." New Jersey's city police departments, along with most others around the country, were completely unprepared for the nationwide racial storm that would burst in just a few years. The New Jersey survey did not mention the issue of controlling police officer discretion and the growing problem of police-community relations, two issues that would soon be at the center of the national police crisis. These failures were a major part of the "ambiguous legacy" of the professionalization movement.[8]

The Turbulent 1960s: Civil Rights, Riots, and the Kerner Commission

The Civil Rights Movement and Rising African American Expectations

February 1, 1960, introduced a new era in the American civil rights movement, one that would have a profound impact on the nation and on policing. After a series of long discussions in their dormitory rooms about racial segregation and other urgent social issues, four African American students at North Carolina A&T University in Greensboro, North Carolina, decided to act. The next day they conducted an impromptu sit-in at the segregated lunch counter of the local Woolworth's store. Word of their bold action spread like wildfire among African American students across the South. Within a week, sit-ins spread to three other North Carolina cities, and in the next five days sit-ins occurred in thirteen other southern cities. Almost overnight the sit-in movement emerged as an action-oriented, student-led effort that redefined the agenda of the national civil rights movement as demands for immediate reforms.[9]

An even more dramatic civil rights action galvanized the nation a year later. The Congress of Racial Equality (CORE) organized the now-famous Freedom Ride, in which two racially integrated buses departed Washington, DC, on May 4, 1961, and headed south to challenge the racial segregation in interstate bus travel throughout the Deep South. The Freedom Riders included thirteen men in this sexist era (no women were permitted) and consisted of seven African Americans (including John Lewis, who went on to a distinguished career as a member of Congress) and six whites. Their plan was to reach New Orleans on May 17, the seventh anniversary of the historic *Brown v. Board of Education* decision, which had declared racially segregated schools unconstitutional. The buses never reached New Orleans. Some arrests and a few violent attacks by racists occurred in the first ten days while the buses were in the Upper South. On Sunday, May 14, however, Ku Klux Klan-led mobs in Anniston and Birmingham, Alabama, attacked the buses, brutally beating some of the Freedom Riders. In Anniston the mob set the bus on fire. Newspapers and television news broadcasts across the country and around the world presented horrific pictures of bloody Freedom Riders and the burning bus, inspiring civil rights protests around the country. In all of these violent incidents, local and state police officers either stood by passively or joined the mobs themselves.[10]

Two years later, civil rights activism reached an even more dramatic level when Dr. Martin Luther King launched a carefully planned protest campaign challenging racial segregation in Birmingham, Alabama. Local police, directed by the avid segregationist commissioner of public safety Eugene "Bull" Connor, responded with repressive dispersals of crowds and arrests of protesters. On May 2, 1963, King and his aides took the controversial step of organizing a march by young people, who left school to join the protest. Nearly a thousand marched and hundreds were arrested, but both young people and adults continued to demonstrate the next day. The police responded by attacking with fire hoses, police dogs, and physical brutality. Photographs and television news footage of these abusive events shocked the nation and become iconic images of the 1960s civil rights movement. Sympathy demonstrations spread across the country as the momentum of the civil rights movement reached a new level.[11]

At the time of the violent clashes in Birmingham, the civil rights movement was still a largely "southern" phenomenon, confined to the states of the Old Confederacy where legal racial segregation still prevailed. That was about to change very dramatically, as the drama of civil rights protests soon spread to the rest of the country.

President John F. Kennedy, who had done little to support civil rights in his two years and four months as president (the best book on his civil rights record as president is titled *The Bystander*), was alarmed by the Birmingham events and the possibility of protests and violence spreading across the country. Realizing that he needed to take some dramatic action, he went on national television the night of June 11, 1963, and proposed a relatively strong federal civil rights bill. He introduced a civil rights bill in Congress but did not live to see it passed. His successor, President Lyndon Johnson, however, made the bill a top priority and lobbied hard for its enactment. Enacted on July 2, 1964, it became the 1964 Civil Rights Act. It remains one of the most important pieces of social legislation ever passed, ending discrimination in public accommodations and outlawing discrimination in employment, along with other anti-discrimination measures.[12]

Flash Point: The Cop in the Big-City Ghetto and the Riots

The dramatic, transformative, and highly publicized events of the southern civil rights movement provoked a "revolution of rising expectations" among African Americans. The flash point of this activism in big cities became the highly visible figure of the white cop in the African American ghetto, a living symbol of discrimination and racial segregation. Police misconduct in urban African American communities had been widespread and unchecked for many years, and the rising tide of civil rights activism moved it to center stage. Civil rights activists protested police use of excessive force, unjustified fatal shootings, discriminatory arrests, offensive verbal abuse, a lack of public complaint procedures, and racial discrimination in police department hiring. The fuse for an explosion was ready, needing only the smallest spark to ignite. The dramatic events of 1964 made the civil rights movement a national crisis.

The spark came on June 16, 1964, in New York City when several young African Americans got into a dispute with a white building superintendent. An off-duty white NYPD lieutenant happened to be near and intervened in the dispute. A fifteen-year-old African American pulled a knife and the officer shot and killed him. Word quickly spread. Teenagers began smashing windows until a small force of police officers dispersed them. The next day a Marxist African American organization distributed inflammatory leaflets accusing the police of brutality. All was relatively quiet until the following day, when the civil rights group CORE conducted a march. A violent clash with the police erupted, resulting in the death of one person and injuries to nineteen citizens and twelve police officers. Similar clashes continued for several days.[13] No one realized it at the time, but this was the beginning of what became known as the "long hot summers" of 1964 to 1968. The noted African American writer James Baldwin was one of the few who did foresee what was soon to come. In his passionately argued book *The Fire Next Time*, Baldwin expressed his outrage over the long history of oppression of African Americans in the United States. His final words, loosely adapted from the Bible (Genesis 9:17) were prophetic: "God gave Noah the rainbow sign. No more water, the Fire Next Time."[14] And fire there would be.

The relatively small New York City riot was an ominous beginning, although similar clashes also occurred that summer in five other cities, including Chicago and Philadelphia. The incidents of violence that swept the country caused panic among national civil rights leaders, and in late July the major organizations and leaders—including the NAACP, the Urban League, and Dr. Martin Luther King—called for a moratorium on demonstrations until after the November presidential election.[15] They feared a "white backlash" against any further urban violence that would cause white voters to support the conservative Republican Barry Goldwater in the November presidential election and defeat the reelection of the pro-civil rights president Lyndon Johnson. The two most militant groups, SNCC and CORE, however, refused to support the moratorium.[16] Fears of a Goldwater victory proved greatly exaggerated as Johnson won reelection in a huge landslide. Fears of a white backlash against civil rights, however, proved to be quite prophetic in the years ahead, as white support for civil rights weakened in the late 1960s and into the 1970s. Leaders of the African American community, meanwhile, became more disillusioned with the lack of national action on the nation's race crisis.

Although few Americans in the mid-1960s were aware of it, urban race riots had a long history in the United States.[17] In 1919 there were serious riots in Washington, DC, Omaha, and Chicago. The Chicago race riot generated a detailed report in 1922, with recommendations for ending racial tensions, none of which were implemented. A critique of the report in the 1960s observed that it "stopped short of looking hard at the power structure of Chicago, by which change could be induced."[18] Similar criticisms apply to all of the post-riot reports in the twentieth century. The 1921 Tulsa race riot was probably the most devastating of all the pre-1960s riots, with as many as three hundred African Americans killed and 1,200 houses demolished. The African American community of Greenwood was physically demolished. No post-riot remedial actions were taken, however. A brief riot erupted in New York City in 1935, but New York City mayor Fiorello LaGuardia suppressed the report he had commissioned on the incident because it was too "radical" for suggesting an informal process for reviewing citizen complaints against the police. In 1943, in the midst of World War II, riots erupted in New York City, Los Angeles (the famous "zoot suit riots"), and Detroit. Fearful of the impact of racial divisions on the war effort, officials in many cities created interracial commissions that campaigned against racism and discrimination. These were the first-ever interracial efforts committed to fighting for racial justice.[19]

Professor Kenneth Clark, the noted African American psychologist who had contributed to the plaintiffs' brief in *Brown v. Board of Education*, concluded that the 1968 Kerner Commission report on the 1960s riots was seriously inadequate. Testifying before the commission, he explained that he had "read that report . . . of the 1919 riot in Chicago, and it was as if I were reading the report" on the 1935 Harlem riot, the report on the 1943 Harlem riot, and the McCone Commission report on the 1965 Watts riot in Los Angeles. He said that "in candor," it was like seeing "the same moving picture reshown over and over again, the same analysis, the same recommendations, and the same inaction."[20] It was a depressing statement but a correct assessment of decades of inaction on American race relations.

Correctly sensing a shift in the national political mood on crime and race in 1964, President Johnson quickly responded by creating a President's Commission on Law Enforcement and Administration of Justice, which delivered a set of reports in 1967.[21] The commission's 239-page report, titled *Task Force Report: The Police*, presented a comprehensive picture of the state of American policing, finding it unprofessional in almost every area. Without explicitly saying so, the report exposed the shortcomings of over a half century of police professionalization. Recruitment practices failed to attract the best candidates for police jobs, and "few departments have appropriate standards today." Additionally, the training "needs of recruits are inadequately met in most departments." On one very important issue, however, the report made what proved to be the extremely influential recommendation that "current police practices [are] in need of administrative policy formulation." This was the first recommendation by a national group on the subject of controlling police officer discretion, and it would set American policing on the road to controlling police officer discretion.[22]

Task Force Report: The Police devoted sixty-plus pages to the nation's now-raging police-community relations crisis. The picture of police shortcomings was truly alarming. The report cited public opinion surveys that found high levels of distrust of the police among African Americans, including the widespread belief that officers routinely used excessive force. It also found that many police chiefs, insensitive to the rising civil rights demands, did not support the very police-community relations programs they had only recently established in their own departments. Community advisory committees, which typically involved prominent city leaders chosen by the chief, were "seriously deficient" in addressing the basic police problems that underpinned the riots. Field studies commissioned by the task force uncovered the shocking fact that officers "who were acknowledged as among [a] department's worst were assigned to police minority group neighborhoods." Additionally, the field studies found a pattern of discourtesy and verbal abuse by officers, with racial epithets such as "nigger," "coon," and "boy" being "widespread." "Too few" departments, meanwhile, "have adequate procedures for dealing with [citizen] complaints." Both individual officers and departments as a whole "often regard a citizen complaint as an attack on the police." In Philadelphia, it was "standard police procedure to charge a person with resisting arrest or disorderly conduct" if he or she accused the police of brutality.[23]

Few members of the general public read *Task Force Report: The Police*, but knowledgeable police experts certainly did and recognized how serious police problems were. American police departments had been overtaken by the national crisis in race relations and were not equipped to meet the new demands thrust upon them. Major reforms were clearly needed, but in the mid- to late 1960s there were no recognized police experts who thought in terms of attempting comprehensive reform of police departments (an idea that would finally come to fruition with the Justice Department's pattern or practice program in the 1990s). They were accustomed to the piecemeal style of reform in previous decades and beyond that did not know where to begin.[24]

More Riots: Detroit and Newark

If any political leaders hoped that the disturbances and riots of 1963 and 1964 were just a temporary phenomenon that would soon pass, their hopes were dashed in the summer of 1965. On the sweltering night of August 11, a California Highway Patrol officer, working in the Watts District of Los Angeles, a center of the African American community, stopped a young African American driver for speeding. His arrest drew a crowd and more officers were dispatched to the scene. The police soon departed, but then some in the crowd began throwing rocks at passing cars, overturning parked cars, setting them on fire, and beating white drivers. The situation was calm the next day, but thirty hours after the initial incident a full-scale riot erupted. The rioting eventually resulted in four thousand arrests, thirty-four people killed, and $35 million in property destroyed. The Kerner Commission report on the riots found that almost all of the riots began with some "police action [as] the final incident" that precipitated the violence. Most of those incidents, moreover, were minor events such as traffic stops.[25]

The Watts riot was an outburst of anger at the entire structure of racism in American society, and more than any other event made civil rights protests a national phenomenon.

In 1966 there were forty-three documented disturbances or riots, but two riots in 1967 were particularly devastating. In Newark, New Jersey, an angry confrontation occurred over a land use issue that proposed giving over 150 acres of parkland in the heart of the ghetto to the state for a new medical school and dental college. Dispute over the issue continued for three weeks until the night of July 20, when the mounting anger among African Americans erupted into a major riot. In the end, twenty-three people were killed (twenty-one African Americans, one police officer, and one firefighter) and property damage was estimated at $10 million. As with the Watts riot, a seemingly minor incident involving the police triggered the massive riot.[26] The Detroit riot erupted just two days after the Newark riot began and proved to be even more destructive. A Detroit police raid of five "blind pigs," illegal social clubs featuring after-hours drinking and gambling, sparked the riot. Fairly quickly, about two hundred local residents gathered near a club to protest, and when someone threw a bottle at a police car, the riot began. Vandalism, looting, and arson soon escalated. Eventually, more than 7,200 people were arrested, 43 people were killed (33 African Americans and 10 whites), and between $40 and $45 million worth of property had been destroyed. Once again, a relatively minor incident was the spark that set off the anger and violence, a further indication of the intense African American anger at the police, their racist practices, and the entire structure of racial segregation in the country.[27]

The Kerner Commission Report

In response to the continuing pattern of riots, President Johnson appointed the Kerner Commission to study the riots and their causes and to make recommendations for reform. Only one of the seventeen chapters in the final report, however, was devoted exclusively to the police. Johnson appointed a range of liberals and conservatives to the commission, but their very different social and political perspectives almost blocked the commission's work. The liberal members, led by New York City mayor John Lindsay, wanted strong statements about white racism and police misconduct, while conservatives regarded such issues as divisive and wanted more emphasis on what the private sector could do to improve conditions in the cities. There was no agreement on how to pay for the large social programs the commission recommended. The Vietnam War was at its peak, straining federal resources and diverting President Johnson's attention from the racial crisis at home. As a result, the report was silent on the funding issue. At the last minute only a passionate plea from commission director Donald Ginsburg secured a unanimous vote approving the final report.[28]

The report's section on "Police and the Community" was a mixed bag of good recommendations and others that either evaded basic issues or were wishful thinking. Particularly important, it correctly pointed out that "deep hostility between police and ghetto communities [w] as a primary cause to the disorders surveyed by the Commission." "In many ways," it continued, "the policeman only symbolizes much deeper problems." Social scientists had previously made this point, but no one had any concrete suggestions for resolving this problem. The report also pointed out "a relative lack of police personnel for ghetto areas, considering the volume of calls for police," while at the same time noting the negative impact of "aggressive preventive patrol" used by many departments in those same neighborhoods. The observation exposed a deep contradiction at the heart of urban policing in the country. African American neighborhoods simultaneously received both too little and too much policing: a lack of sufficient officers to respond to ordinary social problem and too much policing in the form of aggressive officer actions that included unjustified stops without suspicion, use of excessive force, and illegal arrests.[29]

The commission also identified a disturbing issue that had never received serious attention from police experts. Many of the worst riots, it pointed out, occurred in cities whose police are "among the best led, best organized, best trained and most professional in the country." It did not name the Los Angeles police department, although most police experts understood who the report meant. The issue posed a serious dilemma regarding police professionalization: "professionalism" had come to be defined in terms of strong leadership from a police chief and a well-organized and aggressive approach to crime control.[30] The commission did not explore this problem in detail, but a later generation of police experts recognized it and grappled with it. Fifty years later, a 2018 report titled *Proactive Policing*, published by the National Academies of Science, Engineering, and Medicine, gave much praise to "hot spots" policing, a popular program that focused police resources on high-crime areas, but added a boldface advisory that "there are likely to be large racial disparities in the volume and nature of police-citizen encounters when police target high-risk people or high-risk places, as is common in many proactive policing programs," and that this problem "makes the investigation of the causes of racial disparities a key research and policy concern."[31] The problem of racial disparities in the most important police actions—stops, searches, arrests, use of physical force and deadly force—remain today, although as chapters 4 and 5 argue, consent decree reforms have succeeded in narrowing them.

The Kerner Commission report found that few American police departments had adequate procedures for accepting and investigating public complaints. Its field studies found that the police chiefs in Milwaukee, Wisconsin, and Plainfield, New Jersey, rejected "all complaints out of hand," while a police review board in New Haven, Connecticut, was "worthless" in the eyes of local African American leaders. The commission concluded that "objective evaluation, analysis, and innovation on this subject [citizen complaints] is vitally necessary," and recommended the creation of a "specialized agency" for that purpose, a bold recommendation for its time.[32] Although the report saw the need for police department-based community relations programs, its own field studies had found that most existing "community relations" programs were in fact "public relations" programs with no real impact on day-to-day policing and the problems that had fueled the recent riots.[33]

The most important and influential recommendation by the Kerner Commission was its call for written "policy guidelines" to govern police officer discretion. The President's Crime Commission had made the same recommendation the year before. The lack of controls over police officer discretion was such that in 1964 the noted legal scholar Herbert L. Packer declared that the police "are a law unto themselves."[34] The commission argued that "contacts between citizens and the police in the ghetto require discretion and judgment which should be based upon carefully-drawn, written department policy." Written guidelines, it added, were effective only if they were enforced, and to that end it recommended "a strong internal investigative unit to enforce compliance," leaving unstated the unpleasant fact that few police departments had strong internal affairs units. It noted with disgust that some police departments had guidelines on "the wearing of uniforms—but not for how to intervene in a domestic dispute." It then offered a very short list of different areas of routine police work where written guidelines were needed, including "the circumstances under which various forms of physical force—including lethal force—can and should be applied."[35] The fact that the President's Crime Commission and the Kerner Commission made the same recommendation on the urgent need to control officer discretion within a year of each other reflected the rapidly changing current of thinking among leading police experts on the issue.[36]

On the first page of the report, where few readers would miss it, the Kerner Commission offered a revealing insight into the liberal assumptions guiding the project. In an oft-quoted observation, it declared, "Our nation is moving toward two societies, one black, one white—separate and unequal."[37] The statement originated in one of the drafts of the final report, but two staff members spotted it, liked its boldness, and moved it to a more prominent location in the final report. Bold as the statement was, however, it presented a false view of American society. The United States was hardly "moving" toward two societies; they already existed. It required willful ignorance not to notice the pattern of racial segregation in housing and employment; the racial segregation in churches on Sunday morning; and the racial divisions in the different forms of American popular music (pop, jazz, rhythm and blues, country and western). Many of the commission's leadership, staff, and consultants were undoubtedly aware of these racial divisions, but the subject was not openly discussed in commission deliberations. President Johnson, embattled over the Vietnam War, wanted an optimistic report that was consistent with his Great Society program. A sober, realistic note did, however, slip through in the very last paragraph of the chapter on policing, where the report's authors confessed, "We see no easy solution to police-community relations."[38] It was a blunt and honest statement with much truth to it.

The Kerner Commission also made one invaluable and lasting contribution to the understanding of the American police that has never been properly recognized. Among the field studies it commissioned, the most important involved direct observation of police patrol officers at work in three cities (Boston, Chicago, and Washington, DC) by sociologists Albert J. Reiss and Donald J. Black. It was the first-ever quantitative observational study of police officers at work. Their findings provided pioneering insights into routine policing, including police officers' exercise of discretion and use of force, and inspired a rich new field of police research that continues today. The "research revolution" in policing that soon developed can be traced to this Kerner Commission-sponsored study.[39]

On the negative side, however, the riots of the 1960s provoked a white backlash over civil rights, as civil rights leaders in 1964 had feared, and similar hostility to the mounting protests against the Vietnam War, the growing drug culture among young people, and the new counterculture that rejected the norms of middle-class America. An early sign of the civil rights backlash was a 1966 referendum in New York City over the newly expanded Civilian Complaint Review Board (CCRB). Mayor John Lindsay, a liberal Republican, consulted widely and, following the advice of several people, finally appointed four citizens to the board, giving it a civilian majority. The police union was outraged and immediately sponsored a referendum and skillfully played the "crime card," warning voters of an increase in serious crime if the new CCRB was left standing, and in their view, unduly limited the ability of officers to effectively fight crime. To illustrate its point, it distributed a poster depicting a young white woman exiting the subway alone onto a dark street, obviously worried about being attacked. In November city voters rejected the new CCRB by a two-to-one margin, which indicated that white voters were indifferent to the complaints of the African American community about the police department. The revised CCRB was quickly replaced by one with a majority of police command officers. In the years ahead, the "crime card" became a code phrase for the "race card," reinforcing white stereotypes about African Americans and crime.[40]

"Watchdog": The Supreme Court Intervenes in Policing

The Supreme Court as Watchdog of the Police

The U.S. Supreme Court dramatically entered the world of police reform in 1961 with a highly controversial decision on police search and seizure practices.[41] *Mapp v. Ohio* held that any evidence the police seized in violation of the Fourth Amendment could not be used against a defendant at trial, applying the exclusionary rule to the police in all fifty states through the Fourteenth Amendment. Justice Tom Clark explained that "our holding that the exclusionary rule is an essential part of both the Fourth and Fourteenth Amendments is not only the logical dictate of prior cases, but it also makes very good sense. There is no war between the Constitution and common sense." The exclusionary rule was nothing new in policing. The court had applied it to federal law enforcement cases in *Weeks v. United States* in 1914, and the California Supreme Court applied it to state law enforcement in its state in 1955. The court had issued several decisions against various police practices in the 1950s, but *Mapp* clearly signaled a new departure for the court, assuming the role as the "watchdog" of policing and applying constitutional standards to the police in all fifty states.[42]

The *Mapp* decision provoked a storm of protests from the police and political conservatives, fueling fears among many Americans that the Supreme Court contributed to the rise in crime by being too "soft" on criminals. Police officers and leaders charged that the rule "handcuffed" them in the fight against crime, arguing that good evidence against a criminal defendant should be allowed no matter how the police obtained it. Civil libertarians and many liberals, on the other hand, rejoiced at the Supreme Court's "watchdog" role toward the police and saw the court as the best hope for long-term police reform.[43]

An even greater controversy erupted over the Supreme Court's famous decision in *Miranda v. Arizona* in 1966, in which the court held that people in custody had a right to an attorney and that the police were required to advise detainees of that right. Chief Justice Earl Warren described the *Miranda* warning as meaning that "the person in custody must, prior to interrogation, be clearly informed that he has the right to remain silent, and that anything he says will be used against him in court, . . . that he has the right to consult with a lawyer and to have the lawyer with him during interrogation, and that a lawyer will be appointed to represent him" if he or she is poor and cannot afford one. The *Miranda* warning immediately entered American popular culture and became a dramatic point in movies, television, and ordinary public discourse.[44]

Amid the controversy over the court, the *Mapp* and *Miranda* decisions had an important although less well-known impact on American police departments. Fearing correctly that the exclusionary rule and the *Miranda* warning would cause the dismissal of innumerable criminal cases, some police departments (although not all) scrambled to improve their training on searches and seizures and interrogations. A study of Chicago police department practices regarding the exclusionary rule, based on "extensive, structured interviews with Chicago police department narcotics officers," found that immediately after the *Mapp* decision, "the police department, the state's attorney's office, and the local narcotics courts" began a concerted effort "to ensure compliance with the Fourth Amendment." These changes represented a dramatic shift from the recent past. One veteran Chicago detective, for example, recalled that in 1954 the department offered no training at all on the conduct of searches. To ensure police officer compliance with the court's decisions, the training academy added an in-service training program on search procedures. The use of judge-approved search warrants increasingly replaced searches based on officers' impulsive personal decisions to search.[45]

Skepticism about the Supreme Court's Watchdog Role

While civil libertarians and liberals hailed the advent of the Supreme Court as a watchdog of the police, several legal scholars were deeply skeptical about whether the court could effectively play that role. They pointed out that the Supreme Court lacked the institutional capacity to enforce its own decisions. Enforcement of *Miranda*, for example, requires an arrest, a conviction, and a successful appeal.[46] Equally important, the *Mapp* and *Miranda* decisions covered only a tiny fraction of routine police work, and it is not reasonable to assume that the court would eventually impose constitutional standards on all the other activities.[47] One unfortunate consequence of the Supreme Court's police decisions was that they distorted legal scholarship on policing. Law professor Rachel Harmon in 2012 argued that the preoccupation of legal scholars with Supreme Court decisions fostered the mistaken assumption that "constitutional law [is] the sole or principal source for legal regulation of the police." The result was "tremendous attention to improving [legal] doctrine and remarkable inattention to the problem policing presents." The "problem," Harmon argues, involves the many rules and regulations affecting the police, including civil service laws and collective bargaining agreements, to name only two. The basic problem with a narrow focus on constitutional rights alone, Harmon added, is that "constitutional rights cannot alone protect individuals adequately from police intrusion."[48] The lack of scholarly attention to the other rules and regulations governing the police over the course of several decades had the effect of hindering creative thinking about achieving police reforms without Constitution-based litigation.

The greatest weakness of *Mapp* and *Miranda* has been that police officers soon found clever ways to evade the mandates of both decisions. The exclusionary rule gave rise to the so-called "dropsy" phenomenon in which an arresting officer would claim that the suspect had dropped the drugs on the street and that no search was conducted. In a criminal proceeding it became the word of the suspect against the word of the officer.[49] The *Miranda* warning proved to be even easier to evade. Professor Richard Leo, the leading expert on *Miranda*, found that when conducting interrogations, officers were able to manipulate suspects in many ways: "softening them up" by appearing to be on their side; not using the word "interrogation"; subtly "recasting" an interrogation as a "noncustodial" interview; obtaining "implicit" waivers of *Miranda* rights; deemphasizing the significance of the *Miranda* decision altogether; and in some cases simply lying to suspects about nonexistent evidence against them, such as alleged witness testimony or alleged medical records in rape cases. Suspects in custody, Leo argued, are under extreme stress and studies have found that between 78 and 95 percent voluntarily waive their *Miranda* rights and talk to police interrogators. Leo concluded in his 2008 book that "the scholarly consensus is that *Miranda*'s impact on the real world is, for the most part, negligible."[50]

The severe limitations on the Supreme Court's capacity to enforce its own decisions convinced a number of police experts that the court could not effectively be *the* watchdog of the police, and that police officer conduct could be better controlled through internal police department regulations and administrative rulemaking. Liberal activists, civil libertarians, and civil rights activists in the 1960s, however, did not trust the police to develop and enforce meaningful internal rules and regulations.[51] Events from the late 1960s through the 1980s soon disillusioned those who held hopes for the Supreme Court playing an expanded watchdog role. The first shock was the 1968 *Terry v. Ohio* decision, in which the court upheld the right of police officers to conduct limited detention and frisks of persons they had stopped. To ensure their own safety, the court held, officers could pat down the person's exterior (a "frisk" and not a search) to determine whether he or she had a weapon that might be used against the officer.[52] The retirements of Chief Justice Warren and Justice Abe Fortas in 1969, meanwhile, removed two of the strongest civil libertarians from the Supreme Court, allowing the newly elected president Richard Nixon to appoint conservatives as their replacements, which accelerated the movement of the Supreme Court in a conservative direction.[53] The Supreme Court's abandonment of a vigorous watchdog role over the police only encouraged more legal scholars and police experts to think seriously about a police accountability approach that involved internal police measures.

The Rise of Administrative Rulemaking

Pioneer: Professor Kenneth Davis and the Control of Police Discretion

Never has such a short book had such an important and lasting impact on American policing. University of Chicago law professor Kenneth Davis's *Police Discretion* described the basic framework for administrative rulemaking as a means of controlling police officer discretion.[54] His prescription remains today the basic police management tool for controlling officer discretion and reducing the worst police abuses, curbing even minor misconduct, providing guidance to officers in difficult situations, and helping to ensure equal treatment of all people regardless of race, ethnicity, gender, sexual identity, or social class.[55]

Davis did not invent anything new. He simply borrowed the principles and practices established by the 1946 Administrative Procedure Act, which regulated federal agencies. States eventually followed suit with their own versions of the APA for state agencies.[56] The pervasive use of discretion by American police officers, meanwhile, was literally not "discovered" by police experts until the American Bar Foundation Survey of policing in three states (Michigan, Wisconsin, and Kansas) in the mid-1950s. It was the first-ever direct observational study of police officers at work.[57] The survey's initial findings stunned the project leaders. The observational field research revealed that police officers routinely exercised broad and unchecked discretion, and many of their actions were illegal. The project leaders quickly reorganized the entire project, redefining the planned pilot study as the final study, and attempted to make sense of the rich body of information they had accumulated. Law professor Wayne LaFave's book *Arrest: The Decision to Take a Suspect into Custody* (1965), based on the ABF survey findings, for example, was richly detailed in describing the many forms of uncontrolled police discretion, some of which involved blatantly illegal actions.[58]

Professor Herman Goldstein, who had been a field investigator for the ABF survey, published the first detailed proposal for police administrative rulemaking in 1967. He rejected the idea that legislatures and courts should draft rules for the police, explaining that police chiefs and officers have the necessary experience with the complexity of policing to properly understand what kinds of rules should be drafted. "Police participation," he argued, "would be a valuable contribution" to the effort to control officer conduct. He did concede that police officers "are not considered qualified" to deal with the complex issues that would arise, a point that had much truth to it, given the low educational levels of American police officers at the time.[59]

Goldstein identified areas of policing where rules were needed: arrest decisions, the selection of investigative methods, decisions not to prosecute some arrested people, and several others. Interestingly, he did not mention the decisions of greatest concern to African American community residents and civil rights activists: the use of deadly force and physical force, pedestrian and motor vehicle stops, and frisks and searches. He ended his article by advising his readers that because police departments had no prior experience with a formal rulemaking system for regulating officer behavior, they needed to "develop more adequate systems of control" of officers "to ensure compliance" with a system of written policies. This required the development of a strong policy-making unit within a police department. The advice is still extremely relevant today. Virtually all of the DOJ findings letters on troubled police departments have found officer compliance with existing policies to be weak or nonexistent. Goldstein's article was a major intellectual breakthrough in policing and helped to launch further discussions about a system of administrative rulemaking.[60]

Davis opened *Police Discretion* with twenty examples of Chicago police officers' abuses of discretion, based on the observations of five law students serving as his research assistants. The examples included approaching juveniles drinking alcoholic beverages in public and simply seizing the beverages and pouring them out; arresting prostitutes but not their customers even though both were equally guilty of violating the law; not arresting people who blatantly attempted to bribe them, even when witnesses were willing to testify about the attempt, and so on.[61] Davis pointed out the dangers and the absurdity of the situation. The danger lay in not arresting people who had committed a serious crime and who might go on to commit other crimes. The absurdity was to allow the lowest-ranking officers in a police department to make fundamental policy decisions. The Chicago police department, he pointed out, "has no uniform policy" on basic operations; "policy is made by the patrolmen, not by the top officers"; it is "police [officer] made law." On the fundamental point of controlling officer conduct, Davis was blunt: "Police discretion is absolutely essential. It cannot be eliminated."[62]

Up until this time, police chiefs in the United States had been silent on the issue of officer discretion. It was simply too complex an issue and politically difficult to discuss publicly. (One can only imagine the public outrage if police chiefs admitted that they did not enforce all the laws.) The recognized "bible" on police management since the 1950s was O. W. Wilson's *Police Administration*, which educated more than one generation of police chiefs. The 1977 fourth edition contained not one word on police officer discretion and said nothing about the use of deadly force or physical force and the need to control both.[63] Fortunately, by 1977 a number of police chiefs were already moving beyond this antiquated approach to managing a police department.

As police departments slowly adopted rulemaking in the late 1970s and 1980s, however, they did not follow one aspect of the federal Administrative Procedure Act: a "notice and comment" process through which interested parties can submit written comments on proposed policies.[64] Police chiefs kept the rulemaking process an in-house process, excluding both the public and rank-and-file officers from providing input. This was one of the unfortunate legacies of the professionalization movement. The conventional view of police "professionalism" cast the police, and police chiefs in particular, as experts in their field, with ordinary people having nothing of value to contribute. In 2015, however, the President's Task Force on 21st Century Policing took a very different view, recommending that departments directly "involve the community in the process of developing and evaluating policies and procedures."[65] There are as yet, however, no studies of the extent to which police departments have embraced this recommendation.

Implementing Administrative Rulemaking

The structure of administrative rulemaking sketched out by Davis consists of three basic components: confining, structuring, and checking discretion. The framework remains unchanged today. Written policies *confine* discretion by clearly specifying prohibited actions, for example, deadly force policies prohibiting firing warning shots or shots at moving vehicles. Written policies *structure* discretion by providing officers guidance on handling often ambiguous situations. Vehicle pursuit policies today, for example, advise officers not to undertake high-speed pursuits when roads are unsafe because of rain, snow, or ice. Policies *check* discretion by requiring officers to complete use of force reports and to have them reviewed by their immediate supervisors and then by the department's use of force review board (assuming that the department has created one).[66]

The framework for administrative control of officer discretion outlined by Davis is elegant in its simplicity. Unfortunately, simply having written policies does not automatically ensure compliance by the police officers and supervisors involved. One of the many valuable contributions of the Justice Department pattern or practice program has been the disclosure in its various findings letters of the systematic failure of police departments to ensure that both rank-and-file officers and their supervisors comply with the reporting requirements. Such failures undermine the very principle of accountability in a police department.[67]

Although police officers in consent decree focus groups routinely complain about the "burden" of complex written policies and the reporting requirements, attacking them as "paperwork,"[68] in practice administrative rulemaking makes their jobs much easier. By prohibiting the use of deadly force in certain situations, a well-drafted policy prevents officers from making many decisions that are very likely to cause them grief, through citizen complaints, negative publicity, lawsuits, and internal misconduct investigations. By specifying situations where officers should not pursue a vehicle (as in the case of icy roads, for example), a well-structured pursuit policy helps them make more intelligent decisions and not risk accident, injury, or death to the person being pursued, citizens near the road, and police officers themselves.[69]

The only significant changes in the rulemaking process over the years have been, first, the enormous growth in the number of police activities covered by written policies; and second, the greater detail of almost all policies as they have expanded to cover new perspectives and new issues that have arisen. Essentially, rulemaking has steadily expanded to cover all "critical incidents," defined as incidents that threaten the liberty, well-being, or life of members of the public. The steady growth of written policies, however, has created a new problem of policy and procedure manuals becoming too large and poorly organized and in need of periodic reorganization and revision.[70] Nonetheless, administrative rulemaking triumphed by the late 1980s and early 1990s, Charles Epp argues, and became the basic management tool of today's police departments.[71]

The Great Leap Forward: The 1972 New York City Police Department Deadly Force Policy

The great leap forward in police administrative rulemaking was the new deadly force policy adopted by the New York City police department in 1972. It attracted national attention among police chiefs and police experts and was soon copied, often in modified form, by many departments across the country. The NYPD policy marked the beginning of the revolution in administrative rulemaking and the control of police discretion. Epp labeled the New York policy "the foundation for all subsequent reforms" related to police shootings.[72]

The NYPD TOP 237 (for Temporary Order of Procedure) marked a major advance in the control of police use of firearms in several respects. Most important, it eliminated the "fleeing felon" rule, which was the long-standing national standard that allowed officers to shoot to kill any suspected criminal who was fleeing and replaced it with the far more restrictive "defense of life" standard. The new policy radically confined officer shootings by permitting the use of deadly force only to protect human lives, including innocent bystanders and/or themselves, while also prohibiting warning shots, shots to call for assistance, and shots "at or from a moving vehicle" unless a person or persons in the vehicle were threatening the officer or another person. These prohibitions went a long way toward barring the kind of shots most likely to injure or kill innocent bystanders. Many departments today structure officer use of any force by requiring de-escalation in situations where it is feasible and providing specific tactics that can be used to de-escalate. To check officer discretion, the 1972 New York City policy required officers to file a firearms discharge report after every firearms discharge. These reports were reviewed by the department's Firearms Discharge Review Board, as a further check on officer discretion. Disturbingly, however, Fyfe's important article and Geller and Scott's comprehensive 1992 report *Deadly Force: What We Know* were silent on the responsibilities of sergeants in reviewing officer firearms discharge reports. This was a glaring loophole, one that later was very evident in pattern or practice program findings letters and that consent decrees sought to fix.[73]

Fortuitously, James J. Fyfe, a former NYPD officer, was a PhD student at the State University of New York at Albany and secured permission to study the impact of the new policy. From official NYPD records he reviewed data on 4,904 firearms discharge reports from January 1, 1971, to December 31, 1975. His findings were startling and quickly gained national attention. The total number of firearms discharges declined from a peak of 803 in 1972 to a low of 448 in 1975. Fyfe's inclusion of all firearms "discharges," regardless of the situation, provided a comprehensive picture of the use of firearms by officers. The number of officers reporting firing their weapons per week declined by 29.9 percent, a remarkable achievement in such a very short time. Particularly important, the number of discharges to "prevent or terminate" a crime fell by two-thirds. These are precisely the situations where unnecessary fatal shootings are likely to occur. The number of reported "accidental" shootings increased from 4.5 percent of all discharges before the new policy was implemented to 7.5 percent under the new policy, although this was still a small percentage of all discharges. Overall, Fyfe concluded that "the establishment of clearly delineated guidelines and procedures for the review of officer shooting discretion" resulted in "considerable reductions in police shooting and both officer and citizen injury and death."[74]

The NYPD later began publishing an annual use of force report, which continues today (and is readily available on its website), and the long-term trends are remarkable. The number of persons fatally shot by New York City police officers declined steadily, from a high of ninety-three in 1971 to eleven or fewer between 2012 and 2018. An upturn in the late 1980s and early 1990s was largely attributable to the crack cocaine epidemic that plagued the city; the number of fatal shootings declined when the crack epidemic subsided. The 1972 NYPD policy, in short, had both immediate and long-term positive impacts, clearly demonstrating that administrative rulemaking worked to control the most serious action police officers can take.[75]

Geller and Scott's detailed 1992 analysis in *Deadly Force: What We Know* also identified some important national trends in police shootings, both fatal and nonfatal. Particularly important, they found a major drop in the ratio of African Americans shot and killed compared to whites from 1970 to 1984: from 7:1 in big cities in 1971 to 2:8 in 1979. Cutting the racial disparity in half was a major achievement, as significant as the overall reduction in the number of shootings. Their analysis of the "'long march' toward the defense of life standard" found that, overall, "restrictive policies seem to have worked well where they have been tried."[76]

The adoption of the new NYPD deadly force policy by other police departments stimulated police departments around the country to draft written policies to control officer discretion in other areas of policing. The rise of the women's rights movement led to challenges of the traditional police practice of not arresting husbands or partners who assaulted their wives. A women's rights lawsuit against the Oakland, California, police department alleging failure to arrest male assailants in domestic violence incidents resulted in a settlement that included a new police department policy on arrests in domestic violence situations. The policy stated that "arrest shall be presumed to be the most appropriate response in domestic violence cases which involve an alleged felony." This represented a break with the long-standing sexist practice of American police officers treating domestic violence as not a crime.[77] By the 1990s the three short paragraphs of the Oakland policy had been eclipsed by much longer and more detailed policies in departments across the country. The New Orleans domestic policy, adopted in 2015, for example, was twenty-three pages long, with much detail about the "dynamics" of domestic violence incidents and how to conduct an investigation of an incident.[78] Police departments also began to address the dangers of high-speed vehicle pursuits, which had been almost completely unregulated, and began adopting written policies that restricted them to only the most serious cases.[79] Written policies covering many other police actions would steadily grow from the 1980s onward.

The Push for Administrative Rulemaking

Kenneth Davis's book *Police Discretion* and the 1972 NYPD deadly force policy were major influences on the development of administrative rulemaking, but they were not the only forces at work. In *Making Rights Real: Activists, Bureaucrats, and the Creation of the Legalistic State*, Charles Epp examined the various forces in the 1970s and 1980s putting pressure on police departments "to adopt legal checks on the police" and how in the 1980s "the idea gained widespread support" among a growing number of police chiefs.[80] Progress was by no means an easy task, as it was filled with a mixture of high hopes, uncertainties, frustrating turns of events, and hostility from some influential forces.

Activist civil rights attorneys provided much of the initial impetus as they increasingly recognized that the exclusionary rule was, according to Epp, "no magic lever for reform" and began exploring alternative legal strategies for attacking police misconduct. The National Lawyers Guild took up the issue in the 1950s. The guild's Ann Fagan Ginger co-authored the first-ever *Guide to Police Misconduct Litigation* in 1968, while activist lawyer David Rudovsky conducted the first seminar on the subject at the guild's 1971 convention. Rudovsky and fellow activist attorney Michael Avery, meanwhile, published the first edition of their *Police Misconduct Litigation Manual* in 1978. Both guides provided legal roadmaps for local attorneys across the country and helped spur a tremendous increase in police misconduct lawsuits. The civil rights movement, meanwhile, provided a source of lawyers interested in police misconduct as they added police cases to their existing civil rights law practices.[81]

Some lawyers began to think about pursuing broad injunctive relief against patterns of police misconduct. The Supreme Court, however, ended hopes of obtaining injunctions against abusive police practices in its 1976 *Rizzo v. Goode* decision on the Philadelphia police department. The court held that the plaintiffs had failed to show that the police chief and other top police commanders were responsible for the claimed abuses, or that the officers involved would repeat their abuses sometime in the future. Two years later, however, the court opened a potential new door in *Monell v. New York Department of Social Services*. The decision held that cities were liable for misconduct by their employees where there was a "policy or custom" of violations of federal rights but that individual employees were not liable. In *City of Los Angeles v. Lyons* in 1983, however, the court ruled against Adolph Lyons's attempt to get an injunction against the Los Angeles police department for being stopped and subject to a chokehold on the grounds that he could not show that he was likely to be subject to the same treatment in the future.[82] The *Rizzo* and *Lyons* decisions made it virtually impossible to effect systemic police reform through litigation involving individual cases of police brutality.

One result of the increased litigation and media coverage of police misconduct was a "dramatic upsurge" in lawsuits against police departments. The Americans for Effective Law Enforcement (AELE), a pro-police organization, noted a 446 percent increase in police misconduct suits between 1967 and 1971; by 1976 the number of suits had risen to thirteen thousand nationally, an astonishing increase. The rising number of suits and civil rights activism on police issues reflected the dramatic changes in public expectations about the police. Increased police misconduct litigation made the subject a national news item, and the news media increasingly described police misconduct as both "widespread" and "institutionalized" in many police departments.[83]

Patrick Murphy left the NYPD in 1973 to become head of the new Police Foundation, funded by the Ford Foundation, and began a program of police research and policy advocacy. He and James Fyfe immediately launched a national education campaign among police departments about the need for meaningful policies and training on officer use of deadly force. In 1977 the foundation published *Police Use of Deadly Force*, a short but extremely useful report based on a national survey of forty-five sheriff's and police departments with a list of recommendations, particularly on policy development. The report was influential in the policing world because it represented the authoritative voice of a group of forward-thinking police chiefs and sheriffs at a critical moment when more police departments were revising their deadly force policies. The report recommended prohibitions on shooting "at or from moving vehicles," warning shots, and the "drawing or display" of firearms except where people's lives are threatened. As reform of deadly force policies gained momentum, the International Association of Chiefs of Police (IACP), the principal professional association for police chiefs, struck back. The group's members voted to reject a reform proposal introduced by Patrick Murphy at its 1980 convention by a four-to-one margin. And in a retrograde action the organization endorsed the fleeing felon rule, which many police departments were already rejecting. The IACP also refused an invitation to file an *amicus* brief in the landmark *Tennessee v. Garner* (1985) case, in which the Supreme Court declared the Tennessee law on police shootings unconstitutional where it is used against "an apparently unarmed, nondangerous fleeing suspect." The Police Foundation filed its own brief, written by Fyfe.[84]

By the time of the court's *Garner* decision, an increasing number of police departments had already adopted new deadly force policies based at least in part on the NYPD's 1972 policy. Other police departments adopted revised policies soon after the *Garner* decision in order to comply with the court's mandate. Clearly, a seismic shift in the thinking of police chiefs was occurring regarding the control of officer use of firearms, driven both by the 1972 NYPD policy and the 1985 *Garner* decision. By the 1990s, Epp argues, the idea of written rules to govern police departments and control police discretion had been "transformed from a virtual heresy into a new professional orthodoxy." Three years after the *Garner* decision, the IACP finally yielded to the winds of change and began publishing a series of "Models for Management," presenting specific model policies on a variety of subjects. By the early 1990s the organization had converted the effort into a Law Enforcement Policy Center with model policies on a broad array of issues.[85]

Although administrative rulemaking was firmly established in American policing by the 2000s, a new challenge arose in 2003 with the arrival of the private consulting firm Lexipol, which markets complete policy packages to local police departments and offers training to its clients. As of early 2023, Lexipol had an estimated 8,100 law enforcement agencies as clients, representing about 40 percent of all public agencies; in California alone an estimated 95 percent were Lexipol clients. The appeal of Lexipol's product, especially among small agencies, is that it is easy to understand, as it provides a complete package of policies with updates to agencies that do not have the staff resources to develop their own policies. It also provides a regular flow of daily training bulletins for clients to use with their officers.[86]

Research by law professors Ingrid Eagly and Joanna Schwartz, however, found that Lexipol is not neutral on key policing issues, particularly use of force. The central goal of the Lexipol program is to help its police department clients reduce civil litigation. To that end, its use of force policy rejects most of the currently popular reform proposals designed to reduce officer use of force by controlling their shooting discretion. On the crucial issue of force, Lexipol supports the Supreme Court's *Graham v. Connor* decision, which police reformers and the Police Executive Research Forum regard as far too vague to provide meaningful guidance to officers. Lexipol emphasizes maximizing officer discretion and opposes specific prohibitions on the use of force for the simple reason that if there is no specific policy on a particular police officer action, the officer and the department cannot be sued for a policy violation. These positions place Lexipol at the conservative far end of the spectrum on police reform. Lexipol, as a private enterprise offering services that many departments find attractive, is playing a very important role in undermining important principles of administrative rulemaking.[87]

In an interesting development in 2022, the city of Santa Ana, California, delayed its renewal of the Lexipol contract with a unanimous vote of the city council. The major issue was the Lexipol policy of police officer use of deadly force. One council member argued that "decisions regarding life or death . . . should not be made by a private company, but with community input." Several community members who had lost family members to police shootings added their angry comments to the debate. The Lexipol policy, an ACLU spokesperson explained, was in direct violation of a relatively new California law that changed the standard for police officers' use of deadly force from "reasonable" to "necessary." Lexipol officials (who were not present) claimed that the wording of its policy was not mandatory and could be changed by individual police departments. It is not clear at this point whether the Santa Ana controversy would cause other departments to also reconsider their contracts with Lexipol.[88]

Conclusion

The first seventy years of police reform, from roughly 1900 through 1970, were dominated by the police professionalization movement. The advent of professionalization was a pivotal moment in the history of the American police, as the first serious reform effort. Initially it was a small movement, with reforms in relatively few police departments. The leaders of the movement were serious about what needed to be done and ambitious about achieving it. Their primary goal was to replace the long-standing political influence over police departments with police chiefs who understood what professional management of a large organization consisted of. Across the country, departments created specific recruitment standards, the first formal recruit training programs, and standards of internal discipline. These and other reforms were long overdue, but they scarcely met the demands of the times. Little effort was made on controlling police officer conduct on the streets, and by the post–World War II years, no action was taken on the problem of relations between the police and the growing African American communities in the big cities outside the Southeast. On the eve of the 1960s, virtually all American police departments were completely unprepared for the national racial crisis that was just around the corner. The landmark Supreme Court decisions of the 1960s on policing were an important breakthrough in imposing constitutional standards in policing, but court decisions were piecemeal reforms, covering only the issue at hand in each case. The riots of the mid-1960s created a national crisis, and the leading police experts had few solid reforms to offer. The one important breakthrough in the period covered in this chapter was administrative rulemaking, in which police officer discretion, which had previously been ignored, was covered by a set of written rules. The 1972 New York police department policy on police use of deadly force was a major event and eventually became the primary tool for managing a modern police department.

3

The Creation of the Justice Department's Pattern or Practice Program

The Justice Department's pattern or practice program, the central element of this book, came into being in 1994 amid rising public and congressional concern about crime and conflict between the police and the African American community. The program was authorized by Section 14141 of the Violent Crime Control and Law Enforcement Act. Section 14141 was an unprecedented event in the history of the American police. Never before had Congress authorized federal intervention in local and state law enforcement agencies, with the power to enforce reforms through judicially enforced consent decrees. Surprisingly, there was little congressional debate over Section 14141, which provided the Civil Rights Division of the Justice Department with very little specific guidance on how it should implement the new law. This left the Civil Rights Division on its own in creating the new program from scratch, including the procedures for investigating local police departments and the consent decrees that mandated specific reforms. This chapter also examines the 1991 Christopher Commission, created to investigate the highly publicized beating of Rodney King, an African American, by Los Angeles police officers. The commission's final report proved to be a landmark in the history of American policing, examining virtually all of the Los Angeles police department's major problems from the perspective of organizational transformation. The newly established pattern or practice program embraced the organizational transformation perspective and applied it to the police departments it investigated.

Origins: Rising Congressional Concern about Police Misconduct

Public concern about police misconduct escalated dramatically after the highly publicized beating of Rodney King by Los Angeles police officers on March 3, 1991. George Holliday's home video of the incident was broadcast around the country and aroused national outrage about police misconduct.[1] The vast majority of Americans were not well acquainted with "police brutality," however, and it is likely that relatively few had ever witnessed an actual incident. The video of Rodney King being beaten changed all that.

In Congress, the House of Representatives Subcommittee on Civil and Constitutional Rights wasted no time in holding hearings on police misconduct shortly after the King beating. The Black Caucus introduced the Police Accountability Act of 1991, one section of which allowed the U.S. Justice Department to investigate and bring civil suits against local and state law enforcement agencies and to settle suits through judicially enforced consent decrees. The bill, however, also contained a provision giving private citizens the right to bring suits against police departments, which many members found objectionable, and it was deleted.[2] Civil rights laws were nothing new for Congress. The 1964 Civil Rights Act and the 1965 Voting Rights Act were two of the most important laws in American history. But the 1991 Police Accountability Act was something quite different.

The political climate around the country and in Congress changed significantly with the election of Bill Clinton as president in November 1992. Clinton had developed strong relations with African American leaders early in his political career and was committed to civil rights legislation. Presenting himself as a centrist Democrat, however, he also supported tough anti-crime legislation sponsored by conservative Republicans and many moderate Democrats in Congress. In his 1993 State of the Union address he told the nation, "We must pass a tough crime bill. We need to put 100,000 more police on the street."[3] Democrats and Republicans introduced competing crime bills in September 1993. Senate Republicans found the Democratic bill insufficiently punitive, while Democrats demanded funds for more police officers and legislation addressing crimes against women. In the end, the final bill gave each side something it wanted. Conservatives got very punitive measures, including an expanded federal death penalty; a requirement that states pass laws requiring violent sexual predators to register with state authorities for ten years; and a "truth in sentencing" provision that provided federal funding of prisons in states that required violent offenders to serve 85 percent of their sentence. Democrats got $30 billion to fund

100,000 additional police officers around the country; a violence against women program; grants for "boot camps" for certain prisoners (a fad at the time); an assault weapons ban covering nineteen military-style assault weapons; and an elimination of federal funds for prisoner higher education programs.[4]

The Birth of the Pattern or Practice Program

Section 14141 was tucked into the bill, and there was almost no public debate by members of Congress. This was surprising considering the enormous powers it gave to the Justice Department to intervene in local and state law enforcement agencies. Most likely, members of Congress focused their attention on the other punitive and high-profile parts of the bill. Conservatives wedded to federalism certainly had reasons to oppose federal intervention into local and state law enforcement agencies, but they did not oppose Section 14141. The pattern or practice program was a bold and potentially controversial innovation. Never before had the federal government had the power to bring civil suits against local and state law enforcement agencies and secure consent decrees mandating comprehensive reforms. Yet no significant opposition arose.[5]

Equally surprising, the text of Section 14141 was very short and contained little specific guidance regarding the program it created. The text of the section read:

> (a) Unlawful conduct. It shall be unlawful for any governmental authority, or any agent thereof, or any person acting on behalf of a governmental authority, to engage in a pattern or practice of conduct by law enforcement officers or by officials or employees of any governmental agency with responsibility for the administration of juvenile justice or the incarceration of juveniles that deprives persons of rights, privileges, or immunities secured or protected by the Constitution or laws of the United States. (b) Civil action by Attorney General. Whenever the Attorney General has reasonable cause to believe that a violation of paragraph (1) has occurred, the Attorney General, for or in the name of the United States, may in a civil action obtain appropriate equitable and declaratory relief to eliminate the pattern or practice.[6]

The law contained no specifics regarding the scope or seriousness of violations of constitutional rights necessary to initiate Justice Department intervention in local police departments. Race and ethnicity were not mentioned but were nonetheless implicit in the law's mandate regarding unconstitutional policing. Nor were there any guidelines regarding the nature and limits of the "equitable and declaratory relief" that the Justice Department could seek. As a result, the Justice Department's Civil Rights Division had a virtually free hand in designing the nature and scope of its enforcement program.

Designing the Program

The pattern or practice program was assigned to the Special Litigation Section (SLS) of the Civil Rights Division, which also had sections dedicated to the rights of persons with disabilities, institutionalized persons, juvenile rights, access to reproductive health clinics, and other rights issues.[7]

In creating the pattern or practice program, the staff of the Special Litigation Section was in uncharted waters. No law like this had ever been enacted before. The first task was to define its police reform goals. Section 14141 guaranteed protection against violation of "rights, privileges, or immunities" protected by the Constitution or laws of the United States. Racially discriminatory arrests and stops of people without legal justification are certainly covered by this provision. Other reforms that were included in pattern or practice consent decrees, however, are not, including, for example, public complaint procedures, community engagement programs, and strategies to reform police department policies addressing crime and disorder. The pattern or practice program pursued these goals nonetheless, with the latter two being added later in the program's development.

The staff of the pattern or practice program had a national vision of police reform, which looked beyond its own cases and saw the program influencing reform in police departments beyond the program's reach. In its 2017 report on its work, the program explained that it sought to "help to set a standard for reform" that could influence reform in other departments. To this end, it set out to develop a "common set of substantive reforms" that other departments could adopt. These included restrictive use of force policies with mandatory reporting requirements for officers; reforms designed to reduce if not eliminate discrimination against African Americans, Latinos, women, and other groups; reform of public complaint procedures; mid-management reforms, including use of force review boards (UFRB) and early intervention systems (EIS) to enhance officer accountability, and other reforms. The program staff saw its "cases contribut[ing] to nationwide police reform by promoting a model of constitutional policing."[8]

The Christopher Commission report, discussed later in this chapter, highlighted the profound challenges facing the pattern or practice program regarding the objective of organizational transformation. To successfully combat unconstitutional policing, program staff had to penetrate deep into police organizations and identify their policies and procedures, the existing management culture, and the traditional police officer subculture that supports police misconduct. Police experts have long regarded the traditional subculture as a major obstacle to police reforms over the years. The inertia of all complex bureaucracies is well known, and in policing, the power of the police officer subculture to undermine reforms cannot be underestimated. In a 2015 PERF report titled *Re-Engineering Training on Police Use of Force*, Scott Thomson, then chief of the Camden County, New Jersey, police department, summed up the challenge in a pithy phrase: "culture will trump policy every time." The phrase is essentially a confession of defeat: that the traditional police subculture will find ways to weaken or undermine important new reforms. As will be discussed in chapters 4 and 5, however, a significant body of evidence from the consent decree experience suggests otherwise: that good policies, close supervision, and mid-management review procedures can cause police officers to accommodate themselves to new policies and their strict reporting requirements, with the eventual result that they begin to accept a new view of policing, especially with respect to accountability.[9]

Seven Major Goals of the Pattern or Practice Program

The goals of the pattern or practice program are organized in this book around seven specific goals that are included in consent decrees.[10] Two of these goals are more important than the others. Police officer use of force is the most important, and also the most complex, because it is the most blatant exercise of unconstitutional policing and the one felt most deeply by African American community members. Discrimination is the second most important because it pervades virtually every aspect of policing, from stops and arrests, to officers' use of force, and to police employment practices in recruitment, assignment, promotion, and discipline. This chapter also examines the web of accountability that involves the interactions of officers as a result of program goals. The consent decree-mandated use of force policy, for example, results in close relationships between patrol officers, their supervisors, officers in internal affairs, and the use of force review board. These relationships result in a shared commitment to the principle of accountability, most notably through the requirement that patrol officers must provide complete and honest force reports, and their supervisors are required to critically review those reports. The shared commitments develop and strengthen a department-wide commitment to accountability, an intangible but nonetheless important value that is absent from departments with serious patterns of unconstitutional policing.

Not all of the specific goals discussed in this section are matters of constitutional law. Use of excessive force, traffic or pedestrian stops without proper legal justification, and discrimination against African Americans, Latinos, and women certainly are, but others are not. Procedures for handling public complaints, for example, are not covered by constitutional law principles. The same can be said for mid-management units to enhance accountability, community engagement procedures, and reorienting police department strategies related to crime and disorder. What the pattern or practice program staff understood, however, was that these other reforms were necessary in order to achieve the basic goal of ending unconstitutional policing.[11]

Ending Unconstitutional Policing

The most serious problem in police departments with patterns of unconstitutional policing involves officer use of excessive force. To control use of force, the Newark consent decree, for example, required officers to "use advice, warnings, and verbal persuasion, when possible, before resorting to force"; using de-escalation "as resistance [by a person] decreases"; and not use "neck holds," "head strikes," or force "against persons in handcuffs," except in rare occasions where bodily harm to another person is likely.[12] Other consent decree reforms include restrictive policies to prevent pedestrian and motor vehicle stops where there is no legal justification for a stop. The subject of police use of "force" is richly complex, as chapter 4 will discuss in detail. The Portland, Oregon, consent decree, for example, required a strict use of force policy regarding officer handling of people experiencing mental health crises. It also required the police department to create working relationships with local, state, and private mental health agencies. Engagement with external agencies was seen as a necessary development if the police department was to improve its services to people experiencing mental health crises.[13]

Eliminating Discrimination in Policing

Racial and ethnic discrimination is pervasive in American policing and occurs in virtually all police actions: deadly force, physical force, pedestrian and motor vehicle stops, arrests, and other police actions. Racial and ethnic discrimination has been the most common, but the pattern or practice program also addressed gender discrimination. The New Orleans consent decree sought to end discrimination against women by requiring new "policies and procedures related to sexual assaults and domestic violence."[14]

Improving Public Complaint Procedures

The procedures for receiving and investigating public complaints in the internal affairs units of most police departments have long been dysfunctional, with poor leadership, inadequate staffing, and little in the way of formal policies.[15] This book uses the term "public" complaint procedures because the term "citizen" excludes the many potential complainants who are not officially citizens of this country. Neither police internal affairs units nor the more than two hundred independent civilian review boards that now exist, however, have performed well in terms of sustaining a high percentage of complaints against officers.[16] For this reason, the 1997 Pittsburgh consent decree, the first in the pattern or practice program, devoted twenty-five paragraphs to professionalizing the public complaints process, which is handled by the independent Office of Municipal Investigations (OMI). Reforms included expanding the ways people could file complaints (telephone, mail, and fax); prohibiting "any OMI staff to not accept a complaint"; and having "all interviews of complainants, involved officers, and witnesses be tape-recorded and transcribed," along with many other reforms.[17] All of these reforms were designed to end the willfully indifferent practices of police departments regarding public complaints that were rampant in the 1960s and have continued in many departments. Most of the subsequent consent decrees addressed public complaint procedures, although some did not.[18]

Strengthening or Creating Mid-Management Review Units

Special mid-management level units to investigate all instances of use of force already existed in some police departments, but many others had no such unit. The Newark consent decree required the police department to maintain its existing use of force review board (UFRB) and to expand its role. The decree required that if the review board discovered any "policy, equipment, or training deficiencies . . . the UFRB Chair will ensure that they are brought to the attention of the relevant commanding officer for appropriate action."[19] The corrective actions recommended by UFRBs not only make police departments "self-correcting" organizations but help to sustain consent decree reforms after the consent decree has ended. Early intervention systems, meanwhile, are computerized data systems that allow a police department to identify officers with patterns of problematic performance and then refer them to formal interventions designed to correct officers' problems.

Developing Community Engagement

In police departments with serious misconduct problems, relations between police, community organizations, and relevant social service agencies are typically deeply strained or nonexistent. A commitment to community engagement became a new goal for the pattern or practice program as part of the program's "learning curve" after a few years of experience.[20] The 2017 Civil Rights Division report explained that community linkages are necessary to address "institutional failures outside of police departments, in areas such as social services, medical and mental health care, jails, and court systems."[21] The Seattle consent decree stated that "effective and constitutional policing requires a partnership between the Police Department, its officers, community members, and public officials," and consequently required the city to establish by executive order a Community Police Commission (CPC), which would give members of the community a voice in formulating police department policies and programs. In 2017 the Seattle city council passed an ordinance making the CPC a permanent city agency.[22]

Reorienting Crime and Disorder Control Strategy

Perhaps the boldest pattern or practice program reform goal has involved reorienting police departments' crime and disorder control strategies. No other police reform effort is known to have attempted a similar change. The Cleveland consent decree, for example, required the Cleveland Division of Police to "develop and implement a comprehensive and integrated community and problem-oriented policing model in order to promote and strengthen partnerships within the community, engage constructively with the community to ensure collaborative problem-solving, and increase community confidence in" the police department. Problem-oriented policing programs typically went hand in hand with community engagement and became a requirement in later consent decrees as the pattern or practice program developed.[23]

Developing the Capacity to Sustain Consent Decree Reforms

The 2017 Civil Rights Division report stated that helping departments develop the capacity to sustain consent decree reforms after the decree ended was a major priority.[24] Sustaining reforms has had a long and troubled history in American policing (and is discussed in detail in chapter 4).[25] In pattern or practice program consent decrees, however, there are no specific reforms that explicitly address sustainability. Use of force review boards come closest to that goal, by virtue of the corrective actions those boards are tasked with recommending regarding policy, training, and supervision. Early intervention systems also contribute to sustainability to the extent that they successfully identify officers with performance problems and provide interventions designed to correct those problems.

The issue of sustainability was addressed rather weakly in early consent decrees, but as the pattern or practice program staff developed a better understanding of how it should work, the approach became a more formal method of ensuring compliance with consent decree reforms. In Seattle, for example, a formal memorandum of understanding between the city and the police monitor established a nearly two-year framework during which time "the City will self-assess its sustained compliance with the Consent Decree." The seventeen-page document specified the various audits and reviews that the city was required to undertake.[26] The self-assessment process was essentially a strategy to ensure that a city and its police department assume major responsibility for ensuring that they are in full compliance with the consent decree.

A Work in Progress: The Pattern or Practice Program's "Learning Curve"

Learning on the Job

In its 2017 report on the pattern or practice program, completed just before President Obama's administration left office, the Civil Rights Division declared that "much has changed" in the program since the first consent decree in 1997, referring to two "generations" of settlements, with the consent decrees in the later years representing a "different era" in its police reform work.[27] As pattern or practice program staff members and their consultants gained experience, the program underwent significant changes. Samuel Walker has labeled this the program's "learning curve," the capacity to grow and change in response to new circumstances and ideas.[28]

The learning curve manifested itself in two different ways. The first involved adding additional material to requirements that had appeared in early consent decrees. The second involved adding entirely new goals and programs to newly negotiated consent decrees. The origin of these two developments is not hard to discern. The staff's experience with the initial consent decrees (which were noticeably shorter and less detailed than the later ones) taught the lesson that to address unconstitutional policing, they must also address related issues. The New Orleans consent decree, for example, specified additional responsibilities for sergeants that were not directly related to officer use of force incidents but were mandated by the decree regarding how sergeants were to relate to the community in day-to-day police work.[29] The second manifestations of the learning curve involved establishing entirely new goals in consent decrees, which have included creating new structures for community engagement and also for reorienting police departments' strategies for addressing crime and disorder. The Seattle consent decree, for example, directed the city and the police department to create a community police commission to give members of the community a voice in police policy making.[30] Similar commissions were created by later consent decrees. The driving force behind these new developments was growing recognition among pattern or practice program staff that to achieve lasting reform, they must also seek change in the broader social and departmental contexts in which police departments work.

With respect to setting new requirements for sergeants in reviewing officer use of force reports, the 1997 Pittsburgh consent decree required that "each use of force report . . . shall be reviewed by the reporting officer's chain of command." The decree, however, said not a word about the criteria that supervisors should use when reviewing officer reports, although later consent decrees had very specific requirements. Nor did the consent decree have any requirements related to the duties of sergeants apart from reviewing officer force reports.[31] The New Orleans consent decree, issued fifteen years later, was a dramatic indication of how far the Special Litigation Section had moved in adding new details and requirements to consent decrees. For all but the least serious force incidents, the decree required eight specific steps the sergeants should take, including responding immediately to the scene of the incident, ensuring that the person against whom force was used did not need medical attention, identifying and collecting "all relevant evidence," ensuring that a "canvass" for potential witnesses is conducted, ensuring that all witness officers provide a "Force Statement," and so on.[32] The requirements in the later consent decrees, in short, greatly expanded the routine duties of supervisors and in the process began to reshape the traditional police subculture.

The second manifestation of the pattern or practice program's learning curve involved the creation of two new goals. The first involved developing institutional structures to enhance community engagement. The idea of community engagement was nothing new in policing by the 1990s. It was a central element in problem-oriented policing (POP) programs.[33] In traditional POP programs a police department would establish a partnership with neighborhood residents and/or leaders and together identify a specific crime problem in the area (e.g., street drug dealing or graffiti) and develop a joint program for addressing it. The Cincinnati Collaborative Agreement, discussed below, was a citywide effort.

Problem-oriented policing programs drew upon an idea that had been fermenting in police circles for several years, namely, that the police cannot effectively control crime by themselves and need the active cooperation of neighborhood residents to report problems in the area, report crimes, provide information about suspected offenders, and communicate on other issues. The process of police and community residents working together has been referred to as the "co-production" of police services. The President's Task Force on 21st Century Policing made a strong recommendation that "Law Enforcement Agencies should develop and adopt policies and strategies that reinforce the importance of community engagement in managing public safety."[34] The pattern or practice program's consent decrees, Walker explains, "simply extended the principle of community engagement to accountability-related reforms."[35] The initial consent decree, Pittsburgh in 1997, gave no attention to the police engaging with community groups or leaders prior to the entry of the consent decree, thereby creating the impression both locally and nationally that the decree was a bolt of lightning from above. It is entirely possible that the "backsliding" on reforms that began shortly after the consent decree was lifted was due at least in part to the original failure to develop a community engagement process.[36] Later consent decrees all contained some element of community engagement.

The Cincinnati Collaborative Agreement Model

The inspiration for reorienting police strategies related to crime and disorder came from the 2002 Collaborative Agreement in Cincinnati. The city erupted in protests and violence in April 2001, following the fatal shooting of Timothy Thomas, a nineteen-year-old African American man who a police officer was trying to arrest for several misdemeanor offenses, mainly traffic violations. There had been fifteen fatal shootings of African Americans in the city since 1995, and the shooting of Thomas sparked a riot that lasted for six days, eventually doing over $5 million in property damage, until the mayor finally ordered a citywide curfew. As the Collaborative Agreement was developing, the Justice Department responded to the Cincinnati crisis with a separate pattern or practice investigation of the police department, which concluded with a 2002 Memorandum of Agreement with the city mandating a set of reforms.[37]

The Collaborative Agreement settled several suits charging the Cincinnati police department with racial profiling and other forms of discrimination. Largely through the efforts of an activist federal district court judge, the various parties, including the civil rights litigants, the city, the police department, and the police union, met and negotiated the Collaborative Agreement, which was an unprecedented event in the history of police reform. The core principle of the agreement was that "police officers and community members will become proactive partners in community problem solving." The parties agreed to "implement a policing strategy of community problem oriented policing (CPOP)" as a citywide police strategy to respond to crime and disorder.[38] In earlier POP programs, new efforts were directed at specific problems in specific neighborhoods. One of the principal goals in Cincinnati was to end the tradition of aggressive crime-fighting policing (involving high rates of pedestrian and vehicle stops, frisks, and arrests) and replace it with "thoughtful, planned, and collaborative policing."[39]

The Collaborative Agreement dominated both community and national awareness about police reform in Cincinnati, and the pattern or practice program staff began including both community engagement and problem-oriented policing in subsequent consent decrees, including, for example, Albuquerque and Cleveland.[40]

Other New Program Initiatives

Officer wellness was another new goal in the second generation of consent decrees. The pattern or practice program, however, did not take up the issue of officer wellness until relatively late in the program's development. The Civil Rights Division's 2017 report identified "health and wellness" programs in five different consent decree police departments, including Ferguson, Missouri, Albuquerque, and Cleveland. The report noted that much police officer stress was due to the failure of police departments to provide their officers with adequate resources, including modern computer technology, that would make routine police work both more efficient and effective.[41]

An additional new goal in later consent decrees, and an extremely important one in terms of efforts to reform police organizations, involved mandating a major overhaul of the technological infrastructure of certain departments. An unknown percentage of police departments across the country have antiquated recordkeeping systems with, among other problems, no capacity to track officer deployment and performance. This is a special problem in economically hard-hit cities such as Cleveland and Baltimore. The Cleveland findings letter described the utter chaos, inefficiency, and danger that resulted from the lack of up-to-date equipment and resources. Patrol officers were "sent out to perform dangerous jobs without the ability to effectively communicate with the Division or with each other." Additionally, not all of the department's patrol cars had "computers and, of those that do, the computers do not all reliably work." Even the working computers could not provide access to the department's computer assisted dispatch (CAD) system, so that when an officer responded to a call, he or she could not readily obtain vital information "such as the nature of the call, whether anyone involved is armed, whether shots were fired, how many officers currently are on scene, [and] a description of any suspects." In short, Cleveland officers could not serve the public or fight crime effectively, and often put themselves in danger handling certain calls for service.[42] The Cleveland consent decree required the police department to "complete a comprehensive equipment and resource study to assess its current needs and priorities" to make it possible for the police department to fulfill its basic mission of serving the community effectively.[43]

The situation was even worse in Baltimore, where the court-appointed monitor in its first report issued a dire warning that the department was "stuck in the dark ages of data collection, record keeping and performance." Unless significant improvements were made, the police department "simply will not be able to come into compliance with the Consent

Decree."[44] This statement was the direst assessment of any police department among all the consent decrees.

By the mid-1990s, police departments were increasingly "data driven," requiring a sophisticated computer infrastructure for basic operations.[45] Some departments had computerized data systems for various operations that were in different technological "silos" and were incompatible with each other. A sophisticated computer infrastructure was not one of the original goals of the pattern or practice program, but by the time of the second generation of consent decrees, staff members recognized that it was an essential component of any modern professional police department and needed to be included in several consent decrees.

Sources of the "Learning Curve"

The pattern or practice staff did not create the new goals of the program entirely on their own. The learning curve was aided by several different sources of new ideas. The staff's own experience with the early investigations and consent decrees was particularly valuable in helping them understand the need for certain additional reforms, such as community engagement, which had been missing in earlier consent decrees. The Civil Rights Division's 2017 report explained that the staff "learned from its own experience enforcing Section 14141." Staff members also received feedback from law enforcement officials, consent decree monitors, consultants, and community stakeholders in cities they were investigating or where a consent decree already existed. Additionally, the staff kept abreast of "developments in the social science of police reform," such as de-escalation and procedural justice.[46] Finally, the incoming staff under President Barack Obama in 2009 received a report from an informal working group of police experts that met in Pittsburgh and drafted a set of recommendations for strengthening the pattern or practice program. The thirteen recommendations included providing the program with "adequate resources"; obtaining subpoena authority from Congress to facilitate the collection of documents from police departments and local courts; developing a program of "regular conferences to promote best practices regarding [police] accountability"; and making "special efforts to engage members of local communities." The recommendation on engaging community members was the one the pattern or practice program most actively pursued.[47]

The most visible indicator of the impact of the pattern or practice program's learning curve was the increased length of both findings letters and consent decrees to accommodate both greater detail in mandated consent decree reforms and the addition of new requirements. The 1997 Pittsburgh consent decree, the first in the program's history, contained 83 paragraphs, while the 2013 New Orleans decree contained 492, and the 2017 Baltimore decree contained 511.[48] This expansion was an inevitable part of the growing sophistication of the program's staff and their deeper understanding of what reforms are necessary to achieve the basic goal of ending unconstitutional policing.

The Emergence of Organizational Transformation

The Civil Rights Division's 2017 report on two decades of its work emphasized the objective of organizational change. The first page of the report stated that its cases "focus on systemic police misconduct rather than isolated instances of wrongdoing," later adding that the program was "designed to achieve organizational change within police departments where [internal] institutional failures have caused systemic police misconduct." The reference to "institutional failures" made the point that in police departments with continuing patterns of officer misconduct, the problem lay with the top command of the department and was not caused by the proverbial "rotten apple" officers, the traditional scapegoat for incidents of serious misconduct.[49]

Chapter 1 of this book included a definition of organizational transformation as *the sum total of a set of reforms and their impact on a particular organization.* Additionally, it involves the *changes in the most important policies and procedures, which, interacting with each other, result in a new organizational culture, which includes the values, commitments, and working norms of employees throughout an organization.* The idea of organizational transformation in the United States emerged from two principal sources. First, the organizational change movements in medicine, the airline industry, and other organizations were extremely influential. Second, the 1991 Christopher Commission report on the savage beating of Rodney King by Los Angeles police officers provided a model for applying the concept of organizational transformation to police departments.

Organizational Transformation in Areas outside Policing

The Institute of Medicine's 2000 report *To Err Is Human* created a sensation in the medical profession and among members of the public. The long and well-researched report made the shocking estimate that forty-four thousand people die in American hospitals every year because of preventable accidents.[50] Other studies over the years have offered estimates ranging from a low of forty thousand to a high of four hundred thousand a year. The authority of the Institute of Medicine commanded attention and spurred a concerted reform movement to reduce needless hospital accidents and deaths of patients. The medical profession was not alone on the issue. Organizational sociologist Charles Perrow pointed out in his 1984 book *Normal Accidents* that accident-reduction reform was taking place in "chemical plants, airplanes and air traffic control, ships, dams, nuclear weapons, space missions and genetic engineering" (with undoubtedly far more today).[51]

The focal point of organizational transformation is the basic idea that accidents and accidental deaths, whether in hospitals or nuclear power plants, are caused not by incompetent people but rather by problems inherent in complex organizations. Perrow's book *Normal Accidents* argues that in complex organizations, "failures are inevitable" because of a seemingly small problem and/or a series of small problems. To illustrate his point, he described a commonplace "day in the life" scenario of a person missing a job interview because of a string of small failures: locking his car key and house key in his house; being unable to borrow his neighbor's car because its generator had failed, and so on. Perrow's point was that any one of these and other relatively trivial problems might have derailed the job interview, but the cumulative impact of several of them in a dangerous work setting could lead to disaster. Similar kinds of problems occur routinely in policing. The 911 call dispatcher, for example, might fail to inform the police officer of the presence of a weapon at the scene of an incident, or a dispatcher might send an officer to the wrong address. Perrow emphasizes that "great events have small beginnings," many of which are relatively trivial in nature. He also argues that organizations, not individuals, play the central role in "preventing failures—or causing them." "Time and again," he continued, "warnings are ignored, unnecessary risks taken, sloppy work done, deception and downright lying practiced."[52] The problem is in the organization. The law enforcement profession, however, was very slow to embrace the idea of organizational transformation and did not begin to address it until 2018.[53]

The Influence of the Christopher Commission Report

The second source of inspiration for systemic organizational change in policing was the 1991 Christopher Commission report on the Los Angeles police department and the highly publicized beating of Rodney King, an African American, on March 3, 1991.[54] The commission's report exerted a huge influence on the development of the pattern or practice program, setting new standards for comprehensive investigations of police departments and the broad goal of organizational transformation of the department under investigation. These elements were unheard of in the old days of piecemeal police reform.

George Holliday, who lived across the street, caught the beating on his home video camera. He took the video to a local television station the next day and from there it went viral and was broadcast across the country, sparking national outrage. Until that video appeared, very few people had ever seen a recording of a police brutality incident. The Holliday video proved to be a historic event in policing, marking the beginning of the digital age. The new digital age now includes patrol car dashboard cameras, the nearly ubiquitous cell phone cameras in people's hands, and police officer body-worn cameras. Cell phone cameras quickly became important instruments of police accountability, providing visual evidence of police shootings and beatings, shocking the public and stirring many to call for police reform.[55]

Within a month of the Rodney King beating, Los Angeles mayor Tom Bradley appointed a special commission to investigate the incident and the LAPD and to make recommendations for reform of the department. The commission was chaired by the prominent attorney and former secretary of state Warren Christopher, which gave the commission its unofficial name of the Christopher Commission. The commission's letter to the mayor delivering its report explained that "we have sought to examine every aspect of the law enforcement operations and structure that might cause or contribute to the problem" exposed by the King beating.[56]

And examine "every aspect" it did, in a strongly worded, well-documented, and comprehensive 228-page report that examined the close linkages between different issues within the LAPD. Officer use of force, for example, was closely linked to the attitudes and management style of the LAPD's top command. The report noted the department's "apparent failure to control or discipline officers with repeated complaints of excessive force." The woeful standards of both recruitment and training were also closely linked to officer performance on the job. The department failed to screen out job applicants with a "propensity to violence," which only increased the "possibility" that officers "regularly" meted out "street justice" (i.e., physical brutality) to residents. A major problem was "the LAPD's 'culture' and officers' attitudes toward racial and other minorities," which caused street-level supervisors and mid-level command officers to be "indifferent to the problems of discriminatory conduct" toward people of color. The LAPD's aggressive crime-fighting strategy had for decades been a point of pride among department leaders despite its negative impact on racial and ethnic relations in the city. The report offered a long and detailed review of the dysfunctional governance structure of the LAPD, and the troubled relationship between the police department and the Police Commission, its nominal governing body.[57]

The use of excessive force by LAPD officers was not a matter of the proverbial "bad apples" but was a "management issue . . . at the heart of the problem" of officer misconduct. Some rank-and-file officers told commission investigators that "supervisors were not held accountable by their superiors for excessive use of force by their subordinates." The investigation quickly uncovered what proved to be one of the commission's most important findings: the existence of a group of forty-four "problem officers" with particularly high levels of use of force and citizen complaints. (The identification and analysis of these forty-four officers stimulated the emerging idea of early intervention systems in police departments.) Among top-level command officers there was no "overall analysis" of problem officers and evidently no interest in doing one. Some command officers did not even know that the department had a computerized database with data on citizen complaints, use of force reports, and shooting data. The LAPD top command did not regard civil litigation over police misconduct as a "management problem," did not understand that such litigation was "a reflection of the more fundamental problem of excessive force," and did not see the value of utilizing civil litigation data as a potentially valuable resource for managing the department.[58]

Racism pervaded the culture of the LAPD, and verbal harassment and acts of discrimination were directed at members of the public and racial minority officers alike. Commission investigators retrieved MDT (mobile digital transmissions) transcripts where in one case officers entertained themselves by describing patrolling an African American neighborhood as "huntin wabbits"; one officer quickly "corrected" himself by saying, "Actually, muslim wabbits." In another incident, an officer said that his sergeant told him to tell Hispanic residents "to go back to Mexico." The biased treatment of African Americans and others included orders to "prone out" (to lie flat on your stomach with arms extended); traffic or pedestrian stops without legal justification; and the use of canines in which officers ordered the dogs to attack young men who were "already in custody." A consistent source of alienation and anger among African Americans was the "overly aggressive conduct of officers in encounters with members of the public," which was a major part of the "command and control" culture of the department. Officers were "trained to command and to confront, not to communicate," the report explained.[59]

The aggressive law enforcement strategy was reinforced by the LAPD's field training officer (FTO) program, which commission investigators found had serious problems. The program had "no formal eligibility or disqualification" criteria, which meant that many FTO officers, whose job it was to mentor and guide new recruits, had significant performance problems and disciplinary records, including discipline for use of excessive force. The FTO program essentially gave recruits "substantial training about how to use force techniques" but little on "when force is warranted." The department's entire training program on use of force, in fact, was deficient.[60]

The LAPD promotion system was deeply flawed as it did not consider the disciplinary records of candidates for promotion even though the data were readily available. Officer performance evaluations "often paint[ed] unduly favorable pictures of officers," ignoring such relevant information as citizen complaints and use of force incidents. The commission strongly recommended that all officers' "complaint history," including charges that were not sustained, should be included in their personnel files. Existing files on officers were seriously inadequate because of the "problems with the initiation, investigation, and classification of complaints" in the LAPD's citizen complaint process. The Internal Affairs Division actually "investigated only a very small fraction of all excessive force complaints." When investigating officer-involved shootings, LAPD investigators allowed officers who had witnessed a shooting to be interviewed at the scene of the incident "as a group," which gave them an opportunity to "get their stories straight" (that is, concoct an interpretation of the incident that justified the shooting). Finally, investigators found that the "code of silence," which was pervasive in departments across the country, was "perhaps the greatest single barrier" to investigating alleged officer misconduct. The judge in one highly publicized Los Angeles criminal trial was later quoted as stating that police officer witnesses were "clearly lying." The commission, however, did not investigate this issue.[61]

The Christopher Commission's assessment of the governing structure of the LAPD was detailed and highly critical. The Police Commission was created in 1925 as a board of directors for the department, but the Christopher Commission found that its actual authority was "illusory," because it had little power to hold the police chief accountable. It had a small staff and had to depend "heavily on the Commanding Officer," a member of the department, to review information from the department, spot problems, and make recommendations. This guaranteed an LAPD-favorable perspective on the department rather than an independent one. The Police Commission received only limited information on officer use of force and had "no access" to personnel complaint forms or officer use of force reports. With little information about overall LAPD operations, it could not "participate meaningfully in the budget process."[62]

The commission's report concluded with eighteen pages of recommendations on restructuring the governance of the LAPD, including giving the Police Commission more independent authority and additional resources so it could do meaningful oversight of the department. The recommendations led to the creation of an inspector general for the LAPD, as a unit under the direction of the Police Commission. (Within a few years, the LAPD inspector general emerged as one of the most active IGs in the country.)[63]

In the end, the Christopher Commission's report was outstanding in substance and extremely timely, arriving just three years before Congress established the DOJ pattern or practice program in 1994. Law professor Barbara Armacost argues that the commission's treatment of the organizational culture of the LAPD was a "major theme" of the report and it became a major influence on the pattern or practice program.[64] The commission's report provided the first-ever model of a comprehensive assessment of a police department's problems, with recommendations addressing the "problem officer" issue; the department's toxic internal culture; the failure to hold accountable officers at all ranks; and finally, the evident disinterest among top management in these and other issues. Organizational transformation, in short, was needed if the serious problems affecting the LAPD were to be corrected. It is also safe to assume that the Justice Department staff who designed the pattern or practice program understood that organizational transformation was necessary if the goals of their program were to succeed in bringing about comprehensive reforms in those departments where they brought consent decrees.

The Work of Academic Police Experts

Compared with other organizations and professions, police scholars were very late in taking up the issue of organizational transformation as an approach to police reform. Law professor Joanna C. Schwartz in 2018 became the first to address the issue. She began by noting that most responses to the 2014 fatal shooting of Michael Brown by a white police officer in Ferguson, Missouri, indulged in the familiar narrative of "bad apple" officers and focused on piecemeal reforms that were "not enough." (The Justice Department soon initiated its own investigation of the Ferguson police department.) Tragic events, she argued, need to be seen as *systems failures* (italics in original). Noting the tremendous progress that had been made in medicine, aviation, and other complex industries or professions, she bluntly concluded, "It is time for law enforcement to embrace a systems approach." The promise of a systems approach, she added, "is largely unrealized," and in 2018 "policing is where medicine was thirty years ago."[65]

Lawrence W. Sherman, one of the leading police experts, also delved into the subject in 2018. He began by acknowledging his debt to the existing body of research and the organizational reforms in other areas of American life that had successfully reduced unnecessary and often tragic events in medicine and airline traffic. He focused only on officer-involved shootings, however, and not the full range of police activities needing to be covered by organizational transformation.[66] Sherman made the important point that "merely changing policies was not enough" to significantly reduce officer-involved shootings, adding that "no single intervention is likely to have a lasting effect on fatal shootings." He concluded his article with a six-point plan for "redesigning core functions" of police departments to reduce the number of police-public confrontations. The recommendations, however, did not address the broader organizational culture and priorities of police departments that contribute to unnecessary fatal shootings.[67] Professor David Klinger, meanwhile, in an article on "organizational accidents" that lead to fatal police shootings, made the provocative suggestion that the review of shooting incidents should be greatly expanded to involve reviews of *all* police encounters with citizens. He described the potential benefits but did not discuss the enormous costs of such an undertaking on a permanent basis for large and medium-sized police departments.[68]

Professor Franklin Zimring's book on police shootings, *When Police Kill*, offered a specific set of proposals for reorienting routine police work to reduce the opportunities for shootings. Although the book is the best study of police shootings, his proposals are focused only on shootings and do not address the full range of police activities.[69] Law professor David Harris, meanwhile, in an article arguing for either reinforcing or replacing the exclusionary rule, discussed at length the organizational practices that would contribute to replacing the rule, including early intervention systems, encouraging and reviewing citizen complaints, studying "public feedback" on police/citizen encounters, and various other issues. His proposal, however, includes several of the reforms in pattern or practice consent decrees but contains no mechanism for enforcing reforms, such as judicial oversight and/or court-appointed monitors. A better path to meaningful reform would be to simply ignore the exclusionary rule and embrace the full pattern or practice approach to comprehensive organizational reform.[70]

Investigating Police Departments

Conducting Investigations

When the pattern or practice program began operating, it was immediately "flooded" with requests for investigations and consent decrees from local activist groups and individuals. While an unknown percentage of these requests undoubtedly exaggerated the seriousness of the problems in their respective police departments, there was undoubtedly a large number of potentially valid requests, which indicated the pervasive and serious scope of police misconduct across the country and the intensity of community demands for Justice Department action. This presented the program with the challenge of selecting from among all the communities requesting an investigation the few that merited federal intervention. The Civil Rights Division explained that there was no requirement that it respond to "every allegation or request," but a sound selection process was necessary. With a very small staff and limited resources, the program could handle only a few departments at any one time. The very large departments such as the Los Angeles police department and the New Jersey state police were particularly daunting challenges because of their sheer size and bureaucratic complexity.[71]

In the investigative process that developed, pattern or practice program staff and expert consultants initially conducted a preliminary inquiry of a department where they had information about a possible pattern of serious misconduct. These investigations were confidential and relied on a variety of sources of information, including the local U.S. attorney's office, information from "existing lawsuits" against the department in question, and other sources.[72] If the staff felt that the evidence gathered documented a serious problem, a "justification memo" seeking a formal investigation was prepared and submitted to higher officials in the Civil Rights Division. The staff then screened and prioritized departments using a set of criteria they had developed. The staff looked for departments that had problems "common to many law enforcement agencies" (especially patterns of use of excessive force); or had an "emerging or developing issue" where federal intervention "could have an impact" on police departments it did not investigate (e.g., the systemic mistreatment of persons experiencing mental health crises, as with the Portland, Oregon, police department); or departments where intervention "might help set a standard for reform" (for example, the use of retaliatory force against community residents).[73] In order to focus its reform efforts, moreover, the program staff also wanted to know not just whether there is a pattern or practice of police misconduct, but also "*why* observable patterns of police misconduct occur."[74]

Formal Investigations

Once a department is selected for intervention, a formal investigation is launched. These investigations have typically lasted one year or even longer. On-site investigations involve program staff members, the local U.S. attorney, police subject matter experts as consultants, community representatives, police department records, and interviews with key stakeholders: police officials, city officials, community leaders, rank-and-file officers, and their police unions.[75] The Civil Rights Division explained that police unions and "affinity groups" provide "a critical perspective" on key issues such as "why observable patterns of police misconduct occur." Formal investigations are made public in an official findings letter, which is a public document, and through notifications to local officials (the mayor, the police chief, the city attorney). In the later generation of cases there were "almost always" community meetings designed to lay "the foundation for community participation and engagement in the solutions."[76]

In the early pattern or practice cases, the findings letters were very short, describing the police department's current problems but not discussing the history and context of those problems. Later findings letters went to some length to discuss the broader context underlying the need for federal intervention. The Baltimore findings letter, for example, included a three-page discussion of the history of racism and segregation in the city, which contributed to the current race relations problems of the city and the police department. The 2015 Ferguson, Missouri, findings letter explained that "city officials routinely urge [Police] Chief

Jackson to generate more revenue through enforcement." In March 2010, for instance, the city finance director wrote to Jackson that "unless ticket writing ramps up significantly before the end of the year, it will be hard to significantly raise collections next year." The heart of Ferguson's police problem, the findings letter argued, was that "Ferguson law enforcement efforts are focused on generating revenue." Most of the burden fell on the city's African American residents, giving the revenue-generating practice an odious and illegal racial dimension. Professor Christy Lopez argues strongly that the inclusion of both city and police department wrongdoing (as in Baltimore and Ferguson, Missouri) plays an extremely important role in educating the public and local officials about the problems underlying unconstitutional policing.[77] Background information of this sort provides the public and the media with a deeper understanding of the nature and causes of a police department's abusive conduct and helps develop public support for the subsequent consent decree.

In a more general sense, the pattern or practice findings letters have played a special role in exposing the largely hidden world of police misconduct, as was explained in chapter 1. Local African American residents certainly know about patterns of police abuse in their communities, with especially egregious cases in the past becoming part of the community folklore about the police department. Few people, however, have full knowledge about the range and depth of a police department's problems, and in particular the complex internal policies and practices that contribute to and perpetuate systemic misconduct.

Despite their value in documenting patterns of officer misconduct, the findings letters have been almost completely neglected by police scholars. The valuable evidence in these letters, it should be noted, creates significant problems for a major body of police research that relies on official reports of use of force, stops and frisks, and so on. The findings letters evidence of officers not completing reports or of filing seriously inaccurate ones raises serious questions about the reliability of official police reports and research based on those reports. A 2004 article by professors Jon B. Gould and Stephen D. Mastrofski explored this problem and its implications for research. They conducted direct observation of searches in one police department and found that 30 percent of all observed searches involved constitutional violations; this was despite the fact that the authors gave officers the benefit of the doubt in cases where the constitutionality of a search was ambiguous.[78] The inescapable and troubling lesson from the study is that identifying patterns of racial and/or ethnic bias in policing cannot simply be drawn from official police records but must employ more sophisticated means of data gathering in order to capture important officer conduct that is not recorded in official records.

Reaching Settlements

The Variety of Settlements

Following publication of a findings letter, the pattern or practice staff and the local U.S. attorney enter into negotiations with city officials over the terms of a formal settlement. The program has utilized three different types of settlements, and it is important to clarify the distinctions between them because different terms have been used for consent decrees, causing some confusion.

The term *consent decree* in this book refers to a settlement that is a formal legal action accepted by the local U.S. district court as a legally binding agreement. (Some consent decrees are officially titled "settlement agreements" even though they are legally binding consent decrees.) A U.S. district court judge oversees the consent decree and appoints a monitor, who serves as an officer of the court to assess progress toward compliance with the consent decree. The federal judge has the authority to determine whether the police department has reached full compliance and to order that the decree be ended. That decision removes both the judge and the monitor from the case. Judges rely on the recommendation of the court-appointed monitor regarding the degree of compliance and have the authority to extend the consent decree if the monitor reports that the police department is not yet in full compliance.[79]

A second category of settlements involves a *memorandum of agreement* (MOA) or *memorandum of understanding* (MOU) between the Justice Department, the city, and the police department. With only a few exceptions, MOAs do not involve judicial enforcement or the appointment of a monitor, which means that there is no enforcement mechanism for the recommended reforms. There have been important exceptions to this rule, however. The MOAs governing the Washington,

DC, police department and the Cincinnati Collaborative Agreement had both judicial oversight and monitors. Both MOAs included paragraphs giving the judge the authority to convert the MOA into a consent decree in the event the police department was in violation of the terms of the MOA.[80] The Cincinnati Collaborative Agreement provided that if "the [U.S. District] Court finds that any Party has engaged in a material breach of the Agreement . . . the Court may enter the Agreement [and] retain jurisdiction over the Agreement to resolve any and all disputes arising out of the Agreement."[81]

The third category of settlements involves *technical assistance letters* (TA letters). Controversy has surrounded their usage, however. TA letters are sent to the mayor of the city and the police chief. They are short documents that cover only a few police issues and make recommendations for changes related to those issues. TA letters are not legally binding, however, with no judicial oversight or court-appointed monitor. Nor have any TA letters indicated that the Justice Department will revisit the police department to determine whether the recommended changes are being made. TA letters were most heavily used by the administration of President George W. Bush (2001–2009), which was ideologically opposed to federal intervention into local police matters and brought no new judicially enforced consent decrees. (Other presidential administrations, it should be noted, also used TA letters on occasion for smaller departments.)[82]

TA letters raise an important question regarding federal intervention in local and state law enforcement agencies. Put simply, the question is whether the coercive element of a consent decree, with judicial oversight and a court-appointed monitor, is necessary to achieve actual reform in police departments. The cases of both Cleveland and Miami clearly suggest that coercion is indeed necessary. The Justice Department under President George W. Bush investigated both police departments, Cleveland in 2002 and Miami in 2003, and resolved both investigations with TA letters. The March 2003 Miami TA letter consisted of only twenty-four pages, with half (twelve pages) devoted to officer use of force issues, with some attention to the use of canines and Tasers, among other issues. The letter concluded with a friendly farewell, saying that the pattern or practice program staff "look forward to working with you and the MPD in the coming months as our investigation proceeds." There is no evidence, however, of any follow-up investigations.[83] The TA letter to Cleveland was also very short and nonthreatening. It is most likely that few if any serious reforms were made. The performance of both the Miami and Cleveland police departments worsened over the next several years, although it is more likely that the initial investigators simply did not probe very deeply into the two departments' problems. As a result, under President Barack Obama the pattern or practice program staff returned to both police departments and obtained judicially enforced consent decrees in both cases, Cleveland in 2014 and Miami in 2016.[84] Coercion, in short, appears to be necessary to achieve systemic reforms in large police departments.

Law professor Rachel Harmon, who is a skeptic about consent decrees with coercive judicially enforced reforms, in large part because of their costs, has proposed "alternative remedies" to provide federal assistance to reduce officer misconduct and the related costs; these remedies would be voluntary on the part of police departments. She states bluntly that few people believe that Justice Department consent decrees "have solved the problem of police misconduct." (Chapters 4 and 5 of this book present evidence challenging that assertion.)[85] She recommends, for example, that the federal government fund reports that would show police leaders how to successfully adopt early intervention systems (EIS) and "how to conduct internal affairs investigations," and also to fund research on the "causes of [police] misconduct and the effectiveness of other reforms." Harmon's proposal, however, has several basic problems. First, the Justice Department has been supporting academic research on the police for several decades. Many of the sponsored projects have made significant contributions to our understanding of police work and provided the basis for both reforms and further research. There is also no known noncoercive method of making police departments implement reforms that arise from this research evidence, such as a revised traffic stop policy. The problem is especially acute with respect to the most troubled and poorly led police departments with the worst records of police misconduct, because such departments typically also have poor leadership. Nor is there any persuasive evidence of troubled police departments voluntarily adopting reforms designed to make themselves more respectful of people's civil rights. Coerced reforms, it seems, are the only real way to bring systematic reforms to those departments that need it most.[86]

The Many Roles of Monitors and Their Reports

Court-appointed monitors have played an extremely important role in the history of the pattern or practice program, although their work is not well known outside the world of federal oversight of police.[87] Monitors in fact play many different roles. Their basic role is to monitor the progress of police departments toward compliance with consent decrees and to regularly report the findings to the judge. Monitors' reports are official court documents and, therefore, are public documents available to elected officials, the media, community activists, and the public at large. Additionally, monitors provide technical assistance to departments struggling with compliance (for example, with a new use of force policy). This has included providing resources, such as model policies or other relevant information. Monitors' reports typically cite progress toward compliance that is being made, but in several instances they have been sharply critical about a lack of progress. There has been some controversy over the financial costs of monitors, but there is no systematic study of this issue.[88] The eleventh report of the Albuquerque monitor in 2020, for example, found several serious instances of a lack of progress toward compliance, some of which involved backsliding from previous reports, and in one case apparently deliberate sabotage by at least one command officer. Many of these problems had been identified as early as the monitor's fourth report, suggesting a pattern of willful noncompliance.[89]

Because of the controversies about monitors that have arisen in some consent decree cases, over excessive expenses, for example, attorney general Merrick Garland in September 2021 issued a "set of principles and specific recommendations" regarding the role of monitors in all actions involving state and local governments. As this book is being written, it is premature to assess the impact of these new principles and recommendations on the monitoring process.[90]

The reports of court-appointed monitors are easily accessible on the Internet and are another set of valuable documents generated by consent decrees. Typically, they are released semiannually, and they provide illuminating pictures of the consent decree reform process with detailed analyses about whether departments are making progress toward compliance. In some cases, the monitors' reports have provided invaluable insights into the complex dynamics of changing a police department, for example, departments' failures to move forward with required changes and even resistance to implementation on the part of officers at various ranks. The monitor for the Washington, DC, police department, for example, issued a scathing special report on the complete lack of any progress in the first months of the settlement.[91] Early reports by the monitor for the Los Angeles police department identified and sharply criticized public criticisms of the consent decree by LAPD command officers who in fact were members of the implementation team. This problem was quickly corrected, and the department began moving toward full compliance.[92]

The question of what standard should be used to determine "full" compliance, and thus allow for the end of a consent decree, has been a matter of some controversy and confusion. There has not been any rigid standard, such as "100 percent" or "95 percent" compliance. The subject was discussed at a 2012 PERF "Critical Issues" conference devoted to the pattern or practice program. It was revealed that the 95 percent compliance standard was used for the Pittsburgh consent decree and later also applied to a few other decrees. The conference discussion, however, soon fell into an inconclusive debate over such terms as "substantial compliance," "full and effective compliance," and "sustained compliance."[93] The Civil Rights Division's 2017 report states that it does not have fixed deadlines for achieving compliance because it learned from experience that "institutional change presents different challenges to different institutions." In an important shift, the pattern or practice program changed its compliance standard, explaining in 2017 that the "current generation of reform agreements focuses on definite outcome measures." This is reflected in the Memorandum of Agreement with the city of Seattle, which outlines a nearly two-year process with specific tasks for the city to undertake to measure the levels of compliance in various aspects of consent decree reforms.[94]

Conclusion

The creation of the U.S. Justice Department's pattern or practice program in 1994 was an unprecedented event in American police history. Remarkably, in creating the program Congress did not seriously debate it, and the law itself provided no guidance on what the program should do beyond curb unconstitutional policing by local and state law enforcement agencies. Left to their own devices, the program staff created a set of major goals that were embedded in consent decrees. Those goals included ending unconstitutional policing, particularly with respect to officer use of force, and stops and arrests of citizens, curbing racial, ethnic, and gender discrimination, and improving public complaint procedures, along with several other reforms. As the program progressed, the staff discovered additional aspects of day-to-day policing that needed corrective action. A "learning curve" produced a greater awareness of the need to develop formal procedures for community engagement and to also develop new and innovative strategies to address crime and disorder. The program was also deeply influenced by the 1991 Christopher Commission report, which examined the Los Angeles police department following the beating of Rodney King by LAPD officers that year, and the pattern or practice program embraced the concept of organizational transformation in its work. Despite some shortcomings, and a few consent decrees that ultimately failed, the pattern or practice program has had remarkable success in curbing the worst forms of unconstitutional policing, particularly with respect to officer use of force and pedestrian or motor vehicle stops.

4

Putting an End to Unconstitutional Policing

The work of the Justice Department's pattern or practice program has involved investigating and bringing civil suits against police departments where it has found a pattern or practice of unconstitutional policing.[1] This chapter examines that work by focusing on seven major goals of the program as expressed in specific consent decree requirements. No previous police reform effort has ever undertaken such a comprehensive set of reform goals as the pattern or practice program does. The discussion also examines important collateral issues related to several of the goals, including police officer use of force, police organizations, the police officer subculture, and other dimensions of policing.[2] This chapter also discusses two important themes that have been developed by the program: the web of accountability, which has been a product of several specific reforms; and organizational transformation, which involves how several of the program's goals affect police organizations. A 2021 article by professor Michael D. White and colleagues on achieving full accountability in policing outlines "foundational principles" and "strategies" that closely follow the pattern or practice program's approach.[3]

Ending Unconstitutional Police Practices

The explicit mandate of Section 14141 creating the pattern or practice program is to end unconstitutional policing. The major forms of unconstitutional policing involve police officer use of force, including both physical force and deadly force, frisks and searches without legal justification, and both pedestrian and motor vehicle stops. The discussion here focuses on physical force. Deadly force is, of course, a major issue in policing and the national race crisis, but it is not included in DOJ consent decrees, and therefore is not discussed in detail in this book. The consent decree requirements on use of physical force touch on a wide range of issues, including the conduct of rank-and-file police officers and supervisors, alternatives to the traditional use of physical force, and the impact of new use of force policies on police organizations and the police officer subculture.[4]

It needs to be said that not all of the pattern or practice program's goals implicate constitutional rights. Improving public complaint procedures is a program goal, but complaint procedures do not involve any aspects of constitutional law. The same can be said of mid-management level use of force review boards. As we shall see, they make valuable contributions, but if a department abolished its board, there would not be a constitutional law issue. The same can be said of the goal of community engagement. When well designed, community engagement policies make an important contribution to police relations with community members, but again, having or not having community engagement is not a constitutional matter. What appears to have happened is that the staff of the pattern or program staff, putting constitutional issues aside for the moment, concluded that good public complaint procedures and a community engagement process did make an important contribution to improving policing.

Controlling Police Officer Use of Force

Reforming the Use of Physical Force Policies

The Civil Rights Division's 2017 report explained that "addressing systemic excessive force is one of the core functions" of the pattern or practice program.[5] The New Orleans consent decree requirements on officer use of force begin with a statement of principles confining officer discretion: to "use non-force techniques to effect compliance with police orders whenever feasible; use force only when necessary, and in a manner that avoids unnecessary injury to officers and civilians; and de-escalate the use of force at the earliest possible moment." Using the framework of administrative rulemaking, the new policy confines the use of force with a set of specific requirements and prohibitions. Officers are directed to give suspects an opportunity to submit to arrest without the use of force; are prohibited from using "neck holds" and "head strikes"; are prohibited from using force against persons who are handcuffed; and are not to use force to obtain compliance in encounters with members of the public.[6]

The requirement that officers complete use of force reports for each force incident is a cornerstone of police accountability. The New Orleans consent decree requires officers to "notify their supervisors immediately following any use of force incident." Regardless of the level of seriousness, officers are directed to "write a Force Statement before the end of shift."[7] The end-of-shift requirement is crucial because allowing a delay opens the door to several possible problems. An officer may not remember clearly the details of the incident or conveniently "forget" some details as a strategy for avoiding investigation and possible discipline. Additional time also allows the officer to talk with other officers, primarily those who witnessed the incident, to create a false narrative that justifies the officer's use of force.[8]

For their use of force reports, the New Orleans consent decree requires that officers include "a detailed account of the incident from the officer's perspective"; the reason why the officer was present where the incident occurred; "a specific description of the acts that led to the use of force"; the "level of resistance by the person against whom force was used"; and a description of every type of force the officer used. These requirements are designed to end the long history of evasion and deceit by officers in reporting their use of force. (The pattern or practice program findings letters provide rich detail on this phenomenon.) The consent decree specifically prohibits language designed to exaggerate the behavior of the person against whom force was used, or to use vague terms such as an individual's "furtive movement" or "fighting stance" as justifications for using force.[9] Similar prohibitions are included in virtually all pattern or practice consent decrees. The findings letter on the Cleveland police department, for example, describes an appalling record of officer dishonesty in their use of force reports. Cleveland supervisors, meanwhile, made "little effort to determine the level of force that was used and whether it was justified. In some cases, supervisors take steps to justify a use of force that, on its face, was unreasonable."[10] The failures of both officers and their supervisors to comply with consent decree reporting requirements undermine the basic principle of accountability.

The reporting requirement for police officers and the requirement that supervisors critically review those reports serve to form the web of accountability in a police department, binding them together in a commitment to lawful and professional policing.[11] The most important role of the reporting and review requirements is that they fill what some scholars view as an "accountability deficiency" in troubled police departments.[12] They are necessary requirements of the goal of the pattern or practice program, or even of a police department seeking on its own initiative to establish constitutional policing.

The New Orleans consent decree-required use of force policy appears to work. The court-appointed monitor, in the 2017 *Special Report: Use of Force*, found a high rate of officer compliance with the new policy. There were "no incidents" of officers not reporting where "force was used to overcome resistance" by a member of the public, where force resulted in injury, or where use of excessive force was mentioned in use of force lawsuits.[13] The court-appointed monitor in Cleveland, meanwhile, reported in 2020 that use of force incidents, reported crime, officer injuries, and injuries to members of the public had all declined by 2019, indicating a "positive impact of the new consent decree-required force policy."[14]

Supervisors in the New Orleans police department are also subject to a detailed set of new requirements both for responding to the scene of a use of force incident and for routine day-to day policing. At a use of force incident, they are required to check for possible injury to the person against whom force was used; "identify and collect all relevant evidence" about the incident; determine whether the use of force violated department policy, or "raises any policy, training, tactical, or equipment concerns"; canvass the area for possible witnesses to the incident and interview any who are identified; and ensure that witness officers also complete a required "force statement." If a sergeant finds an officer's use of force report inadequate, deliberately false, or indicating a violation of department policy, he or she is directed to refer the report to internal affairs for investigation and possible discipline of the officer.[15]

The responsibilities for day-to-day police work are even broader. Sergeants are required to "respond to the scene of certain arrests; review each arrest report; respond to the scene of uses of force [and] investigate each use of force; review the accuracy and completeness of officers' Daily Activity Reports; respond to each citizen's complaint of officer misconduct; ensure that officers are working actively to engage the community and increase public trust and safety; and provide counseling, redirection, and support to officers as needed."[16] These new requirements for sergeants begin to transform the role of sergeants in routine police work and instill a heightened commitment to accountability and serving the public. Chapter 5 discusses in more detail the impact of consent decree requirements on the traditional police subculture.[17]

The Challenge of Securing Compliance with a New Use of Force Policy

The challenge of implementing a new use of force policy is to ensure that both rank-and-file officers and sergeants comply with their new requirements. Under consent decrees, court-appointed monitors ensure compliance as part of their monitoring responsibilities. The real challenge arises when the consent decree is lifted and both the district court judge and the court-appointed monitor are no longer active. In the worst-case scenario, officers at various ranks begin to shirk their responsibilities, and when other officers join them the entire system of accountability begins to collapse, undermining the basic contribution of a consent decree. The problem is not unsolvable. An alternative process of monitoring already exists in some cities and can be established in others. In several cities, including New York, Chicago, Los Angeles, and Seattle, police departments are subject to review by an independent inspector general.[18] Inspectors general investigate policies and practices in the departments under their authority, identify problems, and make recommendations for change in public reports. In cities where an inspector general does not exist, it is possible for city councils to create one to handle post-consent decree monitoring or to contract with a private consulting firm with sufficient police experience to handle that task.

Other Forms of Use of Force

Police officer use of force is not limited to officers using their fists, police baton, or other prohibited objects (e.g., flashlights). Two alternative forms of force are available in almost all large and medium-sized departments: electronic control weapons (ECWs) and canines.

Electronic control weapons (ECWs), often referred to by the trade name Tasers, originated as a nonlethal alternative to officer use of deadly force, and were widely regarded as a positive step toward reducing officer-involved shootings and cases of excessive physical force.

Considerable controversy arose, however, when ECWs were initially introduced, with reports of indiscriminate deployment in situations not requiring an ECW-type of control. A 2006 report in PubMed found that among seventy-five ECW-involved deaths between 2001 and 2006, an ECW "was considered a potential or contributory cause of death" in 27 percent, a troublingly high figure.[19] Police departments responded with the development of policies and procedures controlling the use of ECWs, which followed the administrative rulemaking framework of confining, structuring, and checking officer discretion. The Police Executive Research Forum in 2011 issued a report with fifty-three separate guidelines on the use of ECWs, covering everything from department policy to training, reporting, and accountability. Subsequent research found that officers in departments with "the most restrictive" policies used their ECWs "less readily" than officers working in departments with "more permissive" policies.[20]

The deployment of canines is generally considered a use of force, and in most departments is subject to a written policy along the lines of the basic use of force policy. Excessive numbers of bites of community residents by police canines have long been a problem, particularly with respect to African Americans. The New Orleans consent decree *confined* the use of canines by requiring that "canine handlers shall limit off-leash canine deployments, searches, and other instances where there is an increased risk of a canine bite to a suspect." The release of canines is confined to "instances in which the suspect is wanted for a violent felony or is reasonably suspected to be armed based upon individualized information specific to the subject." Additionally, canines can be deployed only with the authorization of a canine supervisor, who is a sergeant or of higher rank. Canines can be released and allowed to bite a suspect only when there is imminent danger to the canine officer, other people, or the canine. The deployment of canines is *checked* by the requirement of a review after each canine deployment. The New Orleans consent decree requires that "the involved handler, as well as all other officers who used or observed force, shall complete a Force Statement before the end of shift."[21]

Although not a part of the pattern or practice program, the Los Angeles County sheriff's department, on the recommendation of its special counsel (at the time its external oversight agency), adopted a more restrictive policy regarding the deployment of canines, with the result that canine deployments dropped by more than half between 1991 and 2001, and the number of bites of persons dropped by two-thirds.[22] The administrative rulemaking framework of confining, structuring, and checking the deployment of ECWs and canines, in short, has successfully reduced improper use of both forms of use of force and made a positive impact on police departments' relations with the community.

Alternative Approaches to Reducing Officer Use of Force

A major new strategy for reducing officer use of force involves providing officers with alternative means of resolving potentially dangerous encounters with members of the public. The three alternatives include de-escalation; training officers in "tactical decision making"; and having a department "duty to intervene" policy.

The most popular and now widespread alternative to officer use of force has been de-escalation.[23] The Justice Department included it in its very first consent decree involving Pittsburgh in 1997 and in nearly all of the later decrees. The President's Task Force on 21st Century Policing, meanwhile, recommended that "law enforcement agency policies for training on use of force should emphasize de-escalation . . . where appropriate."[24] De-escalation has been extremely popular among civil rights activists and members of the public as a means of reducing officer use of physical force. Reform-minded police chiefs, meanwhile, see multiple benefits, including reducing use of force incidents and the public controversies that often follow, and decreasing the number of public complaints and lawsuits against the department.

In the Seattle police department, the new consent decree-mandated use of force policy contains a de-escalation component that is notable in several respects. De-escalation is the second item in the basic use of force policy and appears in boldface type: "2. When safe, under the totality of the circumstances, and time and circumstances permit, officers will use de-escalation tactics to reduce the need for force." The prominent placement of de-escalation conveys to police officers the message that it is a priority when dealing with difficult encounters with members of the public. Additionally, the policy does *not* require the use of de-escalation in all encounters but leaves to officers the decision of whether it is appropriate and feasible in particular situations. The details of de-escalation are covered in a separate subsection of the Seattle use of force policy. Particularly important, it *structures* officer discretion by providing officers with specific tactics they can use to de-escalate a difficult encounter. These include using "verbal persuasion"; giving "clear instructions" to the person involved; avoiding language that might offend the person and escalate the encounter; attempting to "slow down or stabilize the situation" so that additional resource can be brought to the scene; and keeping one's distance in order to "maximize tactical advantage."[25]

The question on many police experts' minds, of course, is whether de-escalation works and works consistently in day-to-day policing. A 2017 assessment by the court-appointed monitor of use of force by the Seattle police found a number of promising developments. Instances of use of force had declined without crime rising and without increased injuries to officers. (Some racial disparities among persons against whom force was used remained, however). Officers were "increasingly able to apply de-escalation and tactical skills" to reduce the number of incidents where force might have been used prior to the consent decree. The report concluded that the use of force in the department "has changed in fundamental ways."[26]

The second alternative strategy for reducing officer use of force is the concept of tactical decision making, which involves training officers in a variety of tactics to keep difficult encounters with members of the public from escalating into a use of force. This strategy, also known as the "critical decision-making model," is principle 5 in the influential Police Executive Research Forum report *Guiding Principles on Use of Force*. A detailed description of training over the critical decision-making model, along with de-escalation, is included in the Baltimore consent decree.[27] Tactical decision making was not one of the pattern or practice program's goals. The concept, and training over it, appear to have developed spontaneously in a number of police departments and then gradually spread to many others.

Tactical decision making involves a time-distance-cover-information-backup framework. Officers are encouraged to "slow the action down" in a developing incident and not automatically try to take control of the situation immediately. The impulse to quickly take control of situations has been one of the major elements of the "warrior" mentality among some police officers.[28] (See the discussion of the warrior versus guardian mentality in the next section.) Additional time gives an officer the ability to gather more information about the situation, reassess it if appropriate, and choose the best response to the incident, including calling for backup. Making strategic use of "cover," or "positioning," for example, by standing behind a telephone pole or parked vehicle, helps ensure officer safety. The most controversial tactic is simply withdrawing from the scene. In discussions among PERF members at a national PERF conference, this step was labelled "strategic withdrawal," a deliberate decision by an officer to avoid immediate danger to himself or herself. (Some commentators argue that the fatal shooting of Michael Brown in Ferguson, Missouri, in August 2014 could have been averted if the officer had quickly left the scene and called for backup.) One police chief told a PERF conference on police training, "There is no shame in retreating and calling for backup" in possibly dangerous situations.[29]

The Police Executive Research Forum has been particularly active in seeking ways to reduce officer-involved shootings. Its 2016 report *Guiding Principles on Use of Force* brought together the main points from previous PERF reports on de-escalation, re-engineering police training, and tactical decision making. It also included a sharp critique of the Supreme Court's 1989 decision in *Graham v. Connor*, which it regards as too vague and permissive on officer use of force.[30] The *Graham* decision, it argues, explains "what police officers *can legally do* in possible use-of-force situations, but it does not provide specific guidance on what officers *should do*" (italics in original), by using de-escalation, for example. The result, as many have argued, is some shootings that are "lawful but awful," meaning that they comply with the letter of the *Graham* decision but appear unnecessary and tragic in the minds of the public and many police experts. The PERF report includes thirty guiding principles, with an explanatory discussion for each. Principle 2 states that police department policies should "go beyond the minimum requirements of *Graham v. Connor.*"[31] In the history of police reform, the PERF statement on the *Graham* decision is undoubtedly the first time a leading police professional association has urged police departments to adopt policies more restrictive on police officer conduct than what is required by the Supreme Court.

A third alternative to using force is the recent development of department policies informing officers that they have a "duty to intervene" or "duty to intervene and report" misconduct by other officers.[32] These policies represent a direct challenge to the solidarity of the officer rank and file and the code of secrecy in the traditional police subculture.[33] Under the traditional code of secrecy, officers do not report, either verbally, in reports, or court testimony, misconduct by other officers. In the 1994 Mollen Commission investigation of a major corruption scandal in New York City, one officer testified that if an officer tells on another officer, "he's going to be labeled as a rat."[34] Many police experts regard the code of secrecy as perhaps the greatest obstacle to police accountability for the simple reason that other officers are the best sources of information about officer misconduct incidents. The first study of the police subculture, William A. Westley's *Violence and the Police*, concluded that secrecy was "a shield against the attacks of the outside world" on the police, embodying "loyalty" to other officers and group "solidarity."[35] The code of secrecy has continued largely because over the years police experts and scholars have given it little attention. Rank-and-file officers who do discuss it with the media or outside investigators expose themselves to retaliation by other officers. The 2016 San Francisco Blue Ribbon Panel on the San Francisco police department provides perhaps the best discussion of the many retaliatory tools available to officers who want to silence a potential or actual whistleblower, including but not limited to frequent transfers, desk duty, or assignment to undesirable locations in the city. The Police Executive Research Forum strongly endorsed duty to intervene policies in its 2016 publication *Guiding Principles on Use of Force*.[36]

The Minneapolis police department had adopted a "duty to intervene" policy in 2016, before the 2020 murder of George Floyd. The policy provided that an officer who "observes another employee use any prohibited force, or inappropriate or unreasonable force (including applying force when it is no longer required), must attempt to safely intervene by verbal and physical means, and if they do not do so shall be subject to discipline to the same severity as if they themselves engaged in the prohibited, inappropriate or unreasonable use of force." The nationally publicized death of George Floyd exposed the fact that the other three officers at the scene did not intervene to stop Chauvin.[37] A scathing report by the Minnesota Department of Human Rights in 2022 found that in 76.5 percent of inappropriate use of force incidents, "another officer should have but failed to intervene."[38] The obvious question is, why did they not intervene? The most plausible answer is that the department failed to train its officers over the policy. This would have included academy training for new recruits, field officer training for new officers just out of the academy, and annual in-service training for all officers. Clearly, there was a breakdown in training and supervision in the department on this very important policy.

A variation on the duty to intervene policy is the EPIC program, developed by the New Orleans police department. (It grew out of the consent decree reform atmosphere in the department but was not mandated by it.) The acronym EPIC stands for Ethical Policing Is Courageous. The choice of the word "courageous" represented a shrewd strategy. Stopping misconduct by another officer and reporting it directly challenge the norms of the traditional police subculture, with its emphasis on secrecy, group solidarity, and not reporting misconduct by other officers.[39] The term "courageous" conveys an image of strength. An officer could stop another officer's unlawful conduct and take pride in having done so. A key element of the EPIC program involves "redefin[ing] critical loyalty": loyalty to the department and the mission of the police, and not just to fellow officers.[40]

The EPIC program includes "train[ing] officers and supervisors to identify danger signs" in other officers who might be likely to engage in some form of misconduct; equipping officers "with the skills they need to intervene before problems occur/escalate, and to do so safely"; "support[ing] and protect[ing] officers who do the right thing," which is extremely important given the lack of whistleblower protection in American police departments; and finally, providing officers with "resources to help them make ethical decisions."[41] Intervening to stop another officer's misconduct is essentially a "whistleblower" action. The leaders of the law enforcement profession, academics, and journalists, however, have given almost no attention to the crucial issue of protecting police whistleblowers.[42] The EPIC program quickly gained considerable national publicity, and a number of police departments adopted it. At this point, however, there is no independent research on the extent of the usage of the EPIC program or duty to intervene policies and their effectiveness in reducing police misconduct. Nonetheless, it is an extremely important innovation with respect to controlling the use of force in policing while also cultivating higher ethical standards among officers. The EPIC program was soon joined by the ABLE (Active Bystander in Law Enforcement) program. Training in the ABLE program soon reached over two hundred police departments nationally.[43]

The policies discussed in this section indicate that police departments across the country have in recent years adopted alternative strategies to reduce officer use of force. These strategies have widened the subject of the use of force issue by not focusing narrowly on officer use of force incidents and instead providing officers with new tools for resolving problematic encounters. Police departments have widely adopted de-escalation, and the pattern or practice program has included it in many consent decrees. To the extent that new policies and practices are adopted and used by officers on the street, they create a new style of policing, one with fewer incidents of use of force. An important consequence is that members of the community are very likely to begin to notice the change in officer conduct for the better, and this reshapes their image of a police department and their respect for it. Taking the long view, we can see that this is no small achievement.

The three policy changes discussed in this section are admirable efforts to reduce police officer use of physical force. Professor David Thacher proposes a different model for thinking about how they fit into a police department, which he calls the "learning model." The model involves systematic review of *all* incidents of officer use of force, which requires "relentless self-scrutiny" designed to identify systemic organizational flaws. In most police departments today, force reviews are essentially "compliance reviews" to determine whether or not an officer complies with the relevant use of force policy. The learning model approach, on the other hand, looks not just for outright failures but also for "weak signals," defined as departures from official policy that create serious problems. Officer use of physical force can be affected by many different features of a police department: inadequate policies, improper training, poor communications with the 911 call center and other officers, inadequate field training for officers just out of police academy, and a poorly designed in-service training program for all sworn officers.

Systemic review of all use of force incidents can identify these problems in the various parts of the department. (Use of force review boards, discussed later in this chapter, play a similar role.)[44]

The "Culture War" over Police Use of Force

Although enthusiastically adopted by many police departments and embraced by police experts and community leaders, the policies of de-escalation and tactical decision making have serious opponents among some advocates of tough anti-crime policing. These groups, notably the very pro-police Force Science Institute, exaggerate the dangers of day-to-day policing and argue that officers must at all times be on guard against attacks that threaten their safety and even their lives. Professor Seth W. Stoughton explains that the "warrior" mentality emerged in the 1960s and taught officers "to consider each civilian they interact with as a potential threat" and "to approach every civilian interaction as a potential deadly-force encounter." It needs to be said that no research on police use of force supports this nightmarish version of the dangers posed by "each citizen" in police work.[45]

What has emerged in recent years is a "culture war" between the advocates of alternatives to officer use of force whenever possible and the hardline view that officers must always be on guard against attacks from the public. The culture war took on a new dimension with the 2015 publication of the extremely influential report by Sue Rahr and Stephen Rice, *From Warriors to Guardians: Recommitting American Police Culture to Democratic Ideals*. The title of their paper frames the debate in terms of a democratic society and the responsibility of the police to serve the public. It begins by stating bluntly that "protecting constitutional rights is the mission of police in a democracy." To that end, the police should adopt procedural justice in routine police work because "people don't care as much about crime rates as they do about how they are treated by the police." The us-versus-them attitude of the traditional police subculture is antithetical to this proposition. The "guardian" mentality pays dividends in better policing. Positive police-public encounters encourage people to cooperate with the police, in "alerting them to problems in the neighborhood, identifying criminal suspects, and other forms of cooperation."[46]

Organizational Impacts of a New Use of Force Policy

Developing a new use of force policy is no simple matter for a police department. The impacts are many and pose challenges that are felt throughout the department and the community.[47] The first organizational challenge is that changing even one policy affects officers of different ranks and different units. Retraining rank-and-file officers over a new use of force policy needs to be implemented immediately, with a special in-service training session. That process alone is time-consuming and expensive. A new policy needs to be reinforced through annual in-service training for all rank-and-file officers, supervisors, the heads of the various training units, and members of the use of force review board. Additionally, if there is an independent public complaint review board, that agency must also be informed about the new policy. Finally, it is important to also inform community stakeholders and members of the news media in order to alert them to positive changes that are being made in the police department.

New policies on use of force also impact the police officer subculture in profound ways. They clearly tell rank-and-file officers that the old ways of doing policing are no longer acceptable and in this respect begin to reshape how rank-and-file officers and sergeants think about their jobs, police work in general, and how they treat members of the public. A positive change in a department's use of force policy, along with others, contributes to the reshaping of the police officer subculture.[48] Introducing a new use of force policy quietly has the unfortunate effect of failing to persuade community members that the police department is serious about reform and about reducing officer use of force in particular. If they are properly informed, people begin to notice a change in how police officers treat them, especially with fewer cases of excessive force. The change, of course, is most noticeable to African Americans and Latinos, who have been the greatest victims of unconstitutional police practices. The net result is a significant positive gain in community relations, with fewer unlawful police actions, fewer public complaints, and more respectful treatment by officers in routine encounters. It basically represents an overall improvement in a police department's image among members of the public. This is a major achievement for consent decree-related reforms and for American policing generally.

Finally, new policies help to develop a web of accountability among officers with different ranks and in different units. A revised use of force policy, for example, involves new relationships among patrol officers, their supervisors, officers in the internal affairs unit, and officers serving on the use of force review board. These new relationships, the Civil Rights Division explained, have the effect of "improving systems for supervising officers and holding them accountable for misconduct."[49]

Ending Unconstitutional Traffic Stops

Traffic stops have been a major issue in policing for many decades, particularly with respect to race and ethnicity. African Americans have charged that they are stopped because of their race and not because of a violation of the law, and there is substantial research supporting this claim. The issue exploded into a national crisis in the 1990s; law professor David Harris gave it the label of "driving while black," rather than racial profiling.[50] The Justice Department pattern or practice program focused on traffic stops in two of its consent decrees, one with the New Jersey state police (NJSP, which is primarily focused on traffic enforcement) and the other with the East Haven, Connecticut, police department, where the problem primarily involved discrimination against Latino residents.[51]

The New Jersey state police consent decree required an elaborate accountability procedure and data collection system. Data collection and analysis are two of the key elements of the pattern or practice program, giving law enforcement agencies the capacity to analyze patterns and trends and identify patterns of possible racial and/or ethnic discrimination. The data collection procedures transformed the state police into a "data-driven" agency, in which the collection and analysis of data are central to the agency's mission.[52] White and colleagues argue that "without data collection and analyses positive change at both the organizational and individual officer levels would be impossible."[53]

To hold New Jersey state troopers accountable for their conduct and ensure their safety, the consent decree required troopers making a vehicle stop to call in to the communications center "at the beginning of a stop before the trooper approaches the stopped vehicle." The early call-in requirement is designed to prevent officers from making "rogue" or undocumented stops that evade the department's accountability procedures and allow officers to conceal a certain number of stops of African American drivers.[54] Incident documentation also required officers making a traffic stop to report nineteen separate data items. They include, but are not limited to, the name and identification number of the officer initiating the stop; the date, time, and location of the stop; the license plate number and description of the stopped vehicle; the race or ethnicity and gender of the driver and any passengers; the reason for the stop; and whether any persons were arrested and criminal charges filed.[55]

The long list of items to be reported serves two purposes. First, the data hold troopers accountable for their actions in stops. Failure to report a request for a consent search of a vehicle when a search was conducted, for example, would expose a trooper to discipline upon review of the incident by supervisors. Troopers are also less able to disguise the race or ethnicity of the driver and thereby appear to be policing equitably. Second, the rich detail of the data permits close analysis by supervisors and command officers in identifying patterns and trends in vehicle stops, including data on searches, use of force, and the race, ethnicity, and gender of drivers, passengers, and officers who initiated questionable stops. The sophisticated data system makes the New Jersey state police a "data-driven" organization, in step with other modern law enforcement agencies.[56]

The consent decree also required that all stops be recorded on MVR (mobile video recorder) equipment, thereby adding an additional layer of documentation of stops.[57] Each trooper's supervisor is required to review all traffic stop reports within fourteen days of each incident and also to review MVR recordings on a random basis. If a supervisor identifies a stop that appears to involve a possible violation of department policies, he or she is directed to refer the case to the agency's Professional Standards Bureau for investigation and a determination of whether a formal intervention is needed for the trooper involved.[58]

As an additional layer of accountability, the NJSP consent decree requires the department to develop and implement an early intervention system (named the Management Awareness Program, or MAP, in the NJSP).[59] The MAP includes data on stops, searches, and arrests; data on both public compliments and misconduct investigations; and civil suit data involving troopers, among other items.[60] On a quarterly basis, supervisors are required to analyze the MAP data, with a special focus on patterns and trends regarding the racial, ethnic, and gender patterns in stops. Analyses are also required to "include evaluations of trends and differences over time and evaluations of trends and differences between troopers, units, and subunits." Each supervisor is then authorized to implement any appropriate changes or remedial measures indicated by the MAP data.[61]

Despite many important gains through the consent decree, troubling questions remain about whether the consent decree reduced racial and ethnic disparities in persons who are searched. Professors Jeffrey Fagan and Amanda Geller analyzed data on 275,000 vehicle stops by NJSP troopers on the New Jersey Turnpike and, focusing on searches only, found that African American and Latino drivers who were stopped were "more than twice as likely as White drivers to be searched regardless of officer race." They concluded that "despite institutional reforms" under the consent decree, there were "no tangible gains in distributional equity" with respect to searches. Racial and ethnic disparities in searches continued and the authors suggest that a "failure to attend to race" in traffic stops has allowed the disparities to continue. They then made the provocative comment that there is a "residual component of [officer] discretion that is beyond the reach of training, oversight, and institutional design" that is responsible for the disparities, adding that "bias reflects bad habits of mind, which are not easily broken by a dose of training."[62] The evidence indicates that racial and ethnic biases may be far more deeply rooted in policing than most reformers want to believe and cannot be reduced or eliminated by changes in policies or training. This troubling issue presents a challenge for other police reforms, whether under a consent decree or not. (The following section includes a discussion of professor Jennifer Eberhardt's provocative argument on this issue.)

Ending Discrimination in Policing

Ending discrimination based on race, ethnicity, gender, or sexual orientation is a high-priority goal of the pattern or practice program. The 2017 report by the Civil Rights Division labelled it "a long-standing priority."[63] Given this country's historic race problem and the continuing problems today in police relations with African Americans and Latinos, this priority is hardly surprising. Pattern or practice consent decrees have adopted two different strategies for ending discrimination and creating bias-free policing: formal policies prohibiting the use of race or ethnicity in routine police work, and training programs on how officers are to conduct themselves in encounters with members of the public.

A Bias-Free Policing Policy

The consent decrees for several departments contain a formal statement prohibiting the improper use of race or ethnicity in routine police work. The consent decree over the Newark, New Jersey, police department, for example, provides that the police department "will prohibit officers from considering any demographic category when taking, or refraining from taking, any law enforcement action, except when such information is part of an actual and credible description of a specific suspect in an ongoing investigation that includes other appropriate non-demographic identifying factors." The language of the policy is taken directly from the influential 2001 Police Executive Research Forum policy statement on racially biased policing, which states that "officers shall not consider race/ethnicity in establishing either reasonable suspicion or probable cause." It adds the important clarifying exception that "officers may take into account the reported race or ethnicity of a specific suspect or suspects based on trustworthy, locally relevant information that links a person or persons of a specific race/ethnicity to a particular unlawful incident(s)."[64] The PERF policy statement and the Newark policy, in short, use an administrative rulemaking framework to *confine* officer discretion by specifying prohibited actions and to *structure* discretionary decisions by specifying circumstances when racial or ethnic factors can legitimately be used.

Bringing Procedural Justice to Police Stops

The most creative bias-free training program is in the New Orleans police department consent decree. The required training for officers on how to conduct a stop incorporates the basic principles of procedural justice. Officers are required to "introduce themselves" at the beginning of a stop; explain the reason for the stop; ensure that the stop is not unnecessarily long; and act with "professionalism and courtesy throughout the interaction regardless of any provocation." This language is taken from the academic literature on procedural justice, which has had a significant influence on policing in recent years.[65] The explicit warning about not responding to provocation is designed to end the long police tradition of retaliating against any hostile words or conduct by persons being stopped. (Police officers have long labelled such behavior as "contempt of cop" and deserving of retaliation.) A nearly identical procedural justice training on stops is also included in the consent decree over the Los Angeles County sheriff's department.[66]

Introducing procedural justice as a requirement in making stops contributes to the process of reshaping the traditional police officer subculture with respect to how they treat people in the community, including those people they believe may be violating the law. The old police adage that rank-and-file officer "culture trumps policy" and thereby undermines reform efforts is not necessarily true. The example of procedural justice training for police-public encounters suggests just the opposite: that policy can reshape the police officer culture.[67] Additionally, if officers fully embrace procedural justice, members of the public will eventually begin to notice and begin to tell friends and acquaintances about this new phenomenon. Over time, the result will be a new culture of officer-community member interactions.

The Challenge of Unconscious Bias

The issue of unconscious bias, or implicit bias, related to race, ethnicity, immigration status, sexual orientation, social class, and other factors has become a much-discussed topic in American society. Inevitably, it has also become an issue in policing (although it has not been a part of the various consent decrees). Lorie A. Fridell, founder and director of Fair and Impartial Policing (FIP), an organization devoted to training on unconscious bias, explains that the "key characteristics" of implicit bias involve "categor[izing] individuals and link[ing] them to the stereotypes associated with their groups"; this categorizing occurs "outside of conscious awareness."[68] Eberhardt, a prominent expert on bias, argues that negative stereotypes about different groups are deeply rooted in the history and culture of people around the world and that the United States is no exception to that rule. In American policing, a common implicit bias is the association of young African American men with "danger" and crime, an association that underpins aggressive policing.[69] Criminal justice scholars have documented the racial and ethnic disparities that exist throughout the criminal justice system, from police stops and use of force, to bail decisions and sentencing decisions. Law professor Michelle Alexander's enormously successful book *The New Jim Crow* argues that the nation's huge prison population was built on a set of racially biased decisions throughout the justice system.[70]

Many American police departments have embraced the issue of unconscious bias and sought out training to prevent it from adversely affecting police officer conduct. The Fair and Impartial Policing project offers an array of twenty-nine different courses covering police officers, firefighters, emergency medical service personnel, prosecutors, juvenile justice officers, and probation officers, and has trained officers in police departments across the country. Training on Fair and Impartial Policing principles, for example, was a requirement in the 2017 Baltimore consent decree.[71]

Eberhardt, the leading expert on the subject of bias, is, however, highly skeptical about the possibilities for reducing unconscious bias among police officers through training. Based on her experience with a police training program on bias, she confessed in her book *Biased* to feeling "helpless" after watching videos of high-profile police shootings. She fears that "people put too much faith in the power of these trainings." They "can educate," she concluded, but "not eradicate" the various forces that shape individuals' unconscious beliefs about the world and people.[72]

Eberhardt then made an observation that has profound implications for the goals of the pattern or practice program and other police reforms. "The way to curb bias" in policing, she argues, is not to try to eradicate beliefs that people have held all their lives but "by simply training them [police officers] to do their jobs better."[73] She did not explain what "better" means, but most police experts do understand. Consent decree reforms on police officer use of force, for example, accomplish the task she describes. When police officers comply with a new and restrictive use of force policy by using de-escalation, they are doing their job "better" by not using force in many encounters. When they use principles of procedural justice in making a stop, they are doing their jobs "better." The result will be a reduction in incidents of use of force, especially excessive force, and a reduction in force against African Americans and Latinos in particular. When traffic enforcement officers no longer stop vehicles without proper legal justification, they too will be doing their jobs "better," and the result will be a reduction in racial and ethnic disparities in stops. These examples illustrate the point that written policies, properly enforced by their supervisors, can reshape both police conduct and the traditional police officer culture. Both changes can lead to policing that is more lawful, professional, and respectful.

Ending Discrimination in East Haven, Connecticut

The investigation and consent decree over the East Haven, Connecticut, police department (EHPD) focused primarily on discrimination against Latino residents. East Haven is a town of about twenty-nine thousand people, 10 percent of whom identify themselves as Hispanic or Latino.[74] The Civil Rights Division's findings letter concluded that the department "engages in a pattern or practice of systematically discriminating against Latinos," including "unlawful searches and seizures and use of excessive force." The statistical evidence indicated that "Latino drivers are disproportionally targeted for traffic stops"; that officers use "unacceptable justifications" for stops of Latinos; and that officers retaliate against Latinos who complain of discriminatory treatment.[75]

The East Haven consent decree includes a section on bias-free policing, with a major section on language assistance. The bias-free policing requirement is similar to those found in other consent decrees, with a policy statement based on the 2001 PERF recommendation, that the department prohibits officers from "using [a] demographic category . . . in conducting stops or detentions, or activities following stops or detentions, except when engaging in appropriate suspect-specific activity to identify a particular person or persons."[76]

The consent decree provisions related to language assistance are, arguably, some of the most important parts of the East Haven consent decree. They require the department to "develop and implement a comprehensive language assistance plan and policy" to "ensure that all

EHPD personnel take reasonable steps to provide timely, meaningful language assistance services to LEP [limited English proficiency] individuals they encounter." The department is also required to regularly assess "the proficiency and qualifications of bilingual staff" if they are to become authorized interpreters. Most important in terms of basic police services, the consent decree requires the department to have access to interpreters for 911 calls, for "interrogations and interviews," and also for receiving citizen complaints from individuals not proficient in English.[77] The community engagement section of the consent decree, meanwhile, requires the department to "create robust community relationships and engage constructively with the community to ensure collaborative problem-solving, ethical and bias-free policing."[78] The consent decree requirements related to ending bias against Latino people, in short, are not confined to police patrol activity but extend to all police officer actions, thereby affecting the organizational culture of the entire department.

Ending Gender Discrimination in New Orleans

The pattern or practice program investigation of the New Orleans police department directly addressed the issue of gender discrimination. The findings letter found that "inadequate policies and procedures, deficiencies in training, and extraordinary lapses in supervision have contributed to a systemic breakdown in NOPD handling of sexual assault investigations." There were also "systemic deficiencies in the handling of domestic violence cases, although not to the degree evident in sex crimes."[79] The focus on gender discrimination in the New Orleans police department represented one of the priorities of the pattern or practice program, specifically focusing on "an emerging or developing issue" in policing such that the reform could set an example for other departments across the country.[80]

The resulting consent decree mandated sweeping reforms in both the sexual assault and domestic violence units. The sexual assault unit is required to "develop and implement clear policies and procedures governing its response to reports of sexual assault," clearly indicating that the unit had been operating without clear policies and possibly no policies at all. Officers who are the first responders to sexual assault calls for service are required to document their observations and actions, including statements made by victims, witnesses, or other persons. The department is directed to "provide clear and detailed guidelines for steps at each stage" of responses to reported sexual assaults. These stages include "identifying, locating, and interviewing witnesses and suspects; collaborating with victim advocates; [and] collecting evidence."[81]

The consent decree specifically required the sexual assault unit to undertake a program of community engagement with a variety of stakeholders. These groups included "the DA [district attorney], community service providers, and other stakeholders." The department agreed to create a "committee of representatives from the community," which would review the operations of the sexual assault unit on a semiannual basis, with a special focus on sexual assault calls that had been dismissed as "unfounded" and a random sample of open investigations. The Civil Rights Division viewed the linkages with social service agencies and community stakeholders as fulfilling the goal of "recognizing the links between policing and other criminal justice and social systems."[82] This arrangement represents a form of external monitoring by key community stakeholders and was an important step in the direction of genuine community engagement.

Similar requirements applied to the domestic violence unit. A 2016 report by the court-appointed monitor found substantial improvement of the handling of domestic violence calls and concluded that the department was in "full or near full compliance" with several consent decree requirements. Police investigators, for example, were making "attempts to locate victims"; including the "elements of the crime" in support of the charges against the accused; taking "follow-up action" to provide "safety and/or protection advice" for victims who were at risk after the original incident; and, in general, conducting "professional and proactive" initial investigations. The monitoring team, for example, was able to locate the incident report by the officers who were the initial responders in 93 percent of all cases it examined, indicating a new level of professionalism with regard to recordkeeping.[83]

The New Orleans consent decree addressed gender bias not through a single policy change but by requiring broad changes in the policies and procedures of the two units that deal with women as victims of sexual assault and domestic violence. It also added an important element of external monitoring and community engagement with a range of stake-holders. It is also likely that the new policies and procedures had the effect of reshaping the attitudes toward women among the officers as-signed to the two units.

Improving Public Complaint Procedures

Procedures for handling public complaints against police departments have been a major issue in policing since the 1960s, as discussed in chapter 2. The reports of the 1967 President's Crime Commission and the 1968 Kerner Commission documented the failure of police depart-ment complaint procedures, confirming the criticisms expressed by civil rights activists. The President's Crime Commission put it bluntly: "Too few departments today have adequate procedures for dealing with complaints."[84]

Improving public complaint procedures has been one of the major goals of the pattern or practice program.[85] This book uses the term "public" rather than "citizen" complaints because virtually all U.S. com-munities have potential complainants who are not all officially citizens of the United States. Thus, the more inclusive term is appropriate. Police internal affairs units that investigate public complaints have long been regarded with distrust by civil rights activists because they see police officer investigators as inherently biased in favor of officers under in-vestigation. Until very recently there was no published set of standards for managing police internal affairs units or external public complaint agencies. The Community Oriented Policing Services Office published the first such set of guidelines only a few years ago.[86]

National data on public complaints against the police are incomplete in several respects. The most recent Bureau of Justice Statistics report (published in 2006 with data from 2002) covers only large state and local police departments, omitting data from civilian review boards. Additionally, it only reports complaints about police officer use of force, omitting complaints about other police actions. Thus, the report is not a full accounting of all public complaints. The issue that interests most community activists is the "sustain rate," the percentage of complaints sustained in favor of the complainant. The 2006 BJS report found that 8 percent of use of force complaints were sustained. This is an extremely low figure and does not include data on non-use of force complaints. The data, in short, are not useful for meaningful comparisons of different departments, and the exclusion of citizen review board data only compounds the problem.[87]

Developing and maintaining standards for police department complaint investigation units, however, have proven to be extremely difficult. The New Jersey attorney general took a major step forward in 1991 by promulgating a set of Internal Affairs Policy and Procedures for all police departments in the state, which was then converted into a state statute. (The New Jersey attorney general, it should be noted, has special powers over law enforcement agencies in the state, through the Office of Public Integrity and Accountability.) The New Jersey ACLU in 2009, however, issued a blistering report on the failure of police departments to comply with many of the requirements, finding that 63 percent of police departments required people to file complaints in person; 49 percent refused to accept anonymous complaints; and 79 percent refused to allow juveniles to file complaints unless accompanied by their parents.[88]

A professionalized public complaint process eliminates the various abuses that undermine public trust and confidence in the police: the refusal of a department to accept certain complaints; the failure to fully and objectively investigate complaints; the willingness of officers under investigation to lie about the incident in question; the undermining of standards of discipline; and loss of public trust and confidence in the police department. A professionalized complaint process has just the opposite effect: holding officers accountable for their actions; imposing discipline when it is proven to be appropriate; and building trust and confidence in a police department. Achieving all of these goals would be a major step forward in building positive community relations, but both police departments and civilian complaint review boards are still a long way from that.

Reforming the Pittsburgh Complaint Process

The 1997 consent decree over the Pittsburgh police department devoted much of its attention to the Office of Municipal Investigations (OMI), the external city agency responsible for handling complaints against police officers. (This involved twenty-eight paragraphs out of a total of eighty-three in the consent decree.) The consent decree required the OMI to enter all complaints and investigations since 1986 into a computerized database; to allow complainants to file their complaints in person, by mail, by telephone, or by fax; and to stop requiring complainants "to go to a police station" to file complaints. As an additional accountability measure, the consent decree also required the OMI to notify an officer's supervisor when a complaint involved an allegation of excessive force, improper search or seizure, or racial bias. This provision establishes a crucial link between the OMI and police supervisors, giving complaints more attention and weight. Essentially, the consent decree requirements were designed not to restructure or replace the existing complaint process but to make the OMI a more accessible and professional agency.[89]

Professionalizing the Seattle Office of Police Accountability

The Seattle police department has a unique form of oversight in the Office of Police Accountability (OPA). Created in 2002 in response to earlier public demands, the OPA is housed within the police department but is directed by a non-sworn individual who reports to the chief, the mayor, and the city council, and is limited to two consecutive three-year terms. Thus, it is a unique insider/outsider form of oversight and public complaint review.[90]

The Justice Department findings letter, however, found that the OPA "has not provided the necessary accountability" for the department. In particular, "the quality of the investigations performed by [officers in] the precincts" was poor; precinct investigators, with apparent OPA approval, made excessive use of "supervisory intervention," meaning that cases were investigated and concluded by police officers, an option that typically resulted in no meaningful discipline; and the system of classification of complaints was not transparent and accessible to the public.[91]

The resulting consent decree was oddly far more favorable toward the OPA than the findings letter had been. Its primary requirement was that the department would update the OPA "Training and Operations Manual [and] formalize OPA's procedures, best practices, and training requirements." It listed ten issues that needed revision, including "written protocols" for "investigative practices and procedures"; "case review procedures"; and "communications with complainants and officers."[92] As was the case in Pittsburgh, the Seattle consent decree professionalized the existing OPA rather than making structural changes or seeking to abolish it. Reading between the lines, one can infer that the OPA suffered from serious deficiencies, but the pattern or practice staff chose to focus the consent decree on more serious problems in the police department, notably officer use of force, inadequate supervision of officers who used force, inadequate officer reporting of use of force, and a pattern of bias in routine police work.[93]

Reforming public complaint procedures in policing makes an important contribution to the transformation of police departments. If the complaint process is more accessible to the public, maintains better records of complaints and their outcomes, has trained investigators with written procedures for conducting complaint investigations, and leads to more discipline of officers, members of the public are more likely to trust the department. They are also more likely to file complaints than before. Officers subject to complaints, meanwhile, will experience greater accountability for their conduct and sense that the culture of the entire department is changing. Thus, the improved procedures and culture of the complaint process change the department in a positive direction in the eyes of both complainants and officers.

Alternative Oversight Agencies

The subject of citizen oversight of the police is extremely complex, with two models of oversight and considerable variation within each.[94] The most prevalent form of oversight involves civilian review boards, which focus almost entirely on reviewing individual complaints and concluding that they are either founded, unfounded, exonerated, or not substantiated. (It should be noted that some review boards, the Washington, DC, Office of Police Complaints, for example, also investigate police policies or other issues and publish public reports in addition to investigating complaints.)[95] Some agencies recommend specific discipline to the police chief, while others simply forward their findings to the chief. The other model of oversight involves what are called either "police auditors," "monitors," or "inspectors general," who do not investigate public complaints but have the authority to investigate the policies and practices of the police departments they are responsible for and to issue public reports with recommendations for change.[96]

Research has found that the traditional civilian review boards are very weak in terms of holding both individual officers and police departments accountable for officer misconduct. The available data indicate that complaints are "extremely underreported." The vast majority of people who experience mistreatment by a police officer simply do not file complaints and often only contact family or friends about the incident. Not filing complaints is a strong indicator of public distrust of the complaint process. Many of those who do file complaints either withdraw early in the process or simply fail to respond to requests for an interview, in which case the complaint is dismissed. Among the small percentage of complaints that are investigated, relatively few are resolved in favor of the complainant. Among police internal affairs units, the "sustain rates" of complaints about officer use of force is only 8 percent. Some review boards, meanwhile, are seriously late in completing complaint investigations, taking an average of 3.8 years in Chicago and 19 months in New York City.[97] Unfortunately, complaint data from police departments and citizen review agencies are not useful for comparing the performance of agencies. Agencies use different categories for complaints, and some agencies divide complaints into two categories based on their seriousness. Sustain rates are widely cited by many people, but they are not comparable to other agencies and cannot serve as a valid measure of the extent of police officer misconduct or patterns of disciplinary actions.

Samuel Walker and Carole Archbold argue that inspectors general are a better way to improve police departments than civilian review boards. The inspectors general in New York City, Los Angeles, Chicago, and Seattle have established creditable records of identifying serious problems in police departments.[98] The public reports issued by inspectors general and auditors play an important role in educating the public, elected officials, civil rights attorneys, and the media about the underlying problems in the police issues they investigate.[99] The potential for expanding the role of inspectors general is discussed in greater detail in chapter 6.

Strengthening or Adding New Mid-Management Accountability Units

The pattern or practice program has also sought to enhance officer accountability by creating or strengthening mid-management level units or programs related to accountability. These two units are use of force review boards (UFRB) and early intervention systems (EIS).[100]

The Expanded Role of Use of Force Review Boards

The New Orleans consent decree requires the police department to "develop and implement a Use of Force Review Board to review all serious uses of force." An unknown number of police departments across the country had UFRBs before the pattern or practice program was created, but there is no independent research on their number or operations. The New Orleans UFRB was tasked with reviewing each force investigation conducted by the Force Investigation Team, a specialized investigative team that investigated serious force incidents. If the UFRB finds shortcomings in a force report, it can either demand additional information or refer the case to internal affairs for discipline if the officer had clearly violated department policy.[101]

Far more significant, however, is the responsibility of the New Orleans UFRB to "determine whether a use of force report raises policy, training, equipment, or tactical concerns, and to refer such incidents to the appropriate unit within NOPD to ensure they are resolved."[102] The UFRBs in other departments have a similar requirement. This function makes a UFRB a critical self-policing unit within a police department. To the extent that a UFRB identifies problems and recommends corrective action, it plays a major role in helping to sustain consent decree reforms and other operational matters unrelated to the consent decree.[103] The role of UFRBs in this respect is to help a police department become a "learning organization," which police expert William A. Geller years ago defined as an organization that is "continually expanding its capacity to create its future" by systematically identifying and correcting organizational problems. More recently, White and colleagues define a learning organization as one that "embraces change and continually engages in introspection to identify deficiencies that require modification."[104] To the extent that a UFRB reviews all use of force reports and identifies and reports on problems in other units of the department, it makes a major contribution to the sustainability of consent decree reforms after the decree has been ended. Equally important, the work of a UFRB in this regard contributes directly to the transformation of a police department.

The Challenge of Early Intervention Systems

The pattern or practice program has also included an early intervention system (EIS) in about 75 percent of its consent decrees.[105] An EIS is a computerized database on police officer performance, with the number of officer actions in the database ranging from as low as five to a high of over fifteen. The Newark consent decree, for example, includes data on use of force, public complaints, and disciplinary actions among the eleven indicators.[106] (It needs to be noted that there are no national standards for EIS on this or other issues.) EIS data analysis involves comparing officers' performance records with those of peer officers, defined as officers with comparable assignments in terms of area and shift. Comparing an officer working in a high-crime area, where there are high rates of stops and arrests, with officers working in low-crime middle-class residential neighborhoods is illogical and unfair and not likely to yield meaningful results. Officers initially identified by the EIS data are (in most departments) then reviewed by a department committee, and only some are selected for an intervention to correct the identified performance problem. Problematic officer conduct can include anger management issues, a pattern of disrespect for members of the public, or difficulties in dealing with young men on the street. Interventions may involve counseling by command officers, retraining on a specific police performance issue, referral to professional counseling services, or some other program as determined by the staff of the program.[107]

EIS are potentially very powerful accountability tools, with the capacity to identify the specific performance problem an officer has and refer that officer for corrective action to address that particular problem. EIS are, however, "complex and difficult to maintain, and do not guarantee results," according to White and colleagues.[108] They require careful planning; a well-designed set of thresholds for identifying officers with performance problems; accurate and timely data; and staff who are skilled in handling large and complex computerized databases. Many departments have had difficulties in maintaining an operational EIS.[109] The pattern or practice findings letter on the Seattle police department found the EIS to be "broken." The "thresholds" for identifying officers with performance problems, for example, were too high, allowing many officers to avoid being selected for the program. The Cleveland EIS, meanwhile, was useless because officer participation was "voluntary."[110]

A fully functioning EIS enables police reform by regularly correcting the performance problems of officers identified by the system. In that respect, an EIS contributes directly to improvements in the department's overall performance, helps to sustain consent decree reforms, and by reducing officer misconduct improves the quality of the service delivered to the community. If an EIS is poorly designed and inadequately managed, however, all the potential gains are lost.

Although not included in any pattern or practice program consent decrees, another method of identifying problematic police officers is the so-called "Brady list," a list of officers with records of dishonesty. The name derives from the 1963 Supreme Court decision in *Brady v. Maryland* in which the court ruled that prosecutors must turn over to defense attorneys any evidence that might be favorable to a defendant.[111] Brady lists have reportedly existed in the shadows of the criminal process in various jurisdictions for some time, but there is no published research on the subject. The most systematic approach to implementing the *Brady* decision was created in 2010 by then California attorney general Kamala Harris. The idea of Brady lists has continued to grow. In 2022, for example, the Hennepin County, Minnesota, county attorney created a new written policy on how prosecutors should turn over *Brady*-related material. He argued that his office is "in a unique position" to identify and report police misconduct and that there is now "an expectation" that law enforcement agencies will "proactively and voluntarily" disclose *Brady*-related information. The 2016 Blue Ribbon Panel report on the San Francisco police department discussed Brady lists but found that implementing *Brady* is far more complex than most people realize. Other police departments seeking to adopt a comprehensive approach to a Brady list system have much to learn from the San Francisco experience.[112]

At best, the Brady list concept remains shrouded in semi-secrecy and a lack of a solid body of literature. Media stories are often unclear about whether a particular prosecutor's office does or does not have a functioning list and whether police departments consistently maintain lists. In terms of developing a more professional police, the Brady list is a valuable and long overdue concept. Police departments simply should not tolerate a lack of truthfulness among their officers. Putting an officer on a Brady list effectively bars that person from engaging in routine police work such as stops, arrests, and searches where he or she may fall afoul of the department's Brady list. Many officers placed on a list would be likely to resign and seek a job with a less professional police department. Despite the obvious value of Brady lists, however, there is no evidence of an organized national movement to promote the idea. The Marshall Project does maintain a useful "curated collection of links" on the subject, which is at least a start.[113]

Promoting Community Engagement

Developing greater engagement between police departments and the communities they serve became a major objective of the pattern or practice program in the 2000s. It was not one of the original program objectives but developed as part of the program's learning curve.[114] The pattern or practice program staff increasingly recognized that one of the significant limitations of the early consent decrees was the lack of meaningful engagement with communities most affected by police misconduct, with the result that community residents were often not well informed about the consent decree and the reasons for it, and as a result did not enthusiastically support it. The Civil Rights Division's 2017 report explained that "community engagement, oversight, and democratic processes go hand-in-hand."[115]

The commitment to community engagement has two principal origins. First, civil rights activists since the 1960s had been demanding a meaningful voice in police department policies and practices for racial minority communities, but with little success. In the crisis of the 1960s, some departments created citizen advisory committees. The President's Crime Commission, however, found them to be ineffective, in large part because members were generally part of the community elite, were poorly informed about policing, and were selected by the police chief.[116] Walker extends this analysis more broadly, arguing that through its entire history until the 1970s American police departments were governed by a city's white majority (although the real power often lay with the city's elite), which was serious about fighting crime and indifferent or even hostile to poor communities and communities of color.[117]

Second, the idea of community engagement has been encouraged by a small but growing number of police experts who have argued for greater democratic control of local police departments.[118] The movement toward community engagement represents a rejection of the isolation of police departments that developed in the 1950s on matters of crime-fighting strategies, personnel matters, and other issues. The principle of isolation from the public was one of the unfortunate legacies of the police professionalization movement, particularly in the 1950s and early 1960s. The incoming administration of President Barack Obama in 2009 received a report from an informal working group that met at the University of Pittsburgh Law School and prepared a report to the incoming attorney general on recommendations for improving the program. One of the eleven recommendations called for the pattern or practice program to make "special efforts to engage members of local communities." Community engagement was the main issue that the pattern or practice program quickly embraced.[119]

The Pioneering Cincinnati Collaborative Agreement

The most important model of community engagement was the 2001 Cincinnati Collaborative Agreement, a settlement of several private civil rights suits against the Cincinnati police department. The Collaborative Agreement contained two innovative elements. First, it involved a broad coalition of community groups and public officials, including "African-Americans, social service and religious organizations, businesses and philanthropic groups, police line officers and spouses, City officials, white citizens, other minorities and youth."[120] There was no precedent for a police reform effort giving a formal voice to such a broad community coalition. Second, the agreement included a commitment to changing the police department's crime-fighting strategy to community problem solving, a version of problem-oriented policing, which had been growing in the United States since the early 1980s.[121] Pattern or practice program staff members were evidently impressed with both elements of the Collaborative Agreement and began incorporating them into future consent decrees.

Engagement with Public and Private Agencies

As a community engagement effort, the Portland, Oregon, consent decree requires the police department to establish working relationships with local and state mental health service organizations and other relevant community stakeholders. Specifically, it expects the city of Portland and its partners to "help remedy the lack of community-based addiction and mental health services to Medicaid clients and uninsured area residents." As the 2017 Civil Rights Division's report explained, the Portland community did not have "adequate community mental health services," and the consent decree requirement was designed to help create "better systems to improve health services and reduce the burden on law enforcement."[122] Thus, the consent decree simultaneously promoted both police reform and the reform of community services related to mental health.

Formal community engagement programs give local residents a voice in the policies, procedures, and governance of a police department. The President's Task Force on 21st Century Policing in its 2015 report recommended that "law enforcement agencies should develop and adopt policies and strategies that reinforce the importance of community engagement in managing public safety," and in particular should "work with neighborhood residents to co-produce public safety."[123] Those principles represent major steps toward ending the long-standing isolation of American police departments from the community and contribute directly to the transformation of both the culture and the mission of a police department.

The Problems with Community Input

The concept of community engagement is laudable and potentially of great value, but it is not without its problems. Over the years, there have been many community advisory groups in cities across the country, but they have been criticized because they did not address significant police problems or because police department leaders did not listen to their recommendations. The President's Task Force on 21st Century Policing in 2015 recommended giving community representatives a formal voice in the development of or revision of police department policies.[124] To date, the Seattle Community Police Commission (CPC) appears to be the most active commission, and in 2023 was engaged in a broad range of activity involving Seattle police department policies, police-related legislation in the state legislature, and collective bargaining issues.[125]

In an illuminating study, professor Tony Cheng labeled the process of community input through public meetings "input without influence." Examining seven years of Chicago Police Board monthly meeting transcripts, he found that police officials responded to 74 percent of critical comments by community residents in the audience "with literal silence," and replied to only 26 percent. Moreover, the comments by local residents and responses by police officials at meetings generally involved well-established "scripts," with each side blaming all problems and disagreements on the other side. The end result was no real "constructive discussion" of difficult issues that people in attendance raised.[126] The question of how to achieve community engagement where the police department actually listens and responds with some positive action to community voices is an extremely difficult one that remains largely unresolved.

Creating a formal community engagement structure runs headlong into one fundamental problem inherent in American democracy: Who speaks for "the public" on police issues? Professors Tony Cheng and Jennifer Qu identified three major obstacles to creating community engagement. First, in every American city there is a "multiplicity of community demands toward police." Second, this multiplicity exists because our cities are extremely heterogeneous in terms of race, ethnicity, social class, religion, political views, and other categories. Third, there is the problem of resistance to proposed reforms among those participants "who remain unsatisfied" with them, and there is no shared consensus of opinion on police reform among radical, liberal, and conservative members of the public. The complex entanglements arising from these three factors are not easily resolved.[127]

Reorienting Crime and Disorder Control Strategies

A major component of the Cincinnati Collaborative Agreement involved reorienting the Cincinnati police department's strategy for addressing crime and disorder, directing that the department develop a program of community problem-solving policing. Problem-oriented policing (POP) was nothing new in 2001 and had been adopted by many police departments across the country since the early 1980s.[128] Traditional POP programs work with neighborhood groups to identify particular problems in a specific neighborhood and then jointly develop a strategy to address that problem. A 2017 systematic review of published evaluations of problem-oriented policing programs found that they have "a statistically significant impact on reducing crime and disorder," although the "effect size was small."[129] In 2015 the President's Task Force recommended that police departments adopt the POP framework and work "with neighborhood residents to coproduce public safety."[130]

The Cincinnati program was particularly ambitious because it was a citywide effort, unlike all previous problem-oriented policing programs, which targeted particular problems in specific neighborhoods. The pattern or practice program staff were evidently impressed with both the community engagement and problem-oriented policing elements of the Collaborative Agreement and began including problem-oriented policing in eight other consent decrees, including the decrees in Albuquerque, Baltimore, Cleveland, and Ferguson, Missouri.[131]

The Cincinnati Collaborative Agreement included a contract with the Rand Corporation to conduct a series of evaluations on the impact of Cincinnati's community problem solving on police practices and its impact on the police department's relations with the African American community. The 2009 Rand report, *Police-Community Relations in Cincinnati*, assessed changes arising from the reforms since 2005 and found that "police-community relations in Cincinnati have improved in a number of ways." African American residents reported that the professionalism of the police department had improved; the "perception of racial profiling is on the decline"; and in vehicle stops, both searches and the duration of stops had declined.[132] This was a significant accomplishment for the Collaborative Agreement.

Conclusion

The pattern or practice program's goal of ending unconstitutional policing was not only ambitious, unlike any prior reform effort, but also richly complex. As this chapter has revealed, the reform process involved not just one but a sweeping array of seven different reform goals. You could not end police officer use of excessive force by simply writing a new policy on the subject. Rank-and-file officers needed to be trained on the new policy, particularly on how to write detailed and honest use of force reports. Their supervising sergeants who reviewed officer use of force reports also needed to be trained how to review them. Equally important, they needed to be trained on how to supervise officers about how to maintain order on the streets without resorting to the use of force. New policies on conducting motor vehicle stops or pedestrian stops were equally complex, involving new and sophisticated data collection systems, which required police departments to be equipped with sophisticated computer technology. The goals of the pattern or practice program also included efforts to end discrimination by police officers based on race and ethnicity, and in two specific cases gender discrimination as well. Reform of public complaint procedures was undertaken to address long-standing complaints from the African American community. The program also required the development of mid-management use of force review boards, which were tasked with identifying organizational problems that impeded routine police work and obstructed professionalization. Finally, the later generation of consent decrees initiated the development of community engagement programs to enhance police and community relations, while also creating problem-oriented crime-fighting programs that did not include the traditional aggressive policing consisting of aggressive offensive police tactics. In the end, the reform goals described in this chapter contributed directly to the organizational transformation of police departments that were subject to consent decrees.

5

Resistance, Costs, and Sustainability

The Justice Department's pattern or practice program has confronted challenges on a number of difficult issues during the course of its work. This chapter examines six important issues. The first issue involves resistance to the program, either from politicians at the national or local levels or from police officers at the local level. The second issue involves the obstacles to reform posed by police unions and their collective bargaining agreements. The chapter describes how the pattern or practice program successfully avoided union-based obstacles by doing an "end run" through consent decree reforms that were "management prerogatives" not affected by police union powers. The third issue involves the controversies over the financial costs of consent decrees. The chapter argues that the high implementation costs of consent decrees have been offset by the reduction in litigation expenses and the resulting savings from fewer civil suits as a result of consent decree reforms. The fourth issue involves the findings of published evaluations of consent decrees, two of which are notable for the broad range of issues covered. The fifth issue involves the surprisingly positive collateral impact of consent decree reforms on the traditional police officer subculture and the emergence of more positive police officer attitudes toward their work, their departments, and the public. The sixth and final issue involves the challenging issue of sustaining consent decree reforms once a consent decree has ended. The unanswered question is how best to achieve the goal of sustained police reforms.[1]

Resistance to Federal Intervention: Political, Internal, and External

The pattern or practice program met with resistance from two different sources: political resistance from presidential administrations and from local officials, and internal resistance from both police department leaders and sworn officers at various ranks.

Presidential Administrations and Police Reform

Political resistance from U.S. presidents has followed a clear pattern. Three Democratic presidents, with strong civil rights commitments, enthusiastically embraced the pattern or practice program, while two Republican presidents, with no civil rights commitments, either reduced the program administratively or suspended it completely by order of the attorney general.[2]

President Bill Clinton was in office when Congress created the pattern or practice program in 1994. With a strong commitment to civil rights, he enthusiastically supported the program, which entered its first consent decree in 1997, involving the Pittsburgh police department.[3] By the time he left office in early 2001, the program had four consent decrees in operation and a fifth nearing a settlement.[4] The George W. Bush administration, with no commitment to police reform or to civil rights, drew back from the pattern or practice program and for eight years pursued no consent decrees against any police departments. The program instead used technical assistance letters, which were brief, covered only a few issues, were not judicially enforced, had no court-appointed monitors, and contained no commitment by the Civil Rights Division to return and assess what reforms, if any, were implemented.[5] The technical assistance letters sent to the Cleveland (2002) and Miami (2003) police departments resulted in no meaningful reforms, but the Obama administration later returned to both cities and obtained consent decrees against both departments.[6]

The administration of President Barack Obama made a strong commitment to reviving the pattern or practice program, doubling the size of the staff. The staff had reflected on the program during the Bush years and resumed implementing consent decree reforms and others that were part of its "learning curve." The two most important new goals included building community engagement between police departments and community stakeholders, and reorienting police departments' strategies for fighting crime and disorder. Both programs were inspired by the Cincinnati Collaborative Agreement. As a result of the new issues in the pattern or practice program, the Civil Rights Division's 2017 report on its efforts referred to two "generations" of consent decrees.[7]

President Donald J. Trump's administration was hostile to civil rights enforcement and eager to cultivate political support from the law enforcement community. Consequently, attorney general Jeff Sessions suspended the pattern or practice program in March 2017.[8] His memorandum did not abolish the program, however, and existing consent decrees continued to be implemented. Apart from the lack of new investigations and consent decrees, there was no strong evidence of any serious negative impact on the implementation of existing consent decrees.

President Joe Biden was deeply committed to civil rights enforcement and appointed Merrick Garland as attorney general. Garland acted quickly on police reform and initiated investigations of four police departments: Louisville, Minneapolis, Phoenix, and Columbus, Ohio, with others soon following.[9] He also issued a memorandum clarifying the role of court-appointed monitors in September 2021, resolving some of the questions and controversies that had surrounded some monitors. The memo's principles included, for example, that the role of monitors "should be designed to minimize the financial cost to jurisdictions and to avoid any appearance of a conflict of interest" (with respect to other investigations). It also directed monitors to "assess compliance [with consent decrees] consistently across jurisdictions." These and other issues had been raised over the years, and Garland's memorandum served to provide greater consistency in the role of monitors.[10]

The lesson of the shifting White House political winds with respect to the pattern or practice program is the inescapable fact that in a democratic society the voters elect the president, who has full authority to determine the Justice Department's policy on police reform.

Local Political Resistance

Local resistance to the pattern or practice program occurred in just a few cities and counties. The Civil Rights Division attempted to intervene against the Alamance County, North Carolina, sheriff's department in 2009, but was blocked by the sheriff. The pattern or practice program returned in 2012, however, and in 2016 reached an agreement with the sheriff requiring the development of an anti-bias program.[11] The program also investigated the Columbus, Ohio, police department in 1999, alleging use of excessive force, unlawful stops, and other abuses. The police department and city officials strongly resisted, however, and the impasse was finally resolved by a mutual agreement in 2002. The Justice Department intervened in the Columbus police department in 2021, however, at the invitation of the city.[12] The division also attempted to intervene against the Maricopa County, Arizona, sheriff's department, where a bitter and highly publicized struggle over the department's immigration policies was directed by sheriff Joe Arpaio, a controversial national figure on the immigration issue. A complex legal battle ensued, but the U.S. Department of Justice ultimately prevailed and in 2015 obtained an order finding discrimination against Latinos by Arpaio and Maricopa County.[13] Two of the local resistance efforts, it should be noted, were led by conservative local officials, who, it seems clear, were motivated primarily by their political ideology and only partly by issues related to police practices.

The mayor of Seattle attempted to circumvent the pattern or practice program in 2012 with his own "SPD 20/20" plan for reforming the Seattle police department by the year 2020. The plan included twenty specific reforms in the police department's policies, procedures, and practices and was advertised as avoiding the high costs of a consent decree. The mayor, however, had no realistic proposal for adequately funding the plan and it died a quick death. A consent decree with the Civil Rights Division was soon signed in 2012 and implementation of the decree began.[14]

The very small number of cases of active resistance deserves comment. It appears that officials in most of the cities and counties that were investigated by the Justice Department adopted a "plea bargain" strategy. A legal challenge to federal intervention would be an expensive and risky venture that would revive publicity over past police department misconduct and further aggravate community tensions. A legal challenge, moreover, might well end in defeat, with the city gaining nothing positive. The safe bet was to accept the fact that their police department had serious problems and hope that a consent decree would correct those problems as quietly as possible and reduce police-community tensions.

Internal Police Department Resistance

There are three documented cases of resistance to the pattern or practice program from within police departments. Two cases involved top police department commanders and one involved sworn officers at several ranks.

The Los Angeles case involved LAPD commanders who were members of the consent decree implementation team and who at early public meetings "publicly denigrated the decree and urged the community to be outraged at the cost to taxpayers," along with other criticisms. Members of the monitoring team were present at these meetings, however, and included the officers' remarks in the next monitor's report, which recommended "immediate attention" to the problem. The problem of the dissident commanders was quickly resolved and the LAPD under a new chief proceeded toward implementation of the consent decree.[15] In Cincinnati, the police chief and some top commanders at one point denied the monitoring team access to police records (which the consent decree authorized them to have), and on one occasion a top commander ordered a member of the monitoring team to leave police headquarters. The monitoring team notified the presiding U.S. district court judge, who, in a meeting in her chambers, sternly warned the police chief about the resistance to the monitoring team and then converted the case into a judicially enforced settlement agreement.[16]

The most systematic internal resistance to a consent decree by sworn officers occurred in the Albuquerque, New Mexico, police department. The degree of active resistance by officers was breathtaking. It was far more insidious than the other forms of resistance because it represented a deeply embedded culture of hostility to police reform among officers at several ranks, with the police chief and other top command officers making no effort to exercise strong leadership.[17] The Albuquerque monitor's 2021 report identified serious problems in several important areas of police operations where the consent decree had mandated reforms. The department "overuses force and at times uses excessive force," according to the report, adding that these were the very problems that led to the consent decree in the first place. "It appears to be apparent," the report continued, that the department "does not have the appetite for taking serious approaches" to controlling officer use of force. "Command and control" practices by supervisors in this area "continue to be weak." Systemic problems also existed in the disciplinary system: the department "routinely fails to follow its own written policy and virtually decimates its disciplinary requirements." Investigators, for example, refused to recognize "repeat offenses" by officers or to consider "aggravating circumstances" in "determining appropriate discipline" for officers. Delays in investigations of public complaints, meanwhile, resulted in complaints being dismissed because they missed the union contract deadline for completion specified in the police union contract. The court-appointed monitor publicly speculated that the delays were deliberate and stated bluntly that the department "is willing to go through almost any machination to avoid disciplining officers." The monitor concluded that there was evidence of "deliberate indifference" to consent decree reforms throughout the department. The overall compliance level for the department was actually lower than it had been in the earlier 2019 report.[18]

In 2021 and 2022, however, events took a dramatic turn, as the problems in the department suddenly seemed to be resolved and the department began to move toward successful implementation.[19] The 2022 monitor's report stated that "perhaps for the first time" there was a serious effort on the part of the department to identify and correct officer conduct that was contrary to the consent decree. One positive influence was the role of the External Force Investigative Team (EFIT), an independent consulting group that began training Albuquerque use of force investigators in July 2021. New leaders were also appointed to the department's police academy. The monitor noted that a number of significant problems remain, including "administrative and cultural obstacles that persist," but the police chief was confident that the department would achieve full compliance within two years.[20] The situation remained somewhat ambiguous, however. The 2022 report found that despite important reforms in many areas, a number of "operational compliance" issues remained: supervision remained a "significant problem" and disciplinary practices involved "dissimilar discipline." The monitor recommended "a complete assessment of the current disciplinary system," a task that would be an enormous undertaking in any department.[21]

The best that can be said about the Albuquerque resistance is that it stood alone among all the consent decrees in terms of the degree of systematic resistance on the part of officers at many different ranks. There is no evidence of any other consent decree with similarly widespread resistance among officers. While other consent decrees have at times had various compliance issues, which delayed full implementation, they eventually resolved the problems and began moving toward full compliance.

Overall, resistance to the pattern or practice program was limited to a few cases and has not affected the pattern or practice program as a whole. The hostility to the program by two presidential administrations was temporarily disruptive but not fatal to the program.

The Elephant in the Room: Police Unions

Police Unions as Obstacles to Police Reform

It is the near-universal consensus among police experts and police chiefs that police unions have long been a major obstacle to police reform. Police unions are distinct from private sector unions and are distinct from other public service unions. An estimated 60 percent of police officers in the United States are unionized, compared with 34 percent of other public service employees. This high rate of membership gives them particularly strong power both inside the department and in the external environment.[22] The power of police unions falls into three categories: provisions of union collective bargaining agreements hostile to accountability; the informal power of union members to enforce the well-known "code of silence" among officers; and the political power of police unions to obtain state legislation favorable to their interests, and to influence elections at both the city and state levels.

Until very recently, police scholars and journalists paid little attention to police unions, which created a very serious information gap.[23] It is difficult to understand why police scholars neglected police unions for so long. It is certainly not because it is a controversial subject. Police scholars have been investigating the most sensitive of police issues for decades, including police officer shootings and use of excessive force.[24] The result has been a rich and steadily growing body of research on both subjects. Why scholars neglected police unions until very recently remains a mystery.

The fatal shooting of Michael Brown in Ferguson, Missouri, in August 2014 dramatically changed the political climate regarding police unions, however, and there has since been an upsurge of both news media stories and scholarly articles on police unions. Despite the various powers of police unions, however, and as discussed later in this section, the pattern or practice program developed an effective strategy of doing an "end run" around unions' powers and successfully implementing consent decree reforms that were clearly "management prerogatives" and not employee "conditions of employment" under the terms of collective bargaining law.

When police unions were initially being formed in the mid-1960s and early 1970s, one of the first major goals was the enactment of state law enforcement officers' bill of rights (LEOBOR) statutes. Between fifteen and twenty states enacted such laws, which varied considerably in their content.[25] A 1977 Bureau of Labor Statistics report examined the content of existing police collective bargaining agreements and found none of the offensive anti-accountability provisions that are in union contracts today.[26] With the exception of two state laws, LEOBORs had little impact on holding officers accountable. Contract provisions included the due process rights of officers in disciplinary proceedings and officers' First Amendment rights outside the department. The Rhode Island and Maryland LEOBORs contained the most serious obstacles to accountability, for example, by not permitting individuals who were not sworn police officers to participate in the investigation and questioning of officers. This provision effectively blocked the creation of independent citizen oversight agencies in those states. Maryland, however, repealed its LEOBOR with the 2021 Police Accountability Act, and directed all twenty-three counties in the state and the city of Baltimore to create their own police review boards.[27]

The Problem with Collective Bargaining Agreements

Local police unions changed their strategy in the early 1980s as they discovered that they could gain far more in material benefits (wages, health insurance, retirement plans) and protections for officers through collective bargaining. Contract negotiations are secret, with no public input, and city officials have been unwilling to provoke confrontations with police unions and risk their hostility. Police union leaders, meanwhile, quickly learned that in contract negotiations they could trade inflated demands over wages and benefits in return for concessions on discipline-related procedures.[28]

Until very recently, there had been little research on police union collective bargaining agreements. In 2016 the Black Lives Matter–affiliated group Check the Police published the first national survey of police collective bargaining agreements and identified six provisions that are obstacles to holding police officers accountable for their actions. They include requiring that citizen complaints be filed within a certain number of days after the incident; preventing officers subject to investigations from being "interrogated immediately" after the incident; giving officers subject to complaint investigations "information that civilians do not get"; allowing cities to pay the costs of officer misconduct through paid leave or by paying officers' legal costs (a process known as "indemnification"); keeping information about officers' past misconduct from being included in personnel files; and limiting the capacity of citizen oversight agencies to hold officers accountable.[29]

Law professor Stephen Rushin emerged as the single most important scholar on police unions when he conducted a national survey of 178 collective bargaining agreements in 2017.[30] From this data he identified seven contract provisions that impede police officer accountability: delaying interviews of officers; providing officers subject to complaints with access to evidence about the incident before being interviewed; limiting consideration of an officer's disciplinary history before an officer is disciplined; establishing a statute of limitations after which an officer could not be disciplined for the incident then under investigation; limiting anonymous complaints; limiting citizen oversight in various ways; and allowing the disciplined officer the opportunity to appeal disciplinary actions through arbitration.[31] Individually, no single provision is sufficient to completely impede accountability, but as a group they can effectively delay investigations of officer misconduct and cause chiefs to make compromises in particular discipline cases.

The provisions benefitting officers facing investigation and possible discipline are essentially "special privileges" for police officers that do not exist in other employment contexts. One such special privilege was an agreement between the city of New York and the rank-and-file officer union, by which the city annually contributed to the Legal Services Fund of the Police Benevolent Association; the funds were used to pay the legal expenses of officers who were sued by the city. Taxpayers, in short, were covering the cost of officer actions that harmed individual taxpayers. In other cities where police unions exist, officers are reimbursed for their legal expenses through the process of indemnification.[32]

"The Wall of Secrecy": Informal Police Union Powers

Police unions and individual officers acting on their own exert enormous influence on the rank-and-file officer subculture in ways that over the years have seriously inhibited accountability. The most insidious influence has been the infamous "code of silence" under which officers do not report misconduct by other officers. When the Mollen Commission investigated corruption in the New York City police department in the early 1990s, one officer told the commission that the code of silence "starts in the Police Academy. . . . It starts with the instructors telling you never to be a rat."[33] The impact on officer accountability has been devastating, in large part because the best evidence on officer misconduct comes from other officers who witness or have knowledge about the incidents in question. Yet that invaluable information is denied to police investigators, prosecutors, the media, and the public. In oral testimony, in written reports, and in court testimony, officers simply deny that they saw any misconduct, thereby compounding the accountability problem by lying.

Police lying eventually became so commonplace that it gave rise to the term "testilying."[34] Lawyer and activist attorney Paul Chevigny in 1969 declared that "there can be no doubt that police lying is the most pervasive of all [police] abuses."[35] Richard Leo, the leading authority on the impact of the *Miranda* decision on police interrogation of suspects, found in his study of police interrogations of suspects that investigators routinely lied to suspects they interrogate, for example, by falsely telling a suspect that his partner had already confessed. Leo concluded his book on *Miranda* by arguing that there is "only one reason to support the use of deceptive interrogation techniques": the belief that "the ends justify the means," a belief that undermines the fundamental integrity of the criminal process. The corrupt practice of "testilying" has become deeply ingrained in policing and there is no evidence of any serious attempts to end the practice and its corrupting impact on policing and the entire criminal justice system.[36]

Secrecy and lying by officers are reinforced by the powerful threat and practice of retaliation by other officers. In the 1970s police corruption scandal in New York City, officer Frank Serpico was shot and wounded while conducting a drug raid. Rumors spread that he was set up by other officers in retaliation for his public revelations about corruption in the department.[37] The 2016 San Francisco district attorney's report on the San Francisco police department provided rich detail on the methods of retaliation in that department. One former officer reported that officers "who spoke out against the SFPD and/or their supervisors were ostracized; isolated; and faced retaliatory actions like frequent transfers, desk duty, and work in undesirable locations or units."[38] The Chicago Police Accountability Task Force that same year concluded that "the code of silence is not just an unwritten rule, or an unfortunate element of police culture past and present. The code of silence is institutionalized and reinforced by CPD rules and policies."[39]

The Political Power of Police Unions

From the very first years of police unionism in the 1960s, unions were actively involved in fighting police reform measures designed to improve police-community relations. In fact, criticism of the police by civil rights activists was one of the factors that spurred the creation of police unions.[40] The single most important event occurred in 1966 when liberal New York City mayor John Lindsay by executive order converted the existing Civilian Complaint Review Board (CCRB), an internal police department unit, into one with a majority of members who were not police officers. The New York City Patrolmen's Benevolent Association (PBA) struck back immediately by organizing a city referendum on the existence of the new board. In a bitterly fought campaign, city voters abolished the board by a two-to-one margin. The union cynically played the "crime card," leading white voters to believe that the existence of the board undermined effective policing and would result in an increase in crime. Many white voters understood that the "crime card" was really the "race card," a warning that failure to abolish the new complaint review board would limit the ability of the police to fight crime. (There has, in fact, never been a study verifying that claim.) In the years ahead, other police unions across the country learned that the crime card/race card could be used to sway voters, elected officials, and candidates for public office.[41]

At the state level, unions have found that they could use their political clout, which in some states includes ample budgets for lobbying, to gain provisions in state civil service laws that made police disciplinary records confidential, thereby extending the shroud of secrecy to police personnel records. Revision of these laws began only recently. California in 2018 exempted certain categories of disciplinary actions from confidentiality, and New York State in 2020 repealed Section 50-A of its civil service law to make police disciplinary actions public records.[42] (In both states, however, full implementation was delayed by legal challenges by police unions.) Finally, police unions in a number of cities and states, New York and California in particular, exerted enormous influence in state-level elections and built up a solid base of support in state legislatures. One report found that unions nationally spent $48 million in one year on state-level lobbying and another $71 million supporting candidates for state political office. In 2022, for example, the Los Angeles police union placed almost $4 million in a campaign committee for the upcoming mayoral election.[43]

In the end, police unions have enormous powers and have used them for years to block many police reforms, but their powers have been circumvented to a certain degree by two developments. First, pattern or practice program consent decree reforms fall into the category of "management prerogatives," which the unions have not been able to block. Second, as noted earlier, public attitudes have in recent years become critical of police unions' efforts to keep disciplinary files confidential, and legislatures and judges in a few states have been able to make these files public. In response to growing public awareness of the powers of police unions and their adverse impact on police reform, there is some limited evidence that some police unions are willing to make a few concessions in contract negotiations. In San Antonio, for example, a referendum that would have ended the police union's right to collective bargaining lost by a very narrow margin. The narrow margin of victory apparently caused police union officials to be more willing to make at least some compromises in contract negotiations. In the next round of negotiations, the union "tweaked" certain provisions related to arbitration and the discipline process as concessions. There is no firm evidence at this point, however, on how strong anti-union sentiment is nationally.[44]

The Search for Remedies to Police Union Power

Police experts have tried but have been unable to develop strategies to effectively curb police union power. At best, they have been able to recommend reforms that are at the periphery of police union activities rather than striking directly at the real sources of union power.[45]

One strategy involves greater openness and transparency. Law professor Stephen Rushin suggests making "collective bargaining over police disciplinary procedures open to the public." It is not entirely clear, however, whether "open to the public" means that members of the public have a right to attend negotiating sessions, to submit formal proposals for new procedures and/or repeal of old ones, or to have a right to vote on proposals. Rushin also proposes that cities consider "police disciplinary procedures on their own," as a subject for negotiations separate from the basic collective bargaining contract. It is difficult to imagine, however, that police unions would agree to carving disciplinary provisions out of the union contract and negotiating them separately. Rushin's proposal to make contract negotiations open to the public by including "relevant stakeholders" is a laudable step in the direction of transparency but does not in any meaningful way limit the power of police unions.[46]

The most creative approach to challenging collective bargaining provisions is a proposal by University of Chicago law professors Aziz Z. Huq and Richard H. McAdams to challenge certain provisions "as against public policy." Their article focuses on provisions that delay investigations of officer misconduct, but the basic principle is certainly applicable to other contract provisions as well. A number of contracts around the country have or have had waiting periods between the incident in question and the interrogation of the officer involved. (Several forty-eight-hour waiting period requirements have already been eliminated by one means or another in several cities.)[47] Citing a number of lower court decisions on non-police issues, Huq and McAdams argue that "public policy favors detection of law violations," and that this applies to serious misconduct by police officers. A union contract provision that "strengthens the code of silence and impedes the disciplining of officers who engage in excessive force," they conclude, "is void as against public policy." Presumably, other police union contract provisions could also be challenged as violations of public policy.[48]

One of the greatest obstacles to police accountability involves the right of officers who are disciplined to submit their case to arbitration. Rushin studied 624 police arbitration cases from around the country decided between 2006 and 2020. The right of officers to choose arbitration rather than a conventional appeal is guaranteed in many collective bargaining agreements, according to his national survey. In 46 percent of arbitrations involving the termination of an officer, the arbitrator ordered the officer to be reinstated. Having terminated officers "handed back" to police departments has had a serious detrimental effect on the morale of police chiefs and command officers, and undermines the principle of accountability. Rushin makes the very sound proposal that states could revise their arbitration laws to limit the "standard of review" available to an arbitrator and prohibit arbitrators from reopening the entire record in cases. At present, arbitrators are generally "given fairly broad authority to rehear most or all factual and legal disputes" in the cases before them. This authority effectively erases the established record of cases and allows arbitrators to begin anew. Rushin argues that such broad authority "rarely occurs in other appellate contexts."[49] With a well-organized lobbying campaign, Rushin's proposal would appear to be a genuine possibility.

The Pattern or Practice Program's "End Run" around Police Union Power

The pattern or practice program responded to the power of police unions by simply doing an "end run" around it and focusing on reforms that are clearly "management prerogatives" rather than "conditions of employment" in the law of collective bargaining. Police department use of force policies are a clear example of a management prerogative that is not an employee working condition. Consent decrees, as discussed in chapter 4, have mandated more restrictive use of force policies, including a de-escalation option, and strict reporting requirements for both rank-and-file officers and their supervisors. There is no known instance where a police union has successfully blocked the implementation of a specific consent decree reform. To be sure, police departments do not have a completely free hand with regard to officers' use of force. Collective bargaining agreements contain provisions that delay the investigation of officer misconduct and the imposition of discipline, but they do not completely block either one. The pattern or practice program's end run, in short, allows the program to institute important reforms on key issues without any direct interference from police unions and their collective bargaining agreements.

The Financial Costs of Consent Decrees

Consent Decree Costs and Offsetting Gains

Consent decrees are expensive and the cost is borne entirely by the city or county. Local elected officials have repeatedly complained about the financial burden, and the news media have reported these complaints without conducting thorough analyses of the overall costs and benefits.[50] There also have been no comprehensive analyses of consent decree costs by economists. Two important issues, however, have never been thoroughly examined and incorporated into public discussions. The first is that a significant proportion of consent decree costs involve the start-up costs of providing a police department with adequate resources to become a modern-day professional law enforcement agency, particularly with respect to technology and computer infrastructure. The second involves the cost savings in civil litigation resulting from the positive effect of consent decree reforms in reducing lawsuits against the department.[51]

The best analysis of the costs involved in a consent decree experience is law professor Stephen Rushin's study of the Los Angeles police department consent decree in his book *Federal Intervention in American Police Departments*.[52] Much of the rise in the initial costs of implementation, he found, was due to necessary start-up costs of adding sophisticated technology and the associated administrative costs that are necessary to make a police department a modern, data-driven agency. When the LAPD consent decree began, the city was spending $314 per resident annually on policing. The figure rose to $374 in 2008 but then dropped to $317 by 2011. The rise and then fall of these per capita costs, Rushin argues, were related to the onetime start-up costs. Once those costs were taken care of, the overall costs of the department returned to a level very close to what it had been before the consent decree.[53] At the same time, however, an outrageous but largely hidden cost of police misconduct developed in Chicago and some other cities in the form of what was labelled "police brutality bonds." In twelve cities and counties examined by the ACRE Action Center, city and county officials borrowed nearly $878 million to pay for police misconduct-related settlements. In five cities and counties that were studied in detail, the $187 billion in costs included over $1 billion in profit for investors who bought the bonds. The bond process, in short, meant that taxpayers paid for police misconduct while investors profited.[54] The large start-up costs for police departments was the result of a failure to invest in necessary equipment years before, while the huge payouts in police misconduct litigation were the result of the failure of departments to adopt the necessary reforms—strict new policies on use of force, clear rules for supervising sergeants, and a strong and independent internal affairs unit—to curb officer misconduct.

The cost issue is a very different factor in cities that are in serious financial distress and as a result have been unable to provide their police departments with up-to-date equipment. The findings letter on the Cleveland police department noted with alarm that the lack of up-to-date equipment meant that the department was "asking officers to perform their duties without adequate technology, an appropriate staffing plan, a sufficiently professional workspace, or routine and functioning equipment [which] is dangerous to the officer, undermines public safety and is unfair." A similar situation existed in Baltimore. Rushin summed up the issue of the costs of consent decrees bluntly: "Preventing police misconduct costs money."[55]

The Collateral Financial Benefits of Consent Decrees

Almost completely neglected in controversies over consent decree costs is that certain consent decree reforms, notably on officer use of force, reduced officer misconduct and the resulting civil litigation costs. Rushin found that the costs of police misconduct cases against the LAPD stood at $13,187,100 in 2002, before the consent decree was implemented, and fell to $3,325,054 in 2006, after at least three years of reform.

Thus, the initial start-up costs of the consent decree were recouped by the reduction in officer misconduct litigation expenses.[56] This is a significant contribution of consent decree reforms that has gone almost completely unnoticed.

While consent decrees are indeed expensive, the major costs of police misconduct have been reported only occasionally in news media stories. The *Washington Post* in March 2022 published an explosive national-level story reporting that among the twenty-five largest police and sheriff's departments in the country, forty thousand payments in the decade from 2010 to 2020 totaled $3.2 billion in settlements of police misconduct cases. Almost half of that cost involved officers who were involved in two or more settlements. New York City, Chicago, and Los Angeles together accounted for $2.5 billion of the total costs. In one city, six narcotics officers were involved in 173 suits that cost $6.5 million in settlements. And it was not just the big cities with bad records. The Prince George's County, Maryland, police department paid out $54 million in the decade studied.[57] Effectively reducing police officer use of force abuses with new force policies and reporting requirements for both rank-and-file officers and their supervisors is an enormous cost-saving measure, benefitting both police departments and municipal taxpayers. The onetime cost of ensuring accountability of officers pays financial dividends over a period of many years.

Despite the high costs of police misconduct litigation, however, there have not been organized efforts at the city level to reduce police misconduct and the resulting litigation costs. It is truly surprising that local conservatives, for whom the cost of government has long been a major issue, have not organized such efforts. They could easily make the argument that savings from reduced litigation costs could be used to increase a police department's budget, fund after-school programs for children or additional mental health programs, or simply reduce local taxes.[58]

Evaluations of Consent Decrees

The First Evaluations

Several pattern or practice consent decrees have been subject to independent evaluations, although the number of evaluations is extremely low given the importance of the pattern or practice program.[59] One of the major problems with evaluating pattern or practice program consent decrees is that, as explained in chapter 4, the program is enormously complex, with several major goals, each of which typically involves multiple provisions.[60] As a result, social science articles on consent decrees have focused on selected issues (as in use of force incidents and public complaints) and not addressed the program as a whole. Social science journals have strict length requirements that make comprehensive assessments virtually impossible.[61] Another problem with the social science articles discussed here is that studies were conducted while the consent decree implementations were still in progress, and as a result studies were not able to evaluate a consent decree after it had been ended and all the required reforms were fully in place.

Evaluations have generally reported favorable outcomes on the issues studied. Both Rushin's articles and the Harvard evaluations of the LAPD are the best examples. Some evaluations, however, have reported erosion or "backsliding" in certain areas. The existing evaluations are, with one exception, not useful for assessing the sustainability of particular consent decrees. Such assessments would require teams of researchers and would need to be conducted some years after the termination of a consent decree.

The first evaluation examined the Pittsburgh consent decree and was conducted by a team from the Vera Institute of Justice three years after the termination of the decree.[62] The report was highly favorable, concluding that the decree had "dramatically changed the culture" of the police department. The various accountability-related reforms "remained in full force," including the early intervention system, which was "functional" and had helped to create "broad accountability" in the department. Interviews and focus groups with officers, however, found that many officers feared discipline under the new requirements (such as the new use of force policy) and felt burdened by what they saw as excessive "paperwork," obviously referring to the new reporting requirements on use of force and other actions. Although some officers claimed to have deliberately reduced their workload to avoid potentially difficult encounters and possible discipline, the evaluation found that the department's data on officer enforcement activity did not support the officers' claims of "de-policing."[63] Despite these complaints, however, focus groups and interviews with officers also found that some officers were now sensitive to "the appearance of unequal enforcement." Reducing unequal law enforcement, of course, was one of the main goals of the consent decree. Some officers, moreover, were increasingly accepting the new accountability-related procedures. (A later study, discussed below, found considerable "backsliding" in Pittsburgh on important reforms.)[64]

The Two Los Angeles Evaluations

An evaluation of the Los Angeles consent decree by a team from the Harvard Kennedy School of Government is the most comprehensive of all the evaluations, studying a wider range of issues and in greater depth than other published evaluations. The report concluded that the LAPD was "much changed" as a result of the consent decree and that both the "quantity and the quality" of law enforcement activity had "risen substantially." Instead of any de-policing, the evaluation found that stops and arrests of citizens had actually risen and serious crime had fallen during the consent decree years.[65] The increase in stops and arrests was undoubtedly due to the fact that officers were better trained and supervised and, therefore, were making stops and arrests that conformed to consent decree reforms, department policy, and the law. Reducing excessive force incidents and other forms of misconduct meant that they now had more time to focus on crimes where they had proper legal justification to intervene. Thus, as was argued in chapter 1 of this book, consent decree reforms have had an important impact on the LAPD's capacity to fight crime.

The evaluation also found considerable improvement in race relations, which had long been a major problem for the department (as in, for example, the 1991 Rodney King beating, discussed in chapter 2). A community survey found that members of all racial and ethnic groups were hopeful that the LAPD would in the next three years continue "respecting their rights and comply with the law." Some discontent with the department remained, however. A significant percentage of African American and Hispanic residents said they were "unsatisfied" with their experiences with the LAPD, and 10 percent of African Americans reported that "almost none" of the officers they encountered treated them with respect. A separate set of interviews with seventy-one people in detention after having been arrested in the previous three hours was particularly revealing. Over half of the group (thirty-nine of the seventy-one) said that the LAPD was doing a "good" or "excellent" job. It is certainly surprising that a group of people most likely to be critical of the LAPD gave the department such favorable reviews.[66]

As in the Pittsburgh evaluation, LAPD officers in interviews and surveys complained about the burdens imposed by consent decree reforms. In focus groups, officers "commonly said they sometimes avoid contact with citizens and 'look the other way' when observing illegal behavior in order not to create additional work for themselves or provoke the intervention of a sergeant or watch commander." Yet, as noted earlier, the evaluation team actually found an increase in officer enforcement activities, which did not support officers' claims that they "commonly" backed off from involvement in possible crime situations. It is quite possible that they ignored what appeared to be minor criminal activity so that they could concentrate on more serious crimes.[67]

The evaluation also studied the governance of the LAPD, particularly the Police Commission and the inspector general. Members of the mayoral-appointed commission, it found, were taking their positions far more seriously than in the past, and after years of resistance had begun to earn the respect and cooperation of the LAPD top command. The LAPD inspector general, which had only been created four years before the consent decree began, was a unit under the Police Commission, the governing authority for the LAPD. Initially, the IG had a difficult time establishing cooperation from the LAPD in providing data and documents. Under the consent decree, however, the IG began earning the respect of the LAPD top command and issued the first of a series of reports on important issues requested by the Police Commission. In 2016, for example, the inspector general, at the request of the Police Commission, issued a report comparing LAPD policies on use of force, investigations, and training with policies in four other large police departments. The report's findings were mixed, with the LAPD exceeding some departments on certain issues but lagging behind on others. There is no known example of a similar comparative review done by any other police department in the country. By the 2010s, the LAPD inspector general had emerged as a highly effective police oversight agency.[68] Such comparative assessments initiated by other police departments could be a productive means of stimulating reforms in all of the departments studied.

Rushin also evaluated the LAPD consent decree in his book *Federal Intervention in American Police Departments*, finding much to praise. Improvements to the department's early intervention system (known as TEAMS II) helped to make the department a more effective data-driven agency. New procedures for the handling of use of force incidents proved to be the "single most encouraging aspect" of the consent decree, and use of force reporting improved significantly. The consent decree mandated that the department's Internal Affairs Group review a wide range of alleged officer misconduct, including use of force. The result was a decline in the most serious incidents of use of force. Arrests of persons who were stopped by the police were more often accepted for prosecution than before, suggesting that officers were better trained and supervised in making stops and were more often complying with department policy and the law. The consent decree also mandated the creation of a new Audit Unit, which served as an in-house monitor of police operations. The unit was successful and its leaders helped to establish the International Law Enforcement Auditors Association, an association of similar audit units in other large police departments. This step presumably added a new dimension of professionalism not just to the LAPD but also to other departments across the country. Rushin concluded his assessment by arguing that "overall, the LAPD appears to have made significant and meaningful changes" as a result of the consent decree reforms.[69]

Other Evaluations

Professor Joshua Chanin evaluated three departments—Pittsburgh, Washington, DC, and Cincinnati—on the issues of use of force, civil litigation, and public complaints. In Washington, DC, use of force followed a "volatile" pattern, while civil litigation against the department declined and stayed low. In Cincinnati there were significant improvements. Use of force incidents declined by 46 percent between 2002 and 2012, while public complaints about excessive force declined by 36 percent. Moreover, there was "little or no backsliding" on consent decree-required reforms. Pittsburgh was a different story, however. The end of the consent decree coincided with the election of a new mayor, who opposed the consent decree and was supported by the police union. A city budget crisis created additional problems. These factors, beyond the control of federal intervention, caused officer performance in the consent decree-mandated reforms to "erode considerably."[70]

The successes in Cincinnati, however, did not last. In 2018–2019 city officials and the police department, despite published criticisms by police experts who had been involved with the Collaborative Agreement, terminated the agreement. (The separate Memorandum of Agreement with the Justice Department was no longer in force.)[71] This development reveals the fragility of pattern or practice reforms in situations where the necessary support from city officials ends. And in the case of Cincinnati it appears that community leaders and groups also turned against the reforms brought by the Collaborative Agreement. It also raises serious questions about the sustainability of consent decree reforms in the face of a lack of public support.

Zachary Powell and colleagues studied the impact of consent decrees on the filing of Section 1983 civil rights lawsuits alleging police misconduct in twenty-three departments subject to consent decrees.[72] In theory, consent decree reforms should reduce serious officer misconduct, and this reduction would be reflected in fewer Section 1983 lawsuits. The study found that consent decrees were associated with "modest reductions" in the filing of 1983 suits. The problem with the study is that 1983 lawsuits represent only a tiny fraction of police officer activity and only a very small percentage of use of force cases. The subject of 1983 litigation, therefore, is not a useful indicator of the overall success of a consent decree.[73]

A particularly interesting assessment of a consent decree was a 2016 follow-up study of use of force in the Washington, DC, police department by the Bromwich Group, which had been the monitor of the original Memorandum of Agreement. The assessment was done at the request of the city auditor and was conducted seven years after the end of the MOA. The report found "much that is positive" in the department regarding officer use of force, including the continuing commitment of the department's top management to the mandated reforms and resulting reduction in the "most serious types" of use of force, which included use of firearms. Nonetheless, the report found some "serious shortcomings," involving the use of force reporting system and the department's early intervention system (which it labelled a "star-crossed project").

The report concluded with a list of thirty-eight recommendations for change, which raises an important question related to the proper standards for evaluating a police department some years after a consent decree. Virtually all of the recommendations involved relatively minor issues and not fundamental deficiencies requiring a major overhaul of the department's handling of use of force cases. Thus, seven years after the end of the MOA, the department was doing reasonably well, with only a set of minor problems that could probably be corrected without too much difficulty, provided there was sufficient commitment from the top command. Most important, there was no evidence of wholesale "backsliding" on use of force policies, and the department should not be judged a failure with respect to the issue of use of force.[74]

The follow-up assessment of the Washington, DC, police department also raises the question of how cities and counties can continue to monitor their law enforcement agencies after a consent decree ends and the federal judge and the court-appointed monitor are gone. One alternative would be to assign post-consent decree monitoring to a local inspector general's office, if one currently exists. If not, a local city council could create one (as was the case in Seattle), with consent decree-related reforms being only one of its tasks. Alternatively, monitoring could be done through a contract with a private consulting group with an established record in the field of policing. This issue is discussed in more detail in chapter 6.

Police Chiefs' Comments on Consent Decrees

At the 2012 PERF conference on the pattern or practice program, some chiefs and top commanders were effusive in their praise of the consent decree experience. While their comments do not count as formal evaluations, they nonetheless deserve to be taken seriously. Charles Ramsey, who as superintendent of the Washington, DC, police invited the Justice Department to intervene in the deeply troubled department, stated that "the process of having a consent decree can actually be a benefit to your department." It gave the department leverage over the police union, helped reduce shootings by 80 percent, and "gave us credibility with the public." Robert McNeilly, chief of the Pittsburgh police department at the time of the consent decree, explained that it "opened a door [for reform] that my labor union had closed." A Los Angeles police commander added that the costs of the consent decree were "well spent," helping prevent future litigation against the department and giving the department "credibility with the community."[75]

It is noteworthy that these chiefs celebrated the positive effects of the consent decrees on their departments, including leverage over their police unions, reduction in officer-involved shootings, greater trust by members of the community, and reduction in police misconduct litigation and the resulting costs. They neglected, however, to mention the positive effects of consent decree reforms on crime. As was argued in chapter 1, officers were compliant with consent decree policies on use of force and vehicle stops, and the related reporting requirements, and because the policies reduced legally unjustified actions, they had more time to focus on incidents of suspected serious crime.[76]

In the end, the available evaluations of consent decrees have been generally positive. The two LAPD evaluations stand out as the most comprehensive of all the evaluations, and both report successful outcomes on a range of issues. The backsliding and failures that were noted were generally due to a lack of local community and political support, factors that were beyond the direct control of the pattern or practice program.

Consent Decrees That Failed

Not all consent decrees have been completely successful, and it is important to take into account the failures. The collapse of the Cincinnati Collaborative Agreement has already been discussed. The 1997 Pittsburgh consent decree was the pattern or practice program's first case, but the reforms began to erode almost as soon as the decree was lifted. The reasons for this are clear. The end of the decree coincided with the election of a new mayor, who was closely allied with the police union and did not support the consent decree. Additionally, there appears to have been a significant lack of support for the consent decree among the public.[77]

The consent decree over the Detroit police department quickly became a deeply troubled saga, involving a lack of police department leadership, failure to implement required consent decree reforms despite millions of dollars spent on the court-appointed monitor, and a failure of the court-appointed monitor to effectively oversee the consent decree. The court-appointed monitor, in fact, had an affair with the mayor of the city, who in an unrelated scandal was later convicted and sentenced to prison.[78]

The demise of reform in these three police departments was a blow to the pattern or practice program and to the field of police reform. The lack of support from local political leaders was in each case a major factor in the failure of the consent decree. When considered from a broader perspective, however, the losses represent only three of the twenty consent decrees the pattern or practice program negotiated between 1997 and 2017 (a success rate of 85 percent). Given the enormous challenges facing any consent decree, a record of seventeen successes out of twenty is a remarkably strong record.

Positive Collateral Impacts of Consent Decree Reforms

The Impact of New Policies on the Police Subculture

The positive collateral impacts of consent decree reforms have already been touched on in chapters 1 and 4, but the issue is of such importance that it merits further discussion. To date, the issue has been almost completely neglected in the literature on consent decrees. The following section argues that the impact of consent decree reforms on the rank-and-file officer subculture is one of the program's most important successes. Collateral impacts fall into two basic categories: the impact on individual officers and the impact on police departments as organizations.[79]

Consent decree reforms do far more than is required by the specific language in the decrees. New use of force policies, for example, convey principles and values. The Civil Rights Division's findings letter on the Cleveland police department found recurring evidence of officers "hit[ting] people in the head with their guns" and using force "that is disproportionate to the resistance or threat encountered," among other abuses.[80] By prohibiting such actions, a new use of force policy not only set new standards of conduct for officers but also communicated important values to officers: that they may not use a form of force that department policy prohibits and that they will face discipline if they do so.

The requirement that officers complete detailed and honest use of force reports, and that their supervisors critically review those reports, communicates the principle of accountability to both rank-and-file officers and their supervisors.

In the evaluation of the impact of the Los Angeles consent decree, officers in interviews and focus groups complained about the new restrictions on their freedom to act and what they saw as burdensome new paperwork, but the data cited by the evaluation found that officers were now conducting themselves in a more professional manner. It is also very likely that the LAPD officers simply used interviews and focus groups to posture and vent their grievances against consent decree requirements, the department leadership, and city leaders.[81]

The New Orleans consent decree, as discussed in chapter 4, also contained specific requirements, based on procedural justice principles, for how officers are to conduct themselves when stopping a member of the public, including the requirement that they "introduce themselves" at the beginning of a stop and explain the reasons, along with other requirements.[82] The procedural justice element in officer training on making stops helped to reshape officer attitudes about and behavior toward people they stop. This undoubtedly also had the effect of improving relations with members of the community, including gaining their trust and cooperation in dealing with crime and disorder. It is also very likely that many veteran officers, still rooted in the traditional police subculture, simply retired or resigned to take a job with another police department. The departure of these officers actually served to improve the overall quality of policing in the department they left. It is reasonable to assume that the procedural justice training led to fewer confrontational stops, fewer incidents of use of force and arrests, and greater cooperation by the person or persons stopped. It is also very likely that officer job satisfaction improved as a result.[83]

The positive impacts on police officers in New Orleans also affected members of the public and their attitudes toward the police. This resulted in fewer public complaints, unflattering news stories, investigations by internal affairs, disciplinary actions, and lawsuits. It is very likely that members of the public will also be more likely to cooperate with the police in particular situations and be more likely to provide officers with information about neighborhood problems involving disorder, drugs, and crime.[84]

An important caveat to the discussion above is that reforms can easily fade away. (See the discussion of why reforms fail, below.) If a police department's leadership fails to continuously monitor the reforms that the consent decree put in place, officers will soon learn that they can easily slide back into their old pre-consent decree habits with regard to stops, arrests, and use of force. This would be a tragedy, but the history of police reform is filled with such backsliding, and a police chief and other top commanders must be continually alert to prevent it from happening.

Some troubling questions about the impact of procedural justice training were raised in a survey of Baltimore residents around the time of the death of Freddie Gray, an African American who died while being transported to jail after being arrested, and whose death sparked weeks of protests, some of them violent, against the Baltimore police department. At that time, the National Institute on Drug Abuse was funding a community survey that included questions related to perceptions of procedural justice and the police. A small sample had been collected before Gray's death and a much larger sample was collected afterward, thereby creating separate pre- and post-death samples. A total of 3,615 surveys were completed, with a cooperation rate of 72 percent. The changes in people's attitudes on three procedural justice-related measures were "small and insignificant." Overall support for procedural justice was "quite low" among respondents prior to Freddie Gray's death, and there was "no observable change" in the post-death period. These findings contradicted a key theme in the procedural justice literature: that procedural justice training would have immediate or short-term impacts on how police officers conduct themselves in contacts with members of the public. To put it bluntly, perceptions and attitudes of police officers may not be as "malleable" as many people expect.[85]

The study's findings have important implications for David Kennedy's argument about how in routine encounters on the street both young African Americans and police officers bring established "narratives" about the other side, with young men viewing the police as racially biased and often brutal, while police officers view young men as disrespectful of the police and often involved in drugs and crime. The survey's findings do not contradict Kennedy's "narrative" perspective but do supplement it with important new evidence. Authors of the Baltimore study concluded that community residents "maintain historical, almost inherited

attitudes of the police." This is also undoubtedly also true of police officers and the young African Americans they encounter on the street:
stories of past encounters remain strong. The authors of the survey did
not conclude that procedural justice training for police officers is worthless. Instead, they argue that police officers "should aim to be fair, trustworthy and treat citizens with dignity and respect." That alone would be
a significant contribution to improved policing. But we are still left with
the deeply ingrained memories of conflict among police officers and the
young African Americans they encounter, and no serious plan to deal
with the problem.[86]

Policy Reshapes Culture

As was discussed in chapter 1, there is an adage among police leaders
and officers that "culture trumps policy," meaning that the norms of the
traditional police subculture nullify the intent of new police department
policies. The adage was repeated at a PERF conference by Scott Thomson, then police chief of Camden, New Jersey.[87] The sad aspect of the old
adage is that it is a confession of defeat, an admission that the traditional
police subculture cannot be changed, and that hopes for meaningful
police reform are slim. The evidence from the consent decree experience, however, suggests just the opposite. It is more likely that "policy
reshapes culture," meaning that officers subject to new and restrictive
policies accept the new policies, not completely at first, but increasingly
so as time goes by.

How deeply policy reshapes culture and whether the new officer attitudes and conduct become permanent are still uncertain at this point.
Monitors' reports from a number of departments under consent decrees
provide evidence of strong levels of officer compliance with new policies
and improved conduct on the street. In New Orleans, a 2019 monitor's
Comprehensive Reassessment found remarkable progress in a number
of key areas: firearms discharges had dropped from fourteen in 2003
to three in 2017 and one in 2018; canine deployments involving bites
of people fell from twelve in 2014 to none in both 2017 and 2018; vehicle pursuits dropped from seventy-five in 2015 to twenty-one in 2017.[88]
These are dramatic improvements on key issues and could only occur
if many (and possibly most) officers are complying with the new con-

sent decree reforms. A January 2021 media story on the Newark police department, meanwhile, reported that no officer had fired his or her weapon in the entire year of 2020.[89] That result, in a department with a history of very questionable shootings, clearly suggests that officers are complying with the consent decree-required new and restrictive use of deadly force policy.

The positive collateral effects of the police subculture on policing also play an extremely important role in the issue of organizational transformation. In a reformed police department it is more likely the case that "policy transforms culture," and that the consent decree-related policies on officer use of force have succeeded in transforming the working culture of rank-and-file officers. Officers learn that physical force is to be used only in a very limited range of situations. Officers have also learned that they have a professional duty to provide detailed and honest use of force reports. Their supervisors, meanwhile, understand that they are to critically review officer use of force reports. These three elements form the bedrock of a police department's commitment to accountability (a web of accountability, if you prefer), and the extent to which that commitment is sustained over time contributes directly to the transformation of the culture of the organization in which they work.

The Challenge of Sustaining Consent Decree Reforms

Sustaining major reforms has a very troubled history in American policing. "History demonstrates," White and colleagues argue, that meaningful reforms "are difficult to implement and maintain" in police departments. Reforms that were considered pioneering events in their day were allowed to collapse and disappear. It is also a little-studied issue among police scholars.[90]

Why Police Reforms Fail

The most useful framework for examining the problems associated with sustaining police reforms is professor Wesley G. Skogan's article "Why Reforms Fail," in which he identifies eleven factors related to the failure of police reforms. (The article did not examine consent decree reforms, but many of the author's points are relevant here nonetheless.)

The relevant ones include, but are not limited to, resistance by mid-level and top managers, by frontline supervisors, by rank-and-file officers, or by special units within departments; "public unresponsiveness," meaning lack of interest in and support of reforms by civic leaders and/or members of the public; serious police misconduct events that divert the attention of police leaders and the public; and changes in the leadership of a department.[91] Several of these issues have been found to be problems in consent decrees, although of differing levels of seriousness depending on the department. The list is useful with respect to the pattern or practice program as a guide to anticipating certain problems and preparing in advance to address them.

Three Cases of Failed Reforms

One of the most famous examples of a major reform that collapsed involved the anti-corruption program instituted in the New York City police department by then police commissioner Patrick V. Murphy in the early 1970s. A corruption scandal had erupted in the late 1960s, with some officers going public with their revelations. Generally referred to as the "Serpico" scandal (after officer Frank Serpico, who talked publicly about corruption in the department), the scandal achieved national notoriety and was investigated by a special mayoral committee.[92] Amid considerable publicity, Murphy overhauled the department's anti-corruption efforts, decentralizing responsibility for controlling corruption to commanders at the precinct level, with higher-ranking commanders handling the larger and more serious corruption cases. Murphy, however, left the department soon after his anti-corruption program was implemented to become head of the new Police Foundation in Washington, DC, causing a serious lack of continuity in leadership of the NYPD. The lack of leadership continuity proved to be fatal for the anti-corruption program.[93]

Twenty years later, a new corruption scandal erupted in the NYPD and an investigation by the Mollen Commission found that officer corruption had taken on a "new character," involving both corruption *and* brutality. The commission's report found that "cops did not simply become corrupt; they sometimes became corrupt and violent," threatening or beating drug dealers they encountered. Officers protected and assisted some drug traffickers, and some officers became drug dealers and users themselves. Officers covered up their illegal activity through widespread "perjury and falsifying documents." Most important, the entire corruption control system established by Murphy had "collapsed," with "ineffective field supervision," the collapse of the internal affairs division, and flawed "intelligence-gathering efforts," among other problems.[94] The basic problem with Murphy's corruption control program was that there was no independent external accountability agency with sufficient authority to monitor the department and keep the anticorruption program on track.[95]

A second example of a reform that was not sustained was the team policing experiment in the mid-1970s. Team policing embodied several of the ideas that would later be refined and embraced by the community policing movement. It called for decentralizing some police patrol units to the neighborhood level, with a team of officers who would have wide discretion in developing area-specific programs to address crime and disorder. Arising in the aftermath of the devastating riots of the 1960s, team policing was seen by its advocates as bringing the police closer to the neighborhoods where they worked, establishing closer relations with the people they policed, and developing policing strategies relevant to the area. In a burst of enthusiasm, police departments across the country quickly embraced the team policing idea. Unfortunately, there was little planning in the development of local team policing projects; no serious attention was paid to how decentralized units would be integrated into highly centralized and bureaucratized police departments, and how officer discretion would be effectively controlled in a decentralized context. As a result, team policing soon collapsed and disappeared almost as quickly as it had appeared.[96]

The evaluation of team policing in seven cities by professor Lawrence W. Sherman and colleagues identified three major obstacles to effective implementation of the program. The goal of decentralizing decision making undercut the traditional role of middle management, and officers at that level "often impeded their administrators' goals for team policing." Officers in the traditional patrol force, meanwhile, "objected to team policing" as a distraction from their role and resisted it in a variety of ways. Finally, dispatchers in the 911 systems, who had no stake in the new program, "greatly hampered team policing," although "often without intent." In New York City, for example, team policing officers "often spent half their time outside their [assigned] neighborhoods." The quick demise of the team policing experiment was due mainly to the rush to adopt the program, the failure to anticipate the very real organizational problems it created, and then the rush to drop what had become an embarrassing failure.[97]

A third reform that collapsed was the ambitious community policing program by the Chicago police department known as CAPS (Chicago Alternative Policing Strategy), launched in late 1994. The program was applied to five police districts, with considerable variation in their racial and ethnic composition and levels of poverty. A key component of the program was a regular series of "beat meetings" in all five districts, where police supervisors assigned to an area met with residents of that area and discussed problems that needed to be addressed. The program, however, slowly began to deteriorate in the 2000s. It was not abolished; it was struck by a number of factors over which it had no control. The crucial monthly beat meetings "dried up"; community organizers were laid off; the major recession that began in 2008 led to budget reductions and loss of officers; and Rahm Emanuel, who became mayor in 2011, declared crime as his central issue. The ambitious CAPS program survived only in name.[98]

Consent Decrees and Sustainability

The sad history of failed police reforms presented the pattern or practice program with a serious challenge. Nonetheless, the Civil Rights Division pressed forward, stating in its 2017 report that "the aim of the Division's reform agreements is to build capacity within the law enforcement agency to sustain the outcomes of the reform agreement." That aim, however, was not converted into a specific consent decree goal and there were no guidelines on how to achieve sustainability.[99] The "backsliding" and erosion of accountability in the Pittsburgh consent decree and the cancellation of the Collaborative Agreement in Cincinnati were done by local city officials and the police chiefs.[100] These hostile political forces, however, are beyond the control of the pattern or practice program. Despite the collapse of reform in those two cities, there has been no wholesale collapse of consent decree reforms in other pattern or practice cases.

Two consent decree reforms serve a sustainment function even though they are not labelled as such. Use of force review boards, as discussed in chapter 4, are directed to report any problems related to policy, training, or supervision to the police chief and the relevant unit commander with a recommendation for corrective action.[101] This role represents an important "self-policing" function and contributes to sustaining consent decree reforms (and other non-consent decree elements of the department). But it is only one such unit. Early intervention systems also serve a sustainment function, by identifying officers with performance problems and providing interventions designed to correct those problems. It too, however, is also one small unit in a police department. Sadly, sustaining consent decree reforms in a police department requires much more than just these two units.

A Possible Alternative Mechanism for Sustaining Police Reforms

A possible alternative mechanism for sustaining reforms involves creating inspectors general for police departments. IGs do not investigate individual public complaints but instead investigate police department policies and procedures and issue public reports with their findings and recommendations for change. As discussed earlier, the inspectors general in New York City, Los Angeles, Chicago, and Seattle have established very creditable records of investigating specific policies or practices, identifying the problems that exist, and making recommendations for change. The Seattle IG quickly developed an active program of examining the Seattle police department's policies and procedures, issuing fifteen reports, audits, or memoranda in 2020 and 2021.[102] The NYPD inspector general, meanwhile, has issued reports on officer use of chokeholds, the department's use of force policies, and a number of other important issues. In 2022, however, it came to light that the NYPD inspector general had encountered strong opposition from the police department's bureaucracy and that many IG recommendations were never implemented. As this is being written, the future of the NYPD inspector general is uncertain.[103]

As public documents, inspector general reports can make a significant contribution to sustaining consent decree reforms in two ways. First, they have the capacity to ensure that specific reforms are not allowed to slowly erode through inattention. Second, IG reports play an important role in informing the police chief and command staff, public officials, the media, and the general public about police department problems that need to be addressed. Inspectors general exist in only a few cities at present, but it is quite possible for other cities, regardless of their size, to create one. As an alternative, they could contract with private consulting groups with expertise in policing to perform annual audits. To limit costs, they could select a limited number of consent decree issues to be audited each year. In short, there are several ways in which cities or counties could ensure that their law enforcement agencies sustain existing reforms and even move up to a higher level of best practices.

The later generation of consent decrees adopted more formal procedures for ensuring sustainability. The most notable sustainability plan involved the Seattle consent decree. A Memorandum of Agreement on March 2, 2018, required the city to "assess [the police department's] sustained compliance" with consent decree reforms in seven quarterly reports. The reports were to measure achieved compliance, and in addition "drive reform beyond the requirements" of the consent decree into the period "after federal oversight has ended." The reports would assess use of force reporting by officers; the quality of the work performed by the Office of Police Accountability (OPA); supervisors' compliance with consent decree requirements regarding their responsibilities, and six other areas. The statement about moving *beyond* the requirements of the consent decree is pregnant with meaning. It clearly indicates that the authors of the sustainability statement have a vision of police reform that looks beyond the consent decree, with an eye to continuing reform of the Seattle police department after the consent decree has ended.[104]

Sustainability is indeed a serious challenge, and the pattern or practice program was launched without a clear set of objectives regarding how it would be achieved. Nonetheless, programmatic options are available. Chapter 6 discusses these options in greater detail, with a discussion of how they would relate to other police reform efforts.

Conclusion

The pattern or practice program has faced a number of different challenges during the course of its work, along with one important development that has been a great credit to the program. The program has faced resistance to reform from federal and local political figures in several known instances, but the damage done by Republican presidents has been temporary and minimal, while the resistance from local officials has been more significant. Police unions, meanwhile, have traditionally been a major obstacle to police reform and continue to obstruct it, through provisions in their collective bargaining agreements and political influence at the state and local levels. The pattern or practice program, however, has evaded the power of police unions by doing an "end run" around collective bargaining agreements. The consent decree reforms are management prerogatives under collective bargaining law and beyond the power of police unions to prevent or seriously obstruct them. The costs of consent decrees are very high, but police departments have offset those costs through consent decree reforms that reduced police misconduct and the resulting expensive litigation. The various evaluations of consent decrees are a mixed bag, although the two most comprehensive evaluations both found successful results. The most positive gain for the pattern or practice program is the persuasive evidence in some court-appointed monitors' reports that consent decree reforms have had positive impacts on the conduct of police officers and as a result have reshaped the officer subculture in a positive direction. Finally, the issue of sustaining consent decree reforms after a consent decree has ended remains a very difficult issue, about which there is little research. In the end, therefore, it is safe to say that the pattern or practice program has achieved positive gains on three issues: police unions, the costs of consent decrees, and the positive impacts of reforms on the police officer subculture. It seems fair to conclude that these positive gains outweigh the impacts of the other issues discussed in this chapter.

6

The Future of Police Reform

Police reform has a future, a future that most observers of the police have not fully grasped, in large part because recent reform efforts have been so widely dispersed across the country. The previous chapters of this book have examined the work of the Justice Department's pattern or practice program and concluded that, apart from some shortcomings and a few failures, the program has been enormously successful in achieving significant reforms in deeply troubled police departments. The bulk of this chapter involves an examination of the many reform efforts that have arisen in recent years. One is the revival of the Justice Department's pattern or practice program and its companion program, the Collaborative Reform Initiative. Several state attorneys general, meanwhile, have initiated police reform litigation programs of their own and have brought reform to a number of small police departments. State legislatures have been very active in enacting police reform legislation on a variety of issues. City councils have been equally active in passing new laws on police department policies and citizen oversight agencies. One particularly important development at the city level has been the creation of inspectors general to oversee the police departments in their communities. Reform-minded police chiefs, working through the Police Executive Research Forum, meanwhile, have continued their work of publishing valuable reports on critical police issues. The insurance industry has begun to use its financial leverage to force police departments to revise their policies in ways that reduce officer misconduct. Finally, there are promising developments related to collaborative approaches among police departments and private and public service agencies seeking to develop new ways of delivering public safety to the communities they serve. The list of police reform efforts is extensive and holds great promise for the future. This chapter concludes with a discussion of the future of police reform, with a specific emphasis on how local grassroots organizing in cities and towns can become a major instrument for building public support for police reform and changes in local police departments.

The Current Context of Police Reform

We stand at a crucial moment in police reform. Much has been accomplished in recent years to improve American policing. Police departments that have experienced consent reforms have reduced fatal police shootings and reduced officer use of excessive force, along with other reforms. Much remains to be done, however. Out of the eighteen thousand local law enforcement agencies in this country, many remain untouched by meaningful reforms. The police shot and killed 1,176 people in 2022, a record high, with an average of three people per day. African Americans represented 24 percent of the victims. The overall patterns are fairly stable, although with some interesting changes. The number of fatal shootings by sheriff's department officers rose to 416, compared to 277 in 2013 (the first year the national survey was conducted). California deaths dropped by 29 percent since 2013, while Texas deaths rose 30 percent.[1]

The media have produced a steady flow of articles commenting on the alleged "failure" of police reform, particularly the failure of Congress to pass the George Floyd Justice in Policing Act in 2021 (although it was revived after the death of Congressman John Lewis in early 2023) and the failure of President Joe Biden to act decisively on police issues. The $1.9 trillion American Rescue Plan Act (ARPA) had lax requirements for how local governments were to spend the money and, to the great disappointment of police reform advocates, much of it was spent on Tasers, rifles, automobiles, and armored vehicles.[2]

The problem of race/ethnicity and policing continues, however, and we are still a long way from a fully lawful, professional, and respectful policing. It is foolish to believe that police-related racial and ethnic problems can be eradicated in just a few years by a few reforms. It is not foolish, however, to review the accomplishments of the Justice Department pattern or practice program since its inception in 1994 and see the very tangible improvements in controlling officer use of force, ending vehicle and pedestrian stops that lacked legal justification, improving public complaint procedures, and developing community engagement.

Chapter 5 argued that the evidence on many police reforms also had the effect of reducing racial disparities in policing, but more remains to be done. Michael White and colleagues are among the relatively few scholars who have a national perspective on policing and are optimistic. Assessing the national picture in 2021, they concluded that "it is clear that the push for reform has reached a tipping point," that "the momentum for reform is unprecedented," and that there is "a sense of optimism about the potential for real police reform in the immediate to near future."[3]

The Revived Justice Department Police Reform Programs

The Pattern or Practice Program Returns

The Justice Department's pattern or practice program revived in 2021 with Joe Biden as president and Merrick Garland as attorney general. Well before the Biden administration took office in 2021, there was persuasive evidence that pattern or practice program consent decrees had made remarkable progress in transforming troubled police departments. The New Orleans police monitor in January 2019, for example, found sharp declines in firearms discharges, the use of electronic control weapons, and public complaints against the department.[4] In Seattle, meanwhile, the court-appointed monitor's May 2022 *Comprehensive Assessment* of the police department cited a list of important achievements on key issues. Officer use of force had "decreased significantly," with record lows in 2019 and 2021. The "most serious force incidents" had fallen 61 percent since 2014, and the monthly use of electronic control weapons had declined 80 percent between 2001–2010 and 2015–2021. Some racial disparities still existed, however, with African Americans experiencing more serious use of force than whites. The reporting and review of use of force incidents had "improved dramatically" during the consent decree years. Investigations of officer misconduct related to use of force rose "steadily" between 2014 and 2018, but then declined "by more than half" in 2019 and reached a new low in 2021.[5]

While some other police departments are still struggling to implement their consent decrees in mid-2022, they are outnumbered by the success stories. The Justice Department in the spring of 2022, for example, publicly acknowledged that the once deeply troubled Baltimore police department had made progress toward compliance with implementing its consent decree.[6]

One of attorney general Merrick Garland's most important actions upon taking office was to revive the pattern or practice program. The Civil Rights Division responded quickly by opening investigations of the police departments in Louisville, Minneapolis, Phoenix, Columbus, Ohio, and other departments that soon followed. The revival of the pattern or practice program restored to active police reform work the single most important national reform program, which had served as an inspiration and model for other reform efforts discussed in this chapter.[7]

The revival of the pattern or practice program energized the national debate over the proper role for the program. Christy Lopez pointed out in 2022 that "a newer set of critiques" of the program had joined the debate. Police reform "activists and advocates" argue that the program's consent decrees are "inherently ill-equipped to remedy police abuse," and that the entire DOJ process with respect to policing "stands in the way of the more transformative change necessary" to end the "systemic harm" done by policing. Lopez disagrees with that assessment, arguing that it "falls short" in the context of the full range of DOJ activities. Conceding that the "DOJ cannot fix policing on its own," she argues that police racism is deeply embedded in this country's "educational, housing, medical/mental health care systems." But she adds that while the DOJ is selective about "which problems to investigate," it "support[s] the efforts of others working toward the same civil rights objectives."[8] The evidence presented in this chapter supports Lopez's argument. The work of state attorneys general, the emergence of local police inspectors general, and the burst of police reform among state legislatures and city councils are part of a broad national commitment to police reform, on a scale that has never been seen before. In that context, the DOJ pattern or practice program is only one police reform effort, but an extremely important one that has its own special niche in the larger picture.

Rebirth of the Collaborative Reform Initiative

The Justice Department in 2021 also revived the Collaborative Reform Initiative (CRI), which the Trump administration had cancelled. The CRI is a voluntary collaborative program in which local police departments and city officials acknowledge that they have a significant police problem and request federal assistance to help address the problem. The voluntary aspect of the CRI program means that police departments and city officials are committed to improving their police department at the very outset.[9]

The CRI program includes three different options, which were unchanged by the Biden administration. The lowest level of assistance to local departments is the Technical Assistance Center, which has available a wide range of services related to sixty different police issues. The midrange option is the Critical Response program, which responds to requests for assistance regarding a high-profile event, such as a controversial shooting or excessive use of force. The highest level of support is the Organizational Assessments program, through which the Justice Department undertakes in-depth reviews of "systemic issues" in police departments. This part of the CRI program most closely resembles the Justice Department's pattern or practice program, although with no judicial oversight or court-appointed monitor (a point that some police reform activists object to).[10] It is noteworthy that on May 30, 2022, the U.S. Justice Department initiated a CRI Critical Incident Review investigation of the horrific shooting deaths of nineteen young children and two teachers in Uvalde, Texas, just a week earlier. This action demonstrated the capacity of the CRI program to respond quickly to serious events.[11]

The first police department to participate in the original CRI program was the Las Vegas metropolitan police department (LVMPD) in 2012, which had a serious use of deadly force problem. The CRI investigation focused on the policies, training. tactics, and documentation related to deadly force incidents. The CRI final report found that the LVMPD had reached a very high level of compliance with the proposed reforms.[12] The CRI program also investigated the San Francisco police department, but the investigation abruptly ended when the Trump administration cancelled the entire CRI program in September 2017. The findings report and recommendations survived, however, and the mayor of San Francisco and the chief of police successfully petitioned the California attorney general to assume the role of monitor for implementing the reform recommendations.[13]

An independent evaluation of the CRI program in 2017 found that police departments engaged in the program were "motivated" to seek the investigations and that the technical assistance providers "made efforts to understand [the] local context and the complexities" in the departments they investigated. One problem was "a disconnect" in several cases over what "compliance" with recommendations would involve. The evaluation made ten specific recommendations for improving the CRI process, expressing hope that this "new and innovative model" can be a "viable alternative" for achieving police reform.[14]

The great advantage of the CRI program, including all three of its options, is its flexibility in responding to the different needs expressed by local police departments. The Organizational Assessments component of the program is best suited to addressing a complex set of problems in a police department and is far less expensive than the DOJ pattern or practice program. The Technical Assistance Center, meanwhile, is primarily an information center. Some civil rights and civil liberties advocates have argued that without the coercive element of court-mandated reforms, there is no mechanism for enforcing recommended reforms in the CRI program. In the best of all possible worlds, it would be better to have some coercive process, but that is simply not possible given the financial resources currently available.[15] The most important contribution of the CRI program is that it does not detract from the pattern or practice program but supplements it by adding a new instrument of Justice Department police reform, and brings reform to a far greater number of police departments.

Changes in the Social and Political Climate

The prospects for future police reform have been greatly enhanced by three significant changes in American social and political life since the 2014 crises in Ferguson, Missouri, and the murder of George Floyd by a Minneapolis police officer in May 2020. They include a major upsurge in political protests over police misconduct; a parallel change in public attitudes about the police, police misconduct, and police racism; and a significant change in news media coverage of police misconduct incidents. The three changes are closely interrelated, affecting each other in complex ways, as responses to the continuing flow of police shootings and beatings across the country.

Grassroots protest against police misconduct increased to unprecedented levels in the period beginning in 2014. Two separate incidents have fueled these protests. The first was the fatal shooting of Michael Brown in Ferguson, Missouri, on August 9, 2014. The national news media coverage was intense, covering sympathy protests that sprang up across the country and lasted for weeks. The sense of a national police crisis prompted President Barack Obama to create the President's Task Force on 21st Century Policing, which in June 2015 published its *Final Report* with a total of 151 recommendations and action items on legitimacy, procedural justice, and community engagement, among many other issues.[16] The second incident was the murder of George Floyd by a Minneapolis police officer on May 25, 2020, which prompted even more massive national protests.[17] In early July 2020, the *New York Times* published a national map indicating the locations of protests following the George Floyd murder. The *Times* cited a Kaiser Family Foundation poll estimating that 26 million people said they had protested during one week in June. A *Times* writer later wrote that those protests were one of the "biggest protest actions in American history," an astonishing achievement that clearly signaled a new public mood about policing.[18] An important social and political dimension of the demonstrations was that white Americans were a majority of the people in many of those events, clearly indicating that outrage over police brutality and demands for police reform had reached white Americans as never before.

The massive protests over the Brown and Floyd deaths had a profound impact on public opinion about the police and police misconduct. A 2021 Associated Press-NORC poll found that the percentage of Americans believing that police violence was "an extremely or very serious problem rose" from 36 percent in 2019 to 48 percent in 2021, a shift undoubtedly spurred by the Floyd murder.[19] A 2020 Gallup poll, meanwhile, found that the percentage of Americans believing that civil rights for African Americans had improved dropped sharply from a high of 89 percent in 2011 to 59 percent in 2020.[20]

Public attitudes were also reshaped by changing media interpretations of police misconduct. Professors Angela S. Lee, Ronald Weitzer, and Daniel Martinez studied print media coverage of the crises in three cities with controversial police-caused deaths: Ferguson, Missouri; North Charleston, South Carolina; and Baltimore, Maryland. In all three cities they found the press more likely than before to frame their stories in terms of police problems rather than criminal offenders, and to raise questions about the underlying causes of police misconduct, rather than focus on the immediate incident. The published stories discussed police violence, poor police-community relations, and an "accountability deficiency," a situation in which police officers are "rarely held accountable for their misconduct." This perspective was more in line with the views of protesters and other police critics than had been the case in the past and had the effect of giving a "new visibility" to "police wrongdoing." In a separate article, Weitzer argued that as a result of the increase in media coverage of police shooting cases, more recent stories were "now seriously debating a host of reforms in policing." In a third article, Weitzer found that a "large majority of whites support many of the reforms advocated by Black Lives Matter," indicating a significant change in the attitudes of whites about the police and what needs to be done to end the national race crisis.[21]

One significant source of skepticism about the possibilities of future police reform was a disillusionment with both Congress and President Joe Biden's failure to press strongly for police reform legislation.[22] Those criticisms have considerable merit, but the skeptics are looking at only one part of the total police reform picture. This chapter argues that there is considerable police reform activity across the country, rooted in the work of a number of state attorneys general, state legislatures, and city councils, all of whom have undertaken significant police reforms.

The Emergence of State Attorneys General as Police Reformers

On February 5, 2018, the attorney general of California signed a Memorandum of Understanding with the mayor and police chief of San Francisco, agreeing to assume the responsibility of helping the San Francisco police department implement the 272 reform recommendations made in 2016 by the original CRI investigation.[23] The California attorney general's action was extremely important from a national perspective on police reform. While state attorneys general had engaged in occasional police reform actions in earlier years, the San Francisco case marked the arrival of state attorneys general as serious police reform litigators.[24]

The importance of the police reform actions by state attorneys general must not be underestimated. As most observers had noted years earlier, the Justice Department pattern or practice program is small and able to undertake only a small number of cases. The Civil Rights Division reported in 2017 that in a little more than twenty years it had reached settlements with forty law enforcement agencies, twenty of which involved judicially enforced consent decrees.[25] The involvement of state attorneys general theoretically multiplies the potential number of litigation agencies by a factor of fifty. To be sure, conservative Republican attorneys general are not likely to take on police reform, but their liberal Democratic counterparts are more likely to do so. Importantly, state attorneys general are more accessible to city and state-level police reform activists seeking investigation of local police departments. Additionally, should a Republican be elected president in 2024 and cancel the DOJ pattern or practice program as previous Republican presidents have, state attorneys general could fill the void.[26]

One potential problem for state attorneys general is the ambiguity of their legal authority in either their constitutions or state statutes.[27] White and colleagues in 2021 recommended federal and state legislation "conferring standing upon state attorneys generals to sue and obtain equitable relief in federal court against police departments in their jurisdictions to remedy and prevent violations of constitutional rights."[28] Then California attorney general Xavier Becerra in June 2020 had previously acted on this point with a letter to the Democratic and Republican leaders in both houses of Congress urging an amendment to the 1994 Violent Crime Control and Law Enforcement Act to give "clear statutory authority" to state attorneys general to "investigate and resolve patterns or practices . . . of unconstitutional policing by local police departments."[29]

The Police Reform Work of the California Attorney General

Becerra initiated what quickly became the most active police reform program among state AGs. On June 15, 2020, he issued a statement setting forth a broad police reform agenda, including a duty of officers to intervene to stop misconduct by other officers; a ban on chokeholds and carotid restraints; a de-escalation requirement; a prohibition on shots at moving vehicles, and five other reforms. He also sought legal authority to review and "proactively help" law enforcement agencies "reform their policies and practices."[30]

By 2022, the California attorney general's office had investigated twelve local law enforcement agencies. The reports and recommendations emerging from those investigations were comprehensive and detailed, resembling the Justice Department pattern or practice findings letters and consent decrees. One of Becerra's first actions, as discussed earlier, was to assume responsibility for monitoring reforms in the San Francisco police department. Implementation went well, and to cite one important development, between June 2018 and May 1, 2019, no San Francisco police officer fired his or her weapon—a sure sign of progress in controlling police officer conduct. In a second major case, the attorney general's office investigated the Sacramento police department and in 2019 issued a ninety-seven-page report with recommendations for a new use of force policy, the reporting and investigation of officer use of force, "incident reviews" of officer-involved shootings, and community engagement and transparency.[31]

A notable feature of the California attorney general's efforts included the investigations of the police departments in the cities and towns of Bakersfield, Guadalupe, Maywood, Torrance, Tustin, Vallejo, the Kern County sheriff's department, the gang records and policies of the Los Angeles police department, the Los Angeles County sheriff's department, the Stockton school district, and the Santa Clara County sheriff's department. It is important to note the range in the size of the departments investigated: from the largest department in the state, the LAPD, to departments in very small cities such as Tustin (population 77,765), Maywood (population 27,703), and Guadalupe (population 7,160). The capacity of state attorneys general to bring police reform to very small towns across the country greatly expands the scope of police reform litigation, supplementing the work of the U.S. Justice Department's pattern or practice program. The work of the California attorney general caught the attention of attorneys general in other states, and in January 2023 the newly sworn in Maryland AG announced his plan to seek authority from the governor and the state legislature to enforce federal and state laws related to civil rights violations and police misconduct.[32]

The Illinois Attorney General and the Chicago Police Department

Illinois attorney general Lisa Madigan took the most aggressive action by a state attorney general when her office investigated the Chicago police department and secured a consent decree under her authority. When the Trump administration suspended the pattern or practice program, Madigan recalled, "With no other framework in place to secure necessary reforms, we were left with no other choice. We sued the City of Chicago in federal court."[33] Her effort is notable for several reasons. First, she stepped in and pursued a consent decree when the arrival of President Donald Trump's administration made it impossible for the outgoing Obama administration to finalize a consent decree, even though it had an agreement in principle with the city of Chicago.[34] Second, she achieved a new dimension in community engagement in policing by successfully arranging for two community coalitions, which were suing the Chicago police department, to be accepted by the federal district court as formal parties to the consent decree. Finally, she and her staff obtained a consent decree in the face of delay and dissembling by then Chicago mayor Rahm Emanuel and also the fierce opposition by the Fraternal Order of Police, the rank-and-file officer police union, which tried to sabotage the consent decree.[35]

In conducting its own investigation of the Chicago police department, the attorney general's office made "community engagement and feedback the central focus" of its program. It organized roundtable discussions across the city to "hear from the community members most impacted" by the police, and also organized focus groups with police officers to gain their perspective. The attorney general offered the Fraternal Order of Police a formal role in the consent decree, but the union rejected it. A draft of the proposed consent decree was finally released on July 27, 2018. The federal judge overseeing the case encouraged public input regarding the proposal, and over five hundred letters or memos were filed. The district court approved the consent decree on January 31, 2019.[36]

The inclusion of two community coalitions as formal partners in the consent decree was a historic moment in the history of police reform. No similar event had occurred in the Justice Department's pattern or practice program or any other known police reform effort. The two coalitions, the *Campbell v. City of Chicago* plaintiffs and the *Communities United v. City of Chicago* plaintiffs, signed a Memorandum of Agreement with the Illinois attorney general and the city of Chicago in March 2018. The two groups, referred to as "the Parties," gained, among other things, an opportunity to make presentations to the negotiating teams from the city and the attorney general if they felt that certain issues were being neglected, and the right to file motions to enforce provisions of the consent decree if they felt it necessary.[37] Thus, the two community groups gained a genuine voice in the implementation of the consent decree and established a new dimension of community engagement in police reform.

The Colorado Attorney General

The attorney general of Colorado joined the police reform effort with a 2021 investigation of the Aurora, Colorado, police department and fire safety department. By April 2022, the AG's office was swamped with nearly two thousand complaints about police misconduct, indicating the extent of police misconduct across the state and the high level of public demand for action. The investigation found that the Aurora police department had "a pattern and practice of engaging in racially biased policing against people of color" and "against black people in particular"; used excessive force; and failed to "document stops as required by law." Recommendations for improvement were made for each problem area, including "improve[d] use-of-force policies to give more specific guidance to support officers." A consent decree between the city and the state attorney general was entered in November 2021, and an independent monitor issued its first report on the police department in July 2022.[38]

A remarkable aspect of the Aurora report, however, was attorney general Philip Weiser's discussion of the need for comprehensive reform of police departments. "How much a city benefits from police reforms," he explained, "depends on how comprehensive those reforms are." This important perspective came from the Justice Department's pattern or practice program, and a glance at the report's footnotes indicates that he and his staff were familiar with not just that program but also the broader literature on police reform. We should note that the reports issued by the California attorney general are also comprehensive and reflect the influence of the Justice Department's pattern or practice program. This would seem to confirm the initial expectations of the pattern or practice program's staff that its work "can inform reform measures in police departments across the country."[39]

The actions of the three state attorneys general indicated that a new legal force for police reform was emerging. If more state attorneys general followed their example, it would greatly increase the number of police reform litigation agencies and in many cases bring police reform to small cities and towns.

New Jersey Attorney General: A Novel Approach

The New Jersey attorney general developed an alternative approach to police accountability compared with his peers in other states. Instead of investigating local police departments and bringing civil suits against them, he established an Excellence in Policing Initiative, which incorporated some previous reform efforts. In December 2019 the initiative published a new edition of its Internal Affairs Policy and Procedures (IAPP) manual. The first edition was published in 1991 and in 1996 the state legislature passed a law requiring all law enforcement agencies in the state to adapt their own policies to be consistent with the IAPP. The 2021 edition of the IAPP contained sample forms for public use in filing complaints against a police department. (The forms were in ten different non-English languages.) Following an earlier attorney general directive, all state law enforcement agencies were required to submit a Major Discipline Reporting Form, reporting all disciplinary actions in the previous six months. The attorney general's initiative also included an Internal Affairs Dashboard, which included summary data on all currently open internal affairs investigations.[40]

Other Police Reforms at the State Level

A Burst of Police Reform Legislation by the States

Almost lost in the ongoing national controversy over police misconduct has been the significant police reform activity by state legislatures. A major outburst of new laws followed the 2014 fatal shooting of Michael

Brown in Ferguson, Missouri, and was given a further boost by the recommendations of the 2015 report of the President's Task Force on 21st Century Policing. The Vera Institute of Justice surveyed state legislative activity in 2015 and 2016 and found that thirty-four states and the District of Columbia passed a total of seventy-nine bills, executive orders, and resolutions relating to police reform. In the previous three years, only twenty such bills had become law.[41]

The Vera report *To Protect and Serve* divided the seventy-nine legislative actions into three broad categories: policing practices, documenting police actions, and police accountability. The single most popular idea was requiring police departments to equip their officers with body-worn cameras. Twenty-seven states passed thirty-three laws on this issue. A Connecticut law, for example, mandated the use of body-worn cameras and required the development of guidelines on the retention of body-worn camera footage.[42] The next most popular category involved curbing racial profiling, with seven states enacting laws. A California law expanded the number of demographic categories to be covered by the term "profiling" to include race, color, ethnicity, national origins, gender identity or expression, sexual orientation, and three other categories. An Oregon law required all law enforcement agencies in the state to have written policies and procedures on profiling.[43] Six states, meanwhile, enacted laws controlling how police respond to vulnerable populations and/or mandating the development of crisis intervention programs for incidents involving people experiencing mental health crises. An Indiana law required the state law enforcement training academy to have a mandatory training program on responding to people with mental illness, addictive disorders, developmental disabilities, and other disorders.[44]

Interestingly, only four states enacted laws involving the control of officer use of force. Colorado limited the use of chokeholds by police officers, while Illinois prohibited their use altogether. With respect to police accountability, several states enacted new laws requiring independent investigations (that is, independent of the department where the incident occurred) in the event of a serious injury or death at the hands of local police officers. Hawaii created a Law Enforcement Officer Independent Review Board to investigate deaths of persons in the custody of law enforcement and all deaths by officer-involved shootings.[45]

The Vera report is significant for two reasons. The sheer volume and national scope of the legislation are particularly impressive and clearly reflect a shift in public attitudes about police misconduct and police racism. Far more people were willing to lobby the legislatures on police reform than ever before. Also important is the sophistication of most of the laws; they were not poorly drafted statutes enacted in the heat of the moment. The final report of the President's Task Force on 21st Century Policing in June 2015 had recommendations on all the major issues covered in the new state legislation and undoubtedly influenced the content and the language of proposed bills.[46]

State legislatures continued their police reform activity after the 2015–2016 period. The *New York Times* reported in the fall of 2021 that since the murder of George Floyd in May 2020, thirty states had enacted 140 pieces of police reform legislation. One commentator called it "a remarkable, nationwide, and in some places bipartisan movement that flies directly counter to years of deference to the police." The continuing high level of activity by state legislatures on police reform clearly confirms the optimism about the future of police reform expressed by White and colleagues in 2021.[47] The National Conference of State Legislatures gave a strong boost to police-related legislation with a series of useful background reports, including a 2022 report titled *Investigation and Prosecution of Use of Force* and a Statutory Database with details on approaches to different police-related issues in all fifty states.[48]

Making Public Officer-Involved Shooting Data and Police Disciplinary Records

The states of Texas, California, and New York between 2015 and 2020 passed extraordinary laws that represented major steps forward in police transparency and accountability. Texas in 2015 passed a law requiring all law enforcement agencies in the state to report all officer-involved shootings to the state attorney general's office. Remarkably, HB 1036 was passed by a vote of 133–0 in the House of Representatives, with one legislator voting "present."[49] The list of shootings by department and year is available to the public on the attorney general's website and adds a new dimension to the transparency on the most sensitive of all police issues.

California and New York, meanwhile, each passed laws stripping confidential status from at least some police disciplinary files. A 2018 California law eliminated confidentiality protection from selected parts of police officer disciplinary files, including investigations of officer shootings and other major incidents of use of force, alleged sexual assault by officers, and officers lying on duty. The latter provision marked the first serious effort anywhere in the country to investigate and take action against the scourge of police officers lying. In 2022 the legislature went even further, enacting SB 16 making an even broader range of police actions public records and requiring police departments to keep better records on cases of police misconduct and subsequent investigations.[50] The city of San Jose, meanwhile, took an additional step forward in 2022 with respect to transparency on police misconduct records. It created a web portal through which citizens could access closed misconduct case information held by the city's independent police auditor. The auditor receives complaints from members of the public and reviews the police department's internal affairs investigations. Any person is free to access the auditor's records. Stephen Caines, the police department's deputy chief innovation officer, explained that the department needed to go beyond providing traditional police services and have "robust oversight mechanisms." (The term "innovation officer" added a new and quite possibly influential concept into the world of American policing.) The San Jose mayor added that the new portal was "critical to transparency."[51]

In June 2020, meanwhile, the New York legislature repealed Section 50-A of the state civil rights law. Passed in 1976, Section 50-A shielded from public scrutiny the disciplinary records of police officers, firefighters, and correctional officers in the state. Police reformers and civil rights activists had for years argued that by shielding data on police misconduct, the law was a major barrier to police accountability. Release of the once confidential data, however, was delayed by strong resistance from police unions. In late 2022 the New York Civil Liberties Union was suing nearly a dozen police departments in its effort to obtain once secret disciplinary files.[52]

In an even broader decision, the New Jersey Supreme Court in 2022 unanimously ruled that the public had a "broad right of access to certain information about serious police misconduct." The decision involved a public records request for an internal affairs report in the Elizabeth, New

Jersey, police department. The court based its decision not on a state law but on the common law, which requires courts to balance public interest against police departments' interest in confidentiality. It remains to be seen whether courts in other states will follow the New Jersey Supreme Court reasoning on the scope of the common law.[53] In the spring of 2022, meanwhile, a Maine judge ordered the state police to "unredact" certain police disciplinary records and release them to the news media.[54]

By 2020 the political winds had shifted dramatically in the direction of transparency, and police unions had lost much of their political clout on issues such as keeping police disciplinary files confidential. The decisions to open police officer disciplinary records to public scrutiny in California, New York, New Jersey, and Maine were major victories in the struggle for greater transparency and accountability and provided models for other states to follow. A June 2022 editorial by the editorial board of USA Today declared that "making police disciplinary records public is a critical part" of ensuring police accountability and building community trust. The editorial was a clear indication that the issue had become national in scope. Journalists funded by the Pulitzer Center in Washington, DC, published an invaluable report on police misconduct records laws in all fifty states. It is clearly a useful resource for further efforts to make public these disciplinary records.[55] The question of the confidentiality of police officer disciplinary records remains bitterly contested, however, with police unions exercising all their lobbying power to keep the records confidential.

A National Movement for Police Transparency?

The Texas, California, and New York state laws are important steps forward with respect to increasing the transparency of American police departments and ending the long-standing practice of refusing to make information about police operations open to the public. A 2022 report by the Cronkite School at Arizona State University strongly suggests that there is a growing public interest in greater transparency. That belief was confirmed by the Justice Collaborative Institute, which in 2020 released national survey data indicating that 66 percent of likely voters supported "making all law enforcement disciplinary records of police officers available to the public"; 73 percent, meanwhile, felt that "the public has a right to know which police officers . . . have records of excessive force, sexual assault, racism, or lying."[56]

The most impressive program cited by the report is the Police Transparency Hub in Houston, Texas, which includes data (updated every two months) on three areas: information on submitting a complaint; a dashboard with data on a range of police activities; and access to police department policies and resources. The dashboard includes data on traffic stops, officer use of force, disciplinary actions, and two other issues. With respect to officer use of force, the dashboard includes data on the total number of incidents (since January 1, 2020), the nature of underlying incidents, the outcome for the subject against whom force was used, and the subject's race or ethnicity. The disciplinary action dashboard, meanwhile, includes the total number of disciplinary actions (347 since January 1, 2020) and the discipline imposed (149 suspensions and 18 written reprimands).[57] The Houston Police Transparency Hub is arguably the most detailed disclosure of information about police actions of any department in the country.

The Chicago inspector general also maintains a public dashboard on police department activity. This includes 911 calls (with data, charts, and maps), arrests, complaints, and investigative stop reports. The data are less detailed than the Houston transparency hub but are nonetheless an important step forward. The Chicago Invisible Institute has archived data on citizen complaints against Chicago police officers from 1988 to 2018, which is the most comprehensive archive of such data in the country.[58]

The number of transparency efforts discussed here and in the Cronkite School report are admittedly few in number. But as the report explains, "efforts come from many directions." They would appear to be harbingers of a broad national movement in the years just ahead.[59]

The Work of Other State Agencies

Other state-level agencies also began to join the police reform effort. Just days after the murder of George Floyd by a Minneapolis police officer, the Minnesota Department of Human Rights filed a charge of race discrimination against the Minneapolis police department. Assisted by the highly respected consulting group 21st Century Policing Solutions, it delivered a blistering seventy-two-page report in 2022. Thorough and well-documented, the report found that Minneapolis police officers consistently used more severe force against African Americans than whites; were more likely to stop vehicles driven by African Americans or Indigenous people; and searched and arrested people of color more than whites. The heart of the problem, the report explained, was an organizational culture that the department's leaders taught, reinforced, and did not attempt to correct. The department trained its officers "to be aggressive towards community members," which led to the use of excessive force, offensive language, and other racially biased conduct. The police department's various training programs reinforced a "warrior" culture, teaching officers to require "instant and unquestioned compliance" from members of the community. Field training officers, who supervised officers just out of the police academy, communicated the same message. The department's early intervention system was judged a "failure," in part because the department "does not collect or consider all relevant data" on police officer performance to make the system work effectively. It should be noted that the findings of the Minnesota Human Rights Department were remarkably similar to the conclusions of the 1991 Christopher Commission report on the Los Angeles police department in terms of its comprehensive organizational perspective.[60]

The report explained that the Department of Human Rights would begin seeking a consent decree to require needed reforms. The U.S. Justice Department was also investigating the department at that time and presumably would also seek a consent decree. Whether the two decrees would be merged into one was not immediately known.[61]

The Washington Coalition for Police Accountability (WCPA), a network of organizations and individuals committed to police reform, was founded after the 2020 murder of George Floyd in Minneapolis. During 2021, its first full year of operation, it helped to enact twelve police accountability laws during the legislative session. Its priorities for 2023 included a law creating an independent prosecutor who would investigate and prosecute officers guilty of misconduct. Its independent status would remove cases from county prosecutors, who in some cases have traditionally been influenced by local political considerations. Another bill would end qualified immunity for all sworn police officers in the state. Ending the protection of qualified immunity had been a goal of police reformers around the country for many years. The work of the WCPA in just its first years provides a model for police reform activists in other states with regard to state-level police reform legislation.[62]

The actions by the state-level agencies in Texas, California, New York, Minnesota, and Washington suggest a promising new element of state-level police reform activity. All states have agencies with some grounds for investigating local police departments and could, with the proper leadership and resources, become significant players in the national police reform effort.

New York Governor's Statewide Police Reform Effort

The single most ambitious state-level reform was New York governor Andrew Cuomo's Executive Order 203, creating the New York State Police Reform and Reinvention Collaboration, issued on June 12, 2020. The order mandated that every local political jurisdiction initiate a planning process, with extensive community input, that would result in a police reform plan. The deadline for the plans was April 1, 2021. Governor Cuomo directed each jurisdiction to review community needs; establish policies "that allow police to effectively and safely perform their duties"; "involve the entire community"; and "offer a plan for public comment." Questions to be addressed included, but were not limited to, defining the role of the police; "whether to deploy social service personnel instead of or in addition to police officers"; strategies "to reduce racial disparities"; and procedures for greater community engagement with the police.[63]

The governor's program was ambitious, but it is not clear that there were enough police experts, knowledgeable about the most recent developments in policing, available to assist in the development of all the four hundred-plus project reports. Cuomo's resignation in August 2021, moreover, clouded the future of the program. A quick scan of a few of the reports selected at random indicated that they were well designed, but it is still far too early to assess how effectively the plans are being implemented.[64]

Police Reform Work by City Councils

An Explosion of Police Policies and Oversight

In the summer of 2020, there was an explosion of police reform legislation among city councils in response to the murder of George Floyd on May 25. An informal survey by the author of this book of the fifty largest cities in the country by population found, remarkably, that 84 percent of city councils enacted at least one police reform ordinance between late May and Labor Day of 2020, with several cities enacting several different ordinances.[65]

Eleven cities passed ordinances either creating a new police oversight agency, strengthening an existing one, or creating a task force to consider developing one. Six cities banned the use of chokeholds by the police; three banned "no knock" entries into private dwellings; and three banned the use of chemical sprays and/or the use of tear gas against demonstrators. Only three passed an ordinance requiring the police to use de-escalation (possibly because by the summer of 2020 de-escalation was already adopted by many police departments). No action was taken, however, in several cities where city council sessions were cancelled because of loud and disruptive protests at the session.[66]

The activist group Black Lives Matter contributed to the wave of police reform ordinances with a convenient "8CantWait" list of eight police reform proposals. They included a ban on chokeholds; a de-escalation requirement; verbal warnings before shooting a member of the public; exhausting all remedies before shooting; a duty to intervene where another officer was violating the law or department policy; prohibiting shooting at moving vehicles; requiring police departments to adopt a use of force continuum; and requiring officers to report all incidents of use of force and threats to use force or to point their weapons at people.[67] The eight proposals are all reasonable; some have already been adopted by police departments. The format of the list is clear, concise, and readily accessible to both community activists and city council members.

New Police Oversight Agencies

New police oversight agencies had begun to grow significantly by 2022, according to a survey by law professor Sharon Fairley, who concluded that "civilian oversight has moved into the mainstream as an important component of any police accountability system." Twenty-five new oversight agencies were created in one year; previously it had taken four years to reach that number. Philadelphia created a new Citizens Police Oversight Committee in 2022, with far more powers than the Police Advisory Commission, which it replaced. The powers included subpoena power (which had long been bitterly opposed by police unions); access to crime scenes and records; and the authority to conduct its own investigations.[68] Baltimore, meanwhile, created a new Police Accountability Board in 2022 as mandated by the state's 2021 Police Accountability Act, which required all law enforcement agencies in the state to create an oversight agency.[69] Additionally new oversight agencies continued to be proposed and in many cases adopted through 2023, indicating for the first time a strong feeling across the country that some form of citizen oversight of the police is needed.[70]

The growth of new citizen oversight agencies was a boon for the National Association for Civilian Oversight of Law Enforcement (NACOLE), the national professional association for oversight agencies. Founded in 1995, NACOLE holds an annual meeting, conducts training on a variety of police and oversight issues, and provides support and technical assistance to oversight agencies. The latter two activities contribute significantly to the professionalism of member agencies.[71]

Oversight and Community Input in Chicago: The GAPA Ordinance

The most important development regarding community engagement and the police was the enactment by the Chicago city council of the GAPA ordinance in 2021. GAPA stands for Grassroots Alliance for Police Accountability, a nonprofit activist agency that worked for four years, conducting more than two hundred meetings, to develop the ordinance providing strong powers of oversight and considerable community input into the Chicago police department.[72] The complex structure of the oversight process includes a citywide Community Commission for Public Safety and Accountability. Potential members are nominated by the neighborhood-level district councils, selected by the mayor, and approved by the city council. The commission sets goals and priorities for the superintendent of police, conducts an annual review of the superintendent's performance, works with the police department to set policies, and requires the superintendent and other officials to provide data and reports upon request. These provisions represent a strong and unprecedented element of community input into management of the Chicago police department. The commission selects candidates for superintendent and submits them to the mayor, who can appoint one or reject all of them. The commission can also draft new or revised police department policies, although the mayor can veto them. At the neighborhood level, three-member district councils were created for each of the police department's twenty-two police districts, with members elected by the residents of each district. The councils are tasked with establishing relationships with the police commanders and officers who work in each district and developing community policing initiatives tailored to the crime and disorder needs of each district.[73] Together, the Community Commission and the district councils involve a high degree of democracy and community voice in police issues and are an unprecedented experiment in police governance. Their work is still in the process of development as this book is being written, and implementation has been delayed by the usual Chicago politics. In early 2023, however, mayor Lori Lightfoot failed to win renomination for a second term in office. She was a supporter of the GAPA innovation, and with her loss, the future of this new police oversight process is uncertain.[74]

Inspectors General for Local Police Departments

The most important new police reform institution at the local level has been the inspector general. IGs are independent local agencies that do not investigate public complaints against police officers but instead investigate the policies, procedures, and actions of the police departments they are responsible for. They conclude investigations with public reports on their findings with recommendations for reform. IGs are a particularly important reform instrument as they serve as permanent monitors of local police departments. They are free to choose the issues they investigate, and police departments are required to comply with all requests for information and data. The earliest IGs were established in Los Angeles, New York City, and Seattle; others soon followed.[75]

The public reports issued by IGs can make an extremely important contribution to the public knowledge of the inner workings of police departments. The reports provide key players in the community with valuable information about a variety of police problems. The players include the police chief and top command of the police department (who generally have a right to file a rebuttal to any report), elected local officials, prosecutors and defense attorneys, the news media, public interest groups that address police issues, and the general public. Aside from prosecutors, who can convene grand juries, none of the other stakeholders have the authority or the resources to gather the kind of detailed information about police department operations that an inspector general can. Because of their staff resources and the time to dig deeply into particular issues, inspectors general often report on issues that the various stakeholders were unaware of or only partly aware of. The contribution to public awareness of policing and internal police problems is unmatched by any other criminal justice agency.[76]

Inspectors general are few in number at this point, with relatively new ones in Chicago, Seattle, Louisville, Kentucky, and Columbus, Ohio. Interestingly, the Chicago inspector general issued a report in 2022 sharply criticizing two existing police watchdog organizations: the police department's Bureau of Internal Affairs and the civilian Office of Police Accountability. The report found that both offices lacked policies and protocols for the conduct of their own investigations.[77] The recent addition of new inspectors general clearly reflected growing public demand for greater oversight of the police and an awareness of the special role that IGs can play. One possible future role for local inspectors general, as suggested earlier in this book, would be to serve as post-consent decree monitors for police departments. The monitoring work could involve one or two issues each year, so as to not overload the IG and crowd out its work on other non-consent decree issues.

Police Chief-Led Reform

In the national context of policing, police chiefs across the country contribute to reform by continually revising their policies and regularly adopting new programs or revising existing ones. Chiefs have widely adopted de-escalation and banned officer chokeholds. Chief-led reforms, of course, are piecemeal reforms, with each reform affecting only a part of a police department's operations. As such, they do not attract significant media attention and are little noticed at the national level, but they do have cumulative impacts on individual departments. In their article on how to build accountability into police departments, White and colleagues correctly pointed out in 2021 that there is "momentum within the police profession to institutionalize reform."[78]

The PERF Policy Reports

The real engine of reform within the police profession has been the Police Executive Research Forum (PERF), an association of chiefs and command officers that is a rival to the much larger International Association of Chiefs of Police (IACP), the national professional association for police chiefs and top commanders. PERF has issued a steady flow of reports on issues with recommendations for change over the years. Many of the reports have challenged established police thinking and practices and define new standards for critical issues. PERF reports begin with a one-day conference on a selected issue, with participants including police chiefs, command officers, attorneys with relevant experience, social service providers, and some academics. The key points raised at the conference are then published as reports and are available free online on the PERF website.[79]

The best recent PERF reports include the 2011 report *2011: Electronic Control Weapons*; a 2012 report on de-escalation; a 2013 report on the Justice Department's pattern or practice program that was a candid and mostly favorable discussion of the subject; and a 2014 report on body-worn cameras. The 2015 report *Constitutional Policing as a Cornerstone of Community Policing* was almost certainly the first major report by a national group of police chiefs describing adherence to constitutional principles as a bedrock value for the police profession. As one police chief put it, "The Constitution is our boss. . . . We are not warriors, we are guardians."[80]

The 2015 PERF report *Re-Engineering Training on Police Use of Force* was a shocker for the police profession, documenting the distorted priorities of police training programs with their overemphasis on use of force and other control techniques and very little attention to communication skills. A survey of 280 PERF-member departments found that recruit training programs spent an average of fifty-eight hours on firearms training, forty-nine hours on defensive tactics, and twenty-four hours on use-of-force scenario training, but only ten hours on communication skills and eight hours on de-escalation training. The PERF report included an extended discussion of tactical decision making, with a strong emphasis on training officers to slow down an encounter, keep one's distance from a potentially dangerous suspect, gain time to gather information about the situation, and even disengage from the encounter if necessary. "Time," a Los Angeles police department commander explained, "gives you the ability to communicate with the suspect," "to make a tactical plan," and "to get resources to the scene." Several meeting participants, meanwhile, argued that there is no "shame" in "retreating and calling for backup."[81] The tactical decision-making model provides guidance to officers on how to better control officer response to difficult and often complex incidents and thereby reduce the use of force.

Among all the PERF reports, the 2016 report *Guiding Principles on Use of Force* is arguably the most important and the one with lasting impact on policing. It brings together key points that had been discussed in previous PERF reports, including, for example, the reports on de-escalation and police training, in order to form a comprehensive statement on the subject of police use of force. The stated purpose of the report was "to move policing to a higher standard when it comes to how and when officers use force in situations where they and the public are not threatened by firearms." That higher standard included a sharp criticism of the Supreme Court's 1989 decision in *Graham v. Connor*, the controlling court decision on police officer use of force. The court in *Graham* enunciated a three-pronged "test of reasonableness" that includes "the severity of the crime"; "whether the suspect poses an immediate threat to the safety of officers or others"; and whether the suspect "is actively resisting arrest or attempting to evade arrest by flight." Many police leaders, police reform experts, and court observers have for over thirty years criticized the court's reasonable test as too vague, opening the door for officer shootings in situations where, for example, there is no imminent threat to the life of the officer or some other person. The PERF report argues that the *Graham* decision tells officers what they "*can legally do*" in certain situations but "does not provide specific guidance on what officers *should do*" (italics in original). The result, PERF and other experts have argued, is shootings that are "lawful but awful"— lawful in terms of *Graham* but awful in the eyes of a reasonable person and much of the public.[82]

The remarkable aspect of the PERF discussion of *Graham* is that, probably for the first time ever, a respected police association has argued that police policies on a critical police action should be *more restrictive* than what the Supreme Court requires. The PERF report makes the important point that controlling police officer use of force is not a simple matter of a paper use of force policy, but is richly complex, involving "*how* departments should devise their policies, strategies, tactics, and training." Thus, a revised use of force policy requires changes in all of a police department's training activities: the police academy curriculum, the field officer training curriculum, and the regular in-service training curriculum.[83]

The PERF *Guiding Principles* report promulgated thirty "guiding principles" on officer use of force. Principle 1 states that "the sanctity of human life" is at "the heart of everything" a law enforcement agency does. Principle 2 holds that law enforcement agencies should adopt the best policies, practices, and training on use of force "that go beyond the minimum requirements of *Graham v. Connor*." The fourth principle states that de-escalation should be a formal policy for all law enforcement agencies. Principle 5 calls for adoption of the critical decision-making model as a strategy for officers approaching difficult encounters, including "assessing the situation, threats, and risks"; "identifying options and determining the best course of action"; and continually "reviewing, and reassessing the situation." Principle 6 calls on agencies to adopt "Duty to Intervene" policies that would prevent use of force by other officers. Principle 9 holds that deadly force should not be used "against individuals *who pose a danger only to themselves*" (italics in original). The remaining principles address other aspects of a professionally managed law enforcement agency.[84] All of these principles are directed toward creating a comprehensive approach to reducing police officer use of force, both deadly and nondeadly.[85]

The IACP's Response

The International Association of Chiefs of Police (IACP) in 2017 responded to the PERF *Guiding Principles* report by helping develop a document titled *National Consensus Policy on Use of Force*. In fact, the "consensus" policy was not supported by all law enforcement agencies. Particularly significant, the IACP consensus report opted for keeping the status quo, recommending staying within the boundaries of the Supreme Court's *Graham* decision. The two major national sheriffs' associations, meanwhile, went even further, rejecting the basic idea of a national standard on the force issue because it would not accommodate the views of many of their agencies.[86] That argument undermines the basic principle in all accreditation systems, an argument that would shock leaders and members of all professional associations. The IACP somewhat belatedly developed a Policy Framework for Improved Community-Police Engagement, although the substance of that effort remained extremely weak.[87]

New Approaches to Delivering Police Services

The Insurance Industry and Police Reform

In large part because of the increasingly large jury awards and settlements in police misconduct litigation, the insurance industry has in recent years begun "to force police reform," according to the *Washington Post*. Because of their financial leverage, insurers are "successfully dictating changes to [police] tactics and policies," although mainly in small and medium-sized departments across the country. (Large police departments generally have separate insurance arrangements.) An article published by the Brookings Institution argued that "insurers are the key to progress on police reform." Monetary damage awards, the author adds, "have little impact on police departments" in terms of key policies such as use of force. Insurers have the clout, including the threat of cancelling their policies, to force departments to make substantive changes in policies and procedures that are likely to "reduce both litigation and the resulting costs." Withdrawing from the police field is a realistic option for many insurers, and the number of insurers has been "shrinking."[88]

The current situation of insurers reacting to rising police litigation and costs occurred once before in American police history, in the mid-1970s and 1980s, largely in response to increased litigation over police fatal shootings. In an insightful discussion of this issue in his book *Making Rights Real*, Charles R. Epp argues that in the 1970s police leaders "had no institutionalized understanding of the liability issue" and were essentially learning on the job. Insurers began "to press their organizational clients to adopt policies aimed at reducing their [financial] exposure." The current situation today is essentially repeating that earlier experience.[89]

Collaborative Approaches to Enhancing Public Safety

One of the ironic twists of the massive protests following the George Floyd murder in May 2020 was the response to the calls to "defund the police" by the more radical protesters. The call was nothing more than an empty slogan that expressed deep alienation from the police. There was never any substantive program beyond the vague idea that the police should be replaced by alternative public service agencies or programs. In fact, there was never any meaningful reduction in police department budgets. A 2022 survey of 109 law enforcement agencies by ABC News found only eight whose budgets were cut by more than 2 percent, while 91 agencies had budget increases of 2 percent or more. The Los Angeles police department's budget rose by 9.4 percent in the 2019–2021 period, while Chicago's rose by 15 percent in the same time period.[90]

The angry criticisms of police shootings and brutality by the advocates of defunding the police had the effect of stimulating creative thinking about alternative ways of delivering police services to promote public safety. Across the country, police departments, community activists, and social service agencies began to develop collaborative programs involving the police and social service professionals. The Vera Institute of Justice in 2021 published a challenging report titled *Investing in Evidence-Based Alternatives to Policing*. The report opened with the blunt declaration that "changing the ways police operate in communities is integral to dismantling systemic racism." It explained further that using "police and punitive measures as the primary tools to address health and social issues" simply "funnels millions of people into jails and prisons." It supports its argument with its earlier report *Understanding Police Enforcement: A Multicity 911 Analysis* (September 2020) and a brief report titled *What Happens When We Send Mental Health Providers instead of Police* (May 2021), which comments briefly on programs in Eugene, Oregon, and Denver. It should be noted that the approach advanced by the Vera Institute of Justice resembles in part the work of the Justice Department's pattern or practice program with respect to gender bias in New Orleans and police response to people experiencing mental health crises in Portland, Oregon.[91] The U.S. Justice Department in December 2021 awarded $34 million in grants to police departments engaging in partnerships with health and mental health agencies and other community health providers for programs addressing homelessness, mental health issues, and substance abuse problems. It is still too early in the development of these new programs, but they are a creative way of reorienting the delivery of police services.[92]

Reimagining Public Safety: The Policing Project

The Policing Project, based at New York University Law School and directed by professor Barry Friedman, has engaged in a number of policing projects since its founding several years ago, including neighborhood policing, the 30x30 Initiative for Women in Policing, and regulating the use of technology in policing litigation, along with several others. Its latest and most challenging project involves its Reimagining Public Safety project, which seeks to move away from traditional law enforcement and develop means of providing "vital services to communities that need them." The program's specific goals include "fostering neighborhood safety" and "reducing reliance on police." The program addresses the central problem of the "monumental mismatch between community problems and how the government responds to them." The goal is not to "abolish" the police, as more radical critics of the police demand, but to develop positive working relationships between the police, social service agencies, and neighborhood groups. Friedman argues in his article "Disaggregating the Police Function" that American policing today imposes enormous harms on the communities it serves, including shootings, excessive physical force, stops, searches and arrests, and incarceration. He concludes his article by arguing that "too much of what we treat through the criminal law and agencies of law enforcement are really problems of public health and social welfare. For various reasons, it has become our default to address them with the police power, literally, in the name of 'public safety.' But it is not at all clear we are achieving that safety, and certainly not in optimal ways. We can and must do better." It is clear from the way Friedman presents the issues that he and his colleagues do not have ready-made solutions but plan to use the project as a means of developing new and innovative approaches to developing a new approach to maintaining public safety.[93]

Summary of Police Reform Efforts

The various police reform activities discussed in this chapter clearly indicate that there is a broad spectrum of police reform across the country. These activities include the police reform work by state attorneys general; the significant body of police reform laws by state legislatures and city councils; the important new initiatives making police disciplinary records public; the work of state agencies such as the Minnesota Department of Human Rights; the significant growth of citizen oversight agencies; the growth of inspectors general as local independent monitors of police departments; the continued effort of forward-thinking police chiefs to publish new policies on critical issues; and the emergence of collaborative efforts between police departments and social agencies to better address important social problems. When we step back and gain a national perspective on all these efforts, it is an impressive picture.

Police reform, in short, is far from dead. It is alive and very active. One of the best hopes for the future is that the many efforts will continue to grow, to expand into new areas of policing, and to gain added strength, support, and achievements. The concluding section of this chapter provides a discussion of how the future of police reform can be shaped by vigorous grassroots efforts in every community.

Building the Future of Police Reform

How then are we to build the future of police reform? There is an old political adage that says, "All politics is local." There is much truth in that saying, and there is even more truth in the police adage "Most policing is local." The scenario for future police reform at the local level consists of three different stages: creating an informal community working group and beginning the work on police reform; strengthening and expanding the initial efforts; and finally, creating a formal organization that serves as a permanent community police commission.

Starting from Scratch: Creating a Working Group

An informal working group or task force on police reform begins by bringing together people who have already been active in police issues or at least have a deep interest in police problems. Members can be recruited from neighborhood groups, the faith community, small business owners, representatives of different racial, ethnic, and LGBT groups, lawyers with experience in police issues, and academics with an interest in and/or experience in policing issues. Once established, the working group needs to select a chairperson and to begin developing a plan of action. The initial discussions should focus on what members see as the major problems with their local police department. These problems can include patterns of unconstitutional stops of people, police treatment of homeless people or persons experiencing a mental health crisis, the department's handling of domestic disturbances, and other issues that concern people. From among these issues, the working group can begin to develop a specific reform agenda. It is important to note that cities and communities vary considerably with respect to dealing with the police. Some have well-established networks of reform activists. Others have almost no networks and are quite disorganized with respect to police problems. Each community will have to determine where it stands and how best to build an effective network.[94]

With an agenda in hand, the working group should then announce its presence in the community with a press conference to explain the current problems with the police department and the group's goals for addressing them. Follow-up meetings with neighborhood associations, civic groups, religious institutions, college and university campus groups, and other suitable venues should follow. The working group should also seek meetings, with no media present, with the police chief, the mayor, and city council members. The working group's course of action following those meetings should be shaped by the degree of receptivity, indifference, or hostility expressed by those officials.

Strengthening the Working Group

To expand and strengthen its reach, the working group should at some point begin to create task forces devoted to particular issues such as the handling of domestic violence calls or homeless people. The staff of local social service agencies should be invited to join the subgroup or simply serve as experts. Each subgroup should also begin to develop a library of resource material, including the key policies of the local police department, the policies from other police departments, and relevant articles and reports. On most issues, task force members should review the policies of other police departments (which are conveniently available on the Internet) to help get a picture of the prevailing standards across the country. Once a task force gets a good perspective on the issue it has chosen, it can (and should) recommend that the working group hold a public meeting on the subject. Such a meeting would enhance the visibility and stature of the working group.

Expanding the Working Group's Agenda

As the working group gains experience and a deeper knowledge about police policies and operations, it should begin thinking about expanding its agenda.

One new activity would be to initiate lobbying for the creation of an independent inspector general to oversee the local police department. Inspectors general are mandated to investigate problems in a local police department of its own choosing and to issue public reports on their findings. The inspectors general in Los Angeles, New York City, Chicago, and Seattle have already established substantial records of investigating problems and making sound recommendations for change. A local inspector general would essentially serve as a permanent monitor of the local police department, with the authority to choose which issues to investigate, to obtain police department data and documents (with appropriate confidentiality provisions), and to issue public reports with recommendations for reform.

Another important initiative would be to build a coalition of activist groups in other cities in the state to lobby the state attorney general to develop a program of police reform litigation, as other state attorneys general have already done. Political leaders and civic activists from both major political parties should be lobbied in order to obtain their support for the idea. Increasing the number of state attorneys general involved in police reform litigation would be a powerful supplement to the U.S. Justice Department's pattern or practice program. The statewide coalition should also undertake lobbying the legislature for needed police reform laws. As explained earlier, state legislatures have been extremely active in enacting police reform laws since 2015. Members of the coalition from around the state should meet and agree on a short list of needed state laws and laws that need to be repealed.

Creating a Permanent Community Police Commission

As the working group becomes well established, with some solid accomplishments, it should begin to think about lobbying the city council to create a permanent community police commission to oversee the local police department. A community police commission should be broadly representative of the community, with representatives based on race, ethnicity, gender, sexual orientation, neighborhoods, and so on, and representatives from local civil rights and civil liberties groups. The best example of this is the Seattle Community Police Commission (CPC), which grew out of a history of community activism on police problems. A community police commission began as a requirement in the Seattle consent decree, and in 2017 the Seattle city council enacted an ordinance making the CPC a permanent city agency. Very quickly, the new CPC developed a notable agenda of reform activity, involving Seattle police department issues, including the Seattle police union contract, and state criminal justice issues.[95]

Once established, the community police commission should continue the reform efforts the working group had been doing and strengthen and expand those efforts as needed. It should embark on a public information campaign to inform the community about police problems and the group's reform objectives. This would include press conferences, public meetings, and speaking events hosted by schools, faith organizations, and civic groups.

There is one significant obstacle, however, that prevents many Americans from having an optimistic view of the status of police reform today and the possibilities for the future. Too many people expect that reform efforts will transform police departments quickly, and that there will soon be few if any fatal shootings by police officers; fewer cases of use of excessive force; less discrimination in stops, searches, and arrests, and so on. Knowledgeable police experts, however, know that the idea of quick change in policing is pure fantasy. Police reform requires steady effort and takes time. There are three examples from the last sixty years of American history that illustrate the point: the civil rights movement, the women's rights movement, and the lesbian and gay rights movement. All of them required decades of struggle, with both victories and setbacks along the way. But few of the activists in these movements gave up and walked away from the challenge. And so it is with police reform. Much has been accomplished since the 1970s. But more needs to be done. We cannot walk away from the challenge of creating a lawful, professional, and respectful police across this country.

Conclusion

The evidence in this chapter clearly indicates that a number of police reform movements across the country have appeared in recent years. Some are expansions of older reform efforts, while others are brand-new. The pattern or practice program, which President Donald Trump suspended, and the Critical Response Initiative, which had been abolished, have been revived. These developments are clear causes for optimism about the future of police reform. Particularly important, several state attorneys general have begun to undertake police reform litigation. Both state legislatures and city councils, meanwhile, have enacted a large volume of police reform legislation. Some of those laws have stripped the veil of secrecy away from police disciplinary files, and there appears to be developing a national movement for greater transparency in policing. Citizen oversight agencies continue to grow. The insurance industry has begun forcing police departments to revise certain policies so as to reduce the costs of police misconduct litigation. Some police departments have developed collaborative relationships with community organizations and groups with respect to mental health and related issues. This chapter ended with a discussion of how community groups can organize with the goal of developing an effective lobbying group for police reform and in the future possibly gaining political support for a community police commission. With all of these developments, it seems that the future of police reform across the country looks very good.

Epilogue

Final Thoughts on the Future of Police Reform

The Justice Department's pattern or practice police reform program has no precedent in the history of the American police. Never before has the U.S. Department of Justice had the authority to investigate local and state law enforcement agencies, and where patterns of unconstitutional policing exist, file civil suits against those departments. The suits have ended with consent decrees that mandate sweeping reforms designed to end the abuses of the law. The leaders of the pattern or practice program have both a broad vision and ambitious goals for improving American policing. The overriding goal is to end unconstitutional police practices while at the same time significantly reducing if not eliminating discriminatory practices based on race, ethnicity, and gender. No previous reform effort in the history of the American police has ever had such a vision or goal.

Has the pattern or practice program succeeded in achieving its goals? To a great extent it has. Most of the judicially enforced consent decrees have succeeded in reducing police officer use of force and ending motor vehicle stops that were without legal justification. Several of the departments with the worst records prior to the consent decree have reported significant reductions in use of force and officer misconduct, and a consequent reduction in litigation and savings of millions of dollars. In several departments the program has succeeded in creating formal structures of community engagement, giving community residents a formal voice in police policies and strategies for addressing crime and disorder. These are major accomplishments, unmatched by any previous reform effort reaching back to 1900. The pattern or practice program pursues comprehensive reform of police departments of a sort that past police reforms never imagined.

To be sure, there have been a number of failures. Some departments experienced serious "backsliding" as once implemented reforms began to erode. The most disheartening failure was in Cincinnati, where local political leaders and the police department chief decided to end the Collaborative Agreement that had made significant accomplishments in improving relations between the police department and the African American community. The various failures, however, are only a small part of the overall pattern or practice program's work. The failures account for only 15 percent of all the consent decrees. An 85 percent success rate is a very good record.

Without question, the pattern or practice program's greatest achievement has been to inspire other police reform efforts across the country. One of the program's stated goals in 2017 was to serve as a model and inspiration for other reform programs. Chapter 6 examined the most notable among these: a revival of the Collaborative Reform Initiative, which the Trump administration had abolished; police reform litigation by state attorneys general; a burst of reform laws by state legislatures across the country, with similar activity by city councils; a movement toward public disclosure of police disciplinary files, introducing greater transparency in policing; the creation of inspectors general to serve as oversight agencies for the police in a number of cities; a steady flow of important policy reports by the Police Executive Research Forum, a national group of forward-looking police chiefs and commanders; insurance industry efforts to require stricter policies so as to reduce litigation expenses; and finally, a wave of collaborative efforts between police departments and community groups to establish new ways of enhancing public safety.

The above list of the many police reform efforts is genuinely impressive, involving different public and private organizations in a variety of ways. A similar pattern of active police reform did not exist twenty-five years ago. All of these new efforts, it needs to be said, are independent of the pattern or practice program, which undoubtedly has played a major indirect role in inspiring this broad range of police reform activity. This broad-based foundation serves a very important function. Imagine, if you will, that a conservative Republican is elected president in 2024. And imagine further that he or she directs the attorney general to suspend or even abolish the Justice Department's pattern or practice program. Remember that two previous Republican presidents brought the activity of the pattern or practice program virtually to a halt. Would police reform efforts across the country suddenly shrink in size and level of activity?

Of course not.

The various new police reform efforts would undoubtedly continue and grow. And it is very likely that they would be joined by other new efforts. The pattern or practice program would certainly be missed if it were suspended, but police reform across the country would continue.

The strength of police reform efforts is not simply a matter of organizations. What propels these efforts today is the dramatic shift in public attitudes about the need for further police reform. There is now a deep-seated revulsion among Americans against the continued high level of fatal shootings by police, the unnecessary and often illegal stops of motor vehicles, and the unnecessary beatings of people who have done no wrong. Recall the news media accounts of the massive national protests across the country in the summer of 2020 following the murder of George Floyd in Minneapolis. The *New York Times* mapped the many protests that occurred in just one week. Additionally, the composition of the protesters was quite remarkable: in many protests, the majority of the participants were white. This fact alone marked a major turning point in American attitudes about police misconduct. The demand for meaningful police reforms had moved from the fringe to the forefront of American political life.

This book has provided a detailed examination of the police reform efforts of the Justice Department's pattern or practice program. For the most part, the consent decrees have been successful in ending the worst abuses and establishing more lawful policing. As chapter 6 explained, the pattern or practice program has been joined by a broad range of police reform efforts.

There is good reason to be optimistic about the future of police reform.

The vigorous police reform efforts across the country, this book argues, have created a solid foundation for future reform efforts. The final section of chapter 6 provided a brief outline of how future police reform can be pursued through the creation of local community police commissions. The basis for such a development already exists in many communities. Additional commitment and organizing work can bring more effective police reform to police departments across the country. Only then will we have a lawful, professional, and respectful police in every community.

ACKNOWLEDGMENTS

With respect to my career as a specialist in American policing, I owe my deepest thanks to the late Herman Goldstein, one of the most influential experts in policing in this country. Herman died in January 2020. Our relationship began with him serving as a mentor to me on police issues, and over the years it developed into a deep friendship. He played many important roles in American policing. He was part of the field research team for the pivotal American Bar Foundation Survey of Criminal Justice in the mid-1950s. He later served as an important contributor to the President's Crime Commission's *Task Force Report: The Police* (1967) and the American Bar Association's *Standards Relating to the Urban Police Function* (1973). In all three of these activities, he developed and promulgated new ideas that would soon became major parts of the accepted understanding of American policing. After we first met, he responded to my interest in policing and shared with me his most important ideas and a good bit of gossip about the day-to-day world of policing. Herman was also the founder of the idea of problem-oriented policing, which soon became an important part of American policing. To be honest about it, I think he greatly appreciated my interest in his work because I soon learned that he felt that his law school colleagues were not terribly interested in his ideas or perspective on policing. He was and remains a giant figure in the world of American policing. I owe him very much.

I also want to thank other scholars who shaped my career. Professor David Harris at the University of Pittsburgh Law School introduced me to the world of the Justice Department's pattern or practice program when in 1997 he asked me to read and comment on a draft of the consent decree for the Pittsburgh Division of Police. Soon after that, Professor Christy E. Lopez, who was then a staff member of the pattern or practice program, directly involved me in the program when she retained me as a consultant on the consent decrees for both the Washington, DC, police department and the New Jersey state police. This was my first real taste of the program; it shaped my career and ultimately led to this book. I also owe considerable thanks to a number of people who, like me, regularly attended the annual meetings of the National Association for Citizen Oversight of Law Enforcement (NACOLE). I have always made a point of getting together with them to discuss our mutual insights into the latest developments in the world of policing. My deepest thanks to all of these people.

NOTES

CHAPTER 1. OUR NATIONAL POLICE AND RACE CRISIS

1 Lowery, *They Can't Kill Us All.*

2 President's Task Force, *Final Report.*

3 "Black Lives Matter Puts Another Stamp on History," *New York Times*, July 6, 2020, https://nytimes.com. The *Times* story reported the results of the national surveys of participation in demonstrations.

4 "New Low in U.S. See Progress for Black Civil Rights," Gallup, September 9, 2020, https://news.gallup.com

5 Kennedy, *Don't Shoot*, 124–55 ("Across the Race Divide"). Chapter 5 will discuss an important critical perspective on Kennedy's "narrative" argument. White, Weisburd, and Wire, "Examining the Impact of the Freddie Gray Unrest."

6 Walker, "The Justice Department's Pattern-or-Practice Police Reform Program."

7 Walker, *A Critical History of Police Reform*, 51–106 ("Professionalism Arrives").

8 Abraham, *Justices, Presidents, and Senators.*

9 National Advisory Commission on Civil Disorders, *Report*, 299–322 ("The Police and the Community") (hereinafter cited as Kerner Commission, *Report*); Platt, *The Politics of Riot Commissions.*

10 Davis, *Police Discretion.*

11 Rushin, *Federal Intervention in American Police Departments*, chaps. 2 and 3.

12 Stuntz, "The Political Constitution of Criminal Justice."

13 U.S. Civil Rights Division, *The Civil Rights Division's Pattern or Practice Police Reform Work*, 25; Walker, "The Justice Department's Pattern-or-Practice Police Reform Program."

14 See U.S. Civil Rights Division, *The Civil Rights Division's Pattern or Practice Police Reform Work*, 15–16.

15 Lopez, "DOJ Police Pattern-or-Practice Investigations," 39.

16 The Special Litigation Section (SLS) website, https://justice.gov, contains findings letters, consent decrees, and other legal documents. The "Archives" section contains the same materials from closed cases.

17 U.S. Civil Rights Division, *Investigation of the Cleveland Division of Police* (2014), 14–35.

18 Lopez, *Disorderly (Mis)Conduct.*

19 U.S. Civil Rights Division, *Investigation of the Seattle Police Department*, 4, 5, 12, 13, 14, 17.

20 U.S. Civil Rights Division, *Investigation of the New Orleans Police Department*, 43–51.

21 U.S. Civil Rights Division, *Investigation of the Newark Police Department*, 30–31.

22 U.S. Civil Rights Division, *Investigation of the Portland Police Bureau*, 2.

23 U.S. Civil Rights Division, *Letter to the Honorable Anthony Williams*.

24 U.S. Civil Rights Division, *Investigation of the Baltimore City Police Department*, 149–53.

25 U.S. Civil Rights Division, *Investigation of the Portland Police Bureau*.

26 The term "accountability deficiency" is in Lee, Weitzer, and Martinez, "Recent Police Killings," 204 (table 2). See also the discussion in chapter 6.

27 Walker, "The Justice Department's Pattern-or-Practice Police Reform Program," 27, 37. The most thorough and provocative discussion of organizational policing is Schwartz, "Systems Failures in Policing." See also Walker, "'Not Dead Yet,'" 1818–23.

28 Walker, "The Justice Department's Pattern-or-Practice Police Reform Program," 31–32, 38.

29 U.S. Civil Rights Division, *The Civil Rights Division's Pattern or Practice Police Reform Work*, 2, 12, 14, 20. See also the discussion of organizational transformation in White, Fradella, and Flippin, "How Can We Achieve Accountability," 417–18.

30 Walker, "The Justice Department's Pattern-or-Practice Police Reform Program," 33–34, 38 (calling for more research on the subject).

31 Rahr and Rice, *From Warriors to Guardians*.

32 The original and influential work on the police officer subculture (although challenged, revised, and expanded by much subsequent research) is Westley, *Violence and the Police*.

33 Stone, Fogelsong, and Cole, *Policing Los Angeles*, 19–32.

34 New Orleans Police Department, Office of the Consent Decree Monitor, *Comprehensive Reassessment*. On the quality of police work in the NOPD prior to the consent decree, see U.S. Civil Rights Division, *Investigation of the New Orleans Police Department*.

35 Davis, Henderson, and Ortiz, *Can Federal Intervention Bring Lasting Improvement*.

36 Stone, Fogelsong, and Cole, *Policing Los Angeles*, 19–32.

37 Hannah-Jones, *The 1619 Project*.

38 Fogelson, *Big-City Police*; Walker, *Popular Justice*, 49–79.

39 Kerner Commission, *Report*, 1.

40 Kennedy, *Don't Shoot*, 124–55.

41 Epp, Maynard-Moody, and Haider-Markel, *Pulled Over*.

42 Peffley and Hurwitz, *Justice in America*, 188–93 ("fairness"), 209 ("no easy answers").

43 U.S. Civil Rights Division, *The Civil Rights Division's Pattern or Practice Police Reform Work*.

44 Harmon, "The Problem of Policing," 782–86; Rushin, "Police Union Contracts"; Rushin, "Police Disciplinary Appeals." On non-consent decree police monitors,

auditors, and inspectors general, see Walker, *Police Accountability*, 86–116, 146–57, 183–84.

45 Harmon, "The Problem of Policing," 785.

46 See the brief discussion of the best practices question in Walker and Archbold, *The New World of Police Accountability*, 298–300.

47 Police Executive Research Forum, *Guiding Principles on Use of Force*. This report and others are available online at the Police Executive Research Forum website, www.policeforum.org.

48 Geller and Scott, *Deadly Force*, 248–97.

49 New Orleans Police Department, *Operations Manual*, chap. 41, 13 ("Anti-Bias Policing"); *United States v. City of New Orleans*, Consent Decree (2013), section 181.

50 President's Task Force, *Final Report*, 14 (Action Item 1.5.1).

51 Sam Levin, "'It Never Stops': Killings by U.S. Police Reach Record High in 2022," *Guardian*, January 6, 2023, www.theguardian.com. The most comprehensive analysis of police shootings is Zimring, *When Police Kill*. See also Federal Bureau of Investigation, *Uniform Crime Reports, 2019, Law Enforcement Officers Assaulted and Killed*, https://ucr.fbi.gov.

52 Rashawn Ray, "Five Things John Lewis Taught Us about Getting in "Good Trouble,"" Brookings Institution, July 23, 2020, https://brookings.edu.

53 White, Fradella, and Flippin, "How Can We Achieve Accountability," 450.

54 Hyland and Davis, *Local Police Departments, 2016*, table 2.

CHAPTER 2. A HISTORY OF POLICE REFORMS

1 Fogelson, *Big-City Police*; Walker, *A Critical History of Police Reform*, 3–31 ("The Police Unreformed").

2 Zachs, *Island of Vice*.

3 Walker, *A Critical History of Police Reform*; Fogelson, *Big-City Police*; Miller, *Cops and Bobbies*.

4 Walker, *A Critical History of Police Reform*; Miller, *Cops and Bobbies*; Walker, "Governing the American Police," 616.

5 Walker, *A Critical History of Police Reform*, 53–78; Fogelson, *Big-City Police*.

6 Walker, *A Critical History of Police Reform*, 61–67; Steffens, *The Shame of the Cities*, 134–61 ("Philadelphia: Corrupt and Contented"). On superintendent James Robinson, see Jill LePore, "Invention of the Police," *New Yorker*, July 20, 2020.

7 Domanick, *To Protect and Serve*; Hayde, *My Name's Friday*; *People v. Cahan*, 44 Cal.2d 434, 282 P.2d 905 (1955).

8 MacNamara, *New Jersey Municipal Police Survey*, 10, 28, 32, 53; Walker, "Governing the American Police," 629–31.

9 Schmidt, *The Sit-Ins*, 47–57.

10 Arsenault, *Freedom Riders*. Arsenault also covers the less well-known 1947 Journey of Reconciliation challenging racial segregation in interstate travel in the states of the Upper South.

11 McWhorter, *Carry Me Home*.

12 Bryant, *The Bystander*; Purdum, *An Idea Whose Time Has Come*, 3–33 (Birmingham protests), 34–37, 56–58 (President Kennedy's television speech).

13 Kerner Commission, *Report*, 36–37.

14 Baldwin, *The Fire Next Time*, 120. Biblical source: Genesis 9:17. "God Gave Noah the Rainbow Sign" is the title of a Carter Family song.

15 Drinan, "The Pre-Election Moratorium on Demonstrations."

16 "Key Negro Groups Call on Members to Curb Protests," *New York Times*, July 30, 1964, https://nytimes.com.

17 An excellent collection of original documents on race riots and essays by contemporary historians is Platt, *The Politics of Riot Commissions*.

18 Waskow, *From Race Riot to Sit-In*. Quoted in Platt, *The Politics of Riot Commissions*, 152.

19 Chicago Commission on Race Relations, *The Negro in Chicago*; Brophy, *Reconstructing the Dreamland*. On the suppression of Mayor La Guardia's report after the 1935 New York City riot, see Platt, *The Politics of Riot Commissions*, 159–95. *The Politics of Riot Commissions* also has documents and commentary on the riots in East St. Louis (1917), Chicago (1919), Detroit (1943), and later riots.

20 Clark, testimony, in Kerner Commission, *Report*, 483.

21 President's Commission on Law Enforcement and Administration of Justice, *The Challenge of Crime in a Free Society*, 239–310 (chap. 4, "The Police"). The commission published nine task force reports, including reports on courts, corrections, juvenile delinquency, and a highly influential report on science and technology, which introduced a flow chart on the criminal process that immediately became a standard reference, and introduced the term "criminal justice system" to the lexicon of the field of criminal justice.

22 President's Commission on Law Enforcement and Administration of Justice, *Task Force Report: The Police*, 21–30, 138, 163 (hereinafter cited as President's Crime Commission, *Task Force Report: The Police*). On controlling all "critical incidents" that police officers encounter, see Walker and Archbold, *The New World of Police Accountability*, 296–97 (listed as one of several proposed "best practices").

23 President's Crime Commission, *Task Force Report: The Police*, 156, 165, 194, 195.

24 Walker, "The Justice Department's Pattern-or-Practice Police Reform Program," 31–32, 26–27, 28.

25 Kerner Commission, *Report*, 120. The report on the Watts riot commissioned by the governor of California, generally referred to as the McCone Commission Report, was widely dismissed as inadequate. Governor's Commission on the Los Angeles Riots, *Violence in the City*.

26 Kerner Commission, *Report*, 56–69.

27 Kerner Commission, *Report*, 84–108; Fine, *Violence in the Model City*.

28 Kerner Commission, *Report*, 299–322 ("The Police and the Community"); Gillon, *Separate and Unequal*, 243–46 (the final vote to approve the report).

29 Kerner Commission, *Report*, 209–305; Walker, "The Justice Department's Pattern-or-Practice Police Reform Program," 37.

30 Kerner Commission, *Report*, 299, 301.

31 National Academies of Science, Engineering, Medicine, *Proactive Policing*, 301, 318–19 ("Conclusion 7–1").

32 Kerner Commission, *Report*, 310–11; Walker, *Police Accountability*, 19–49 ("The Rise, Fall, and Revival of Citizen Oversight").

33 Kerner Commission, *Report*, 319–20.

34 Packer, "Two Models and the Criminal Process." The article is a crucial chapter in Packer's enormously influential book *The Limits of the Criminal Sanction*.

35 Kerner Commission, *Report*, 312–15.

36 President's Crime Commission, *Task Force Report: The Police*, 21–30. See also the extremely valuable Epp, *Making Rights Real*, 93–114 (chap. 5).

37 Kerner Commission, *Report*, 1. On the saga of the phrase, see Gillon, *Separate and Unequal*, 227–46 ("Two Societies").

38 Kerner Commission, *Report*, 320. On President Johnson's expectations, the deep divisions among commission staff members, and the resulting compromises, see Gillon, *Separate and Unequal*.

39 Reiss, *The Police and the Public*; Donald J. Black, *The Manners and Customs of the Police*; Walker, *Popular Justice*, 206–8 ("Research Revolution").

40 Flamm, "Law and Order at Large"; Walker, *Police Accountability*, 29–31 ("Crisis in New York").

41 On the court's neglect of the police (apart from a few cases) until the advent of the Warren Court in 1953, see Chemerinsky, *Presumed Guilty*, 39–58 (chap. 4, "Why the Court Ignored Policing for Much of American History"), 59–79 (chap. 5, "Judicial Silence on Constitutional Protections and Remedies before 1953"). The Warren Court is discussed in part 3, 83–137.

42 *Mapp v. Ohio*, 367 U.S. 643 (1961); *Weeks v. United States*, 232 U.S. 383 (1914); Long, *Mapp v. Ohio*; *People v. Cahan*, 44 Cal.2d 434 (1955).

43 The leading conservative academic critic of the Supreme Court and defender of then current police practices was Northwestern University professor of law Fred E. Inbau, *Criminal Interrogation and Confessions*.

44 *Miranda v. Arizona*, 384 U.S. 436 (1966); Baker, *Miranda*.

45 Orfield, "The Exclusionary Rule and Deterrence," 1017, 1028, 1029. Interestingly, the article contained a discussion of police officer lying, suggesting that police perjury was a common practice, but there is no evidence of any action being taken to curb or eliminate it.

46 Goldstein, *Policing a Free Society*, 157–86 ("Controlling and Reviewing Police-Citizen Contacts"); Chemerinsky, *Presumed Guilty*, 131–37 ("Rights Need Remedies").

47 Amsterdam, "Perspectives on the Fourth Amendment," 417–28; Goldstein, *Policing a Free Society*, 93–130 (chap. 5, "Categorizing and Structuring Discretion").

48 Harmon, "The Problem of Policing," 776, 785 ("Constitutional Rights Alone"); 816–817 ("Law of the Police"); Goldstein, *Policing a Free Society*, 93–130 (chap. 5, "Categorizing and Structuring Discretion").

49 Zeidman, "From Dropsy to Testilying"; Leo, *Police Interrogation and American Justice*, 119–64 (chap. 4, "The Structure and Psychology of American Police Interrogation").

50 Leo, *Police Interrogation and American Justice*, 119–64 (chap. 4, "The Structure and Psychology of American Police Interrogation"); 280 (quote).

51 The principal exception on this issue was Goldstein, "Police Policy Formulation." See also Goldstein, *Policing a Free Society*, 178–81; and Harmon, "The Problem of Policing," 765–86.

52 *Terry v. Ohio*, 392 U.S. 1 (1968). The history of the *Terry* case and subsequent stop and frisk actions by the police is in White and Fradella, *Stop and Frisk*, 44–55.

53 Chemerinsky, *Presumed Guilty*, 184–206 (chap. 14, "Eroding Remedies for Police Misconduct"), 243–72 (chap. 18, "The Vanishing Remedies for Police Misconduct"); Abraham, *Justices, Presidents, and Senators*.

54 Davis, *Police Discretion*.

55 Walker, "The Justice Department's Pattern-or-Practice Police Reform Program," 26–27, 28.

56 Davis, *Police Discretion*, 103–7.

57 Walker, "Origins of the Contemporary Criminal Justice Paradigm."

58 LaFave, *Arrest*.

59 Goldstein, "Police Policy Formulation."

60 Goldstein, "Police Policy Formulation." See also Goldstein's subsequent and more thorough discussion in *Policing a Free Society*, 93–130 (chap. 5, "Categorizing and Structuring Discretion").

61 Davis, *Police Discretion*, 3–7.

62 Davis, *Police Discretion*, 11–12, 16; "essential" quote, 140. On the lowest-ranking officers making the most important decisions, see Reiss, *The Police and the Public*, 114–20 ("Discretionary Justice").

63 Wilson and McLaren, *Police Administration*.

64 Davis, *Police Discretion*, 105–7, 140.

65 President's Task Force, *Final Report*, 14 (Action Item 1.5.1.).

66 See chapter 4 of this book for a discussion of use of force review boards.

67 Walker, "The Justice Department's Pattern-or-Practice Police Reform Program," 21–42. See the findings letters on departments subject to consent decrees on the website of the Special Litigation Section, https://justice.gov.

68 Davis, Henderson, and Ortiz, *Can Federal Intervention Bring Lasting Improvement*; Stone, Fogelsong, and Cole, *Policing Los Angeles*, 19–43 ("Claims of De-Policing").

69 Alpert and Lum, *Police Pursuit Driving*.

70 See, for example, chapter 5 of this book on the recurring failures of Albuquerque, New Mexico, police officers and supervisors to comply with the consent decree reforms, despite repeated warnings by the court-appointed monitor. Public Management Resources, *Monitor's Thirteenth Report*, 2, 3, 6.

71 Epp, *Making Rights Real*, 93–114 (chap. 5, "Policing's Epiphany"). A strong critique of administration rulemaking is Ponomarenko, "Rethinking Police Rulemaking," 3. The author's argument, however, does not appear to be practical, largely because it would create an extremely cumbersome bureaucratic process.

72 Epp, *Making Rights Real*, 82.

73 Fyfe, "Administrative Interventions"; Geller and Scott, *Deadly Force*, 248–75 ("Policy Development").

74 Fyfe, Administrative Interventions," 318, table 2 ("Officer-Reported Reasons for Shooting").

75 New York City Police Department, *Use of Force Report 2019*, appendix E, "Subjects Shot and Killed by Officers, 1971 to 2019" (figure 61).

76 White and Fradella, *Stop and Frisk*, 81–115. See also the discussion of de-escalation as a strategy to reduce police officer use of force, with reductions in racial and ethnic disparities, in chapter 4 of this book.

77 Oakland Police Department, Special Order No. 3853 (November 1, 1979), in Loving, *Responding to Spouse Abuse and Wife Beating*; reproduced in Walker, *The Police in America*, 211.

78 See, for example, the lengthy current New Orleans policy on the handling of domestic incidents. New Orleans Police Department, *Operations Manual*, chapter 42.4 ("Domestic Violence").

79 Alpert and Lum, *Police Pursuit Driving*.

80 Epp, *Making Rights Real*, 55–91 ("Liability's Triumph").

81 Epp, *Making Rights Real*, 65, 66, 68; Milton et al., *Police Use of Deadly Force*, 127–47 ("Recommendations").

82 *Rizzo v. Goode*, 423 U.S. 362 (1976); *Monell v. Department of Social Services*, 436 U.S. 658 (1978); *City of Los Angeles v. Lyons*, 461 U.S. 95 (1983).

83 Epp, *Making Rights Real*, 71–72, 75.

84 *Tennessee v. Garner*, 471 U.S. 1 (1985); Milton et al., *Police Use of Deadly Force*; Epp, *Making Rights Real*, 78–81, 83–84.

85 Epp, *Making Rights Real*, 93; see website of International Association of Chiefs of Police, Law Enforcement Policy Center, www.theiacp.org.

86 Eagly and Schwartz, "Lexipol's Fight against Police Reform"; Brandon Pho, "Private Companies or the Public: Who Should Write Santa Ana Police Policies?," *Voice of OC*, September 22, 2022, https://voiceofoc.org.

87 Eagly and Schwartz, "Lexipol's Fight against Police Reform," 35–37; Eagly and Schwartz, "Lexipol: The Privatization of Police Policymaking"; *Graham v. Connor*, 490 U.S. 386 (1989).

88 Pho, "Private Companies or the Public."

CHAPTER 3. THE CREATION OF THE JUSTICE DEPARTMENT'S PATTERN OR PRACTICE PROGRAM

1 Rushin, *Federal Intervention in American Police Departments*, 73–78; Cannon, *Official Negligence*, 125–47.

2 Rushin, *Federal Intervention in American Police Departments*, 72.

3 Clinton, *State of the Union Address*, February 17, 1993.

4 Rushin, *Federal Intervention in American Police Departments*, 67–102.

5 Rushin, *Federal Intervention in American Police Departments*.

6 42 U.S.C. 14141. The law has since been recodified as 34 U.S.C. 12601, https://uscde.house.gov.

7 See the website of the Special Litigation Section, https://justice.gov; Rushin, *Federal Intervention in American Police Departments*, 67–102.

8 U.S. Civil Rights Division, *The Civil Rights Division's Pattern or Practice Police Reform Work*, 1, 2, 6, 20, 25.

9 Scott Thomson, quoted in Police Executive Research Forum, *Re-Engineering Training*, 23; Walker, "The Justice Department's Pattern-or-Practice Police Reform Program," 33–34, 38 (calling for research on this issue).

10 Walker, "The Justice Department's Pattern-or-Practice Police Reform Program," 26–32; White, Fradella, and Flippin, "How Can We Achieve Accountability" (adopting an organizational change framework that closely parallels the Justice Department pattern or practice goals).

11 See the broad discussion of what the pattern or practice program can and cannot do in Lopez, "DOJ Police Pattern or Practice Investigations."

12 *United States v. City of Newark*, Supplementary Motion for Entry of Consent Decree, 25.

13 *United States v. City of Portland*, Amended Settlement Agreement. This is a subsequent amended order.

14 *United States v. City of New Orleans*, Amended and Restated Consent Decree, 54–60. The other pattern or practice effort on gender discrimination involved investigations and settlements of the Missoula, Montana, police department, the Missoula County Attorney's Office, and the University of Montana Office of Public Safety, all of which were involved in some aspect of gender discrimination. See, for example, *United States v. City of Missoula*, Memorandum of Understanding.

15 President's Crime Commission, *Task Force Report: The Police*, 193–97; Kerner Commission, *Report*, 310–12.

16 Walker, *Police Accountability*.

17 *United States v. City of Pittsburgh*, Consent Decree, 23–32.

18 Author's review of Justice Department consent decrees in website of the Special Litigation Section, Conduct of Law Enforcement Agencies, www.justice.gov.

19 *United States v. City of Newark*, Supplementary Motion for Entry of Consent Decree, 36–38.

20 U.S. Civil Rights Division, *The Civil Rights Division's Pattern or Practice Police Reform Work*, 2, 4, 6, 20, 23, 35, 40 (several terms are used, such as "different generation," "different era," but the meaning is the same); Walker, "'Not Dead Yet,'" 1807–18.

21 U.S. Civil Rights Division, *The Civil Rights Division's Pattern or Practice Police Reform Work*, 33. For an administrative rulemaking approach to ensuring stake-

holder participation in community engagement, see Simmons, "The Politics of Policing."

22 *United States v. City of Seattle*, Settlement Agreement, 2–4; Walker, "The Community Voice in Policing."

23 *United States v. City of Cleveland*, Settlement Agreement, 8–10.

24 U.S. Civil Rights Division, *The Civil Rights Division's Pattern or Practice Police Reform Work*, 37; Walker, "The Justice Department's Pattern-or-Practice Police Reform Program," 30, 37 (calling for research to investigate the factors that contribute to or impede sustainability in police organizations).

25 Walker, "Institutionalizing Police Accountability Reforms."

26 *United States v. City of Seattle*, City of Seattle's Memorandum.

27 U.S. Civil Rights Division, *The Civil Rights Division's Pattern or Practice Police Reform Work*, 2, 4.

28 Walker, "'Not Dead Yet,'" 1807–18.

29 *United States v. City of New Orleans*, Amended and Restated Consent Decree.

30 *United States v. City of Seattle*, Settlement Agreement.

31 *United States v. City of Pittsburgh*, Consent Decree.

32 *United States v. City of Pittsburgh*, Consent Decree, 18; *United States v. City of New Orleans*, Amended and Restated Consent Decree, 26–27.

33 Greene, "Community Policing in America"; Scott, *Problem-Oriented Policing*. It is important to note that neither of these two reports discusses organizational transformation.

34 President's Task Force, *Final Report*, 43 (Recommendation 4.1).

35 Walker, "'Not Dead Yet,'" 1809–14.

36 *United States v. City of Pittsburgh*, Consent Decree.

37 "Cincinnati Tops List of Police Killings of Blacks," *New York Times*, April 28, 2001, www.nytimes.com; *In Re: Cincinnati, Collaborative Agreement*, https://cincinnati-oh.gov; U.S. Department of Justice, *Memorandum of Agreement between the United States Department of Justice and the City of Cincinnati*.

38 *In Re Cincinnati, Collaborative Agreement*, 2, 3, 4–5. See also *United States v. City of Cincinnati*, Memorandum of Agreement, www.justice.gov.

39 *In Re Cincinnati, Collaborative Agreement*, 5–6.

40 *United States v. City of Albuquerque*, Settlement Agreement, 79–82; *United States v. City of Cleveland*, Settlement Agreement, 8–10.

41 U.S. Civil Rights Division, *The Civil Rights Division's Pattern or Practice Police Reform Work*, 33.

42 U.S. Civil Rights Division, *Investigation of the Cleveland Division of Police* (2014), 54–57.

43 *United States v. City of Cleveland*, Settlement Agreement, 67–69 (67, quote).

44 Baltimore Police Department Monitoring Team, *First Semiannual Report*, 40.

45 Walker and Archbold, *The New World of Police Accountability*, 25.

46 U.S. Civil Rights Division, *The Civil Rights Division's Pattern or Practice Police Reform Work*, 20.

47 Pittsburgh Working Group, *Report to the U.S. Attorney General*. Copy in possession of this author, who was a member of the working group.

48 *United States v City of Pittsburgh, Pittsburgh Bureau of Police, and Department of Public Safety*, Consent Decree; *United States v. City of New Orleans*, Amended and Restated Consent Decree; *United States v. Police Department of Baltimore City, et al.*, Consent Decree; Walker, "Not Dead Yet," 1808.

49 U.S. Civil Rights Division, *The Civil Rights Division's Pattern or Practice Police Reform Work*, 1, 20. As discussed in chapter 1, White, Fradella and Flippin, "How Can We Achieve Accountability" closely parallels the DOJ pattern or practice program with its emphasis on organizational transformation as a cornerstone of meaningful police reform. Walker, "The Justice Department's Pattern-or-Practice Police Reform Program," 31–32; Walker, "'Not Dead Yet,'" 1818–23.

50 Institute of Medicine, *To Err Is Human*, 1; Allen, "How Many Die From Medical Mistakes."

51 Perrow, *Normal Accidents*, 3; Schwartz, "Systems Failures in Policing," 3–4, 17; Sherman, "Reducing Fatal Police Shootings."

52 Perrow, *Normal Accidents*, 5–9, 10.

53 U.S. Civil Rights Division, *The Civil Rights Division's Pattern or Practice Police Reform Work*, 1, 2, 11, 12, 14, 20; Sherman, "Reducing Fatal Police Shootings."

54 Cannon, *Official Negligence*, 125–47 (discussion of the Christopher Commission).

55 As this book is being written, there is no comprehensive study of the impact of the digital revolution on policing, particularly with respect to holding officers accountable for their on-the-job conduct. But see the enormous impact of the videotape recording of Rodney King by Los Angeles police officers in 1991 in Cannon, *Official Negligence*, 125–47.

56 Members of the Commission, letter to Mayor Tom Bradley, July 9, 1991, in Christopher Commission, *Report of the Independent Commission* (hereinafter cited as Christopher Commission, *Report*). The organizational transformation approach taken by the Christopher Commission stands in stark contrast to the many "blue ribbon" commissions that investigated and issued reports on police departments from the 1920s through 1970s. See Walker, "Setting the Standards."

57 Christopher Commission, *Report*, 17, 183–224 (chap. 10, "Structural Issues—The Police Commission and the Chief of Police").

58 Christopher Commission, *Report*, 31–65 (chap. 3, "The Problem of Excessive Force"), quotes on 31, 34, 38, 60, 63; Walker, *Early Intervention Systems*.

59 Christopher Commission, *Report*, 72, 74–78, 104.

60 Christopher Commission, *Report*, 127, 130.

61 Christopher Commission, *Report*, 140, 142, 153, 154, 161, 168, 170.

62 Christopher Commission, *Report*, 183–85, 188, 190–91.

63 Christopher Commission, *Report*, 206–21. On inspectors general in the United States, see Walker and Archbold, *The New World of Police Accountability*, 214–26. See also the discussion in chapter 6 of this book.

64 Armacost, "Organizational Culture and Police Misconduct," 495 (organizational culture as a major theme).

65 Schwartz, "Systems Failures in Policing," 3–4, 17.

66 Sherman, "Reducing Fatal Police Shootings."

67 Sherman, "Reducing Fatal Police Shootings," 434, 436–37, 439. See also Sherman, "Evidence-Based Policing."

68 Klinger, "Organizational Accidents," 42–43.

69 Zimring, *When Police Kill*, 143–250 (part 2, "Prevention and Control of Police Killings"); Sherman, "Reducing Fatal Police Shootings," 422, 427, 428.

70 Harris, "How Accountability-Based Policing," 165–86.

71 U.S. Civil Rights Division, *The Civil Rights Division's Pattern or Practice Police Reform Work*, 9–11; Walker, "The Justice Department's Pattern-or-Practice Police Reform Program," 24–25.

72 U.S. Civil Rights Division, *The Civil Rights Division's Pattern or Practice Police Reform Work*, 5.

73 U.S. Civil Rights Division, *The Civil Rights Division's Pattern or Practice Police Reform Work*, 6, 9, 9–16 ("Conducting an Investigation"); Lopez, "DOJ Police Pattern or Practice Investigations," 35.

74 U.S. Civil Rights Division, *The Civil Rights Division's Pattern or Practice Police Reform Work*, 6.

75 See the references to key community leaders and organizations cited in almost all of the later consent decrees, Special Litigation Section website, https://justice.gov.

76 U.S. Civil Rights Division, *The Civil Rights Division's Pattern or Practice Police Reform Work*, 9–10, 11, 13–14, 12 (the question of "why").

77 U.S. Civil Rights Division, *The Civil Rights Division's Pattern or Practice Police Reform Work*, 15–16; U.S. Civil Rights Division, *Investigation of the Baltimore City Police Department*, 12–15; U.S. Civil Rights Division, *Investigation of the Ferguson Police Department*, 6–9; Lopez, "DOJ Police Pattern or Practice Investigations," 38–39.

78 Gould and Mastrofski, "Suspect Searches."

79 U.S. Civil Rights Division, *The Civil Rights Division's Pattern or Practice Police Reform Work*, 20–21.

80 U.S. Civil Rights Division, *The Civil Rights Division's Pattern or Practice Police Reform Work*, 21.

81 *In Re Cincinnati Policing, Collaborative Agreement*, 114, 128.

82 Various Technical Assistance letters are listed in the Special Litigation Section's website, under "Cases and Matters," and also in the separate "Archives" section of closed cases, www.justice.gov. Timetables of settlements are found in U.S. Civil Rights Division, *The Civil Rights Division's Pattern or Practice Police Reform Work*, 19, 36, 41–48.

83 Letter, Steven Rosenbaum to Mr. Alejandro Vilarello, City Attorney, in U.S. Civil Rights Division, *Investigation of the Miami Police Department*.

84 U.S. Civil Rights Division, *Investigation of the Cleveland Division of Police* (2002). Subsequent investigations: Civil Rights Division, Letter to Hon. Mayor Tom Regalado, RE: Investigation of the City of Miami Police Department (July 9, 2013); U.S. Civil Rights Division, *Investigation of the Cleveland Division of Police* (2014).
85 Harmon, "Limited Leverage," 38.
86 Harmon, "Limited Leverage," 38, 54–57 (describing the various alternative remedies).
87 Walker, "The Justice Department's Pattern-or-Practice Police Reform Program," 25.
88 U.S. Civil Rights Division, *The Civil Rights Division's Pattern or Practice Police Reform Work*, 21–23; David Nakamura, "Federal Monitors Cost Millions, with Disputed Results. Seattle's Police Watchdog Was a Case in Point," *Washington Post*, August 2, 2021, https://washingtonpost.com.
89 Public Management Resources, *Monitor's Thirteenth Report*.
90 Attorney General Merrick Garland, *Memorandum for Heads of Civil Litigating Components*.
91 Bromwich Group, *Special Report of the Independent Monitor*.
92 Kroll Associates, *Report of the Independent Monitor*.
93 Police Executive Research Forum, *Civil Rights Investigations of Local Police*, 32–34.
94 U.S. Civil Rights Division, *The Civil Rights Division's Pattern or Practice Police Reform Work*, 35; *United States v. City of Seattle*, City of Seattle's Memorandum.

CHAPTER 4. PUTTING AN END TO UNCONSTITUTIONAL POLICING
1 This book does not examine the consent decrees involving the police departments in Puerto Rico or the Virgin Islands. *United States v. Commonwealth of Puerto Rico*, Settlement Agreement; *United States v. Territory of the Virgin Islands*, Consent Decree.
2 The evidence and argument in this chapter represent an expanded and revised version of an earlier article: Walker, "The Justice Department's Pattern-or-Practice Police Reform Program."
3 White, Fradella, and Flippin, "How Can We Achieve Accountability." See also U.S. Civil Rights Division, *The Civil Rights Division's Pattern or Practice Police Reform Work*.
4 Walker, "The Justice Department's Pattern-or-Practice Police Reform Program," 26–27.
5 U.S. Civil Rights Division, *The Civil Rights Division's Pattern or Practice Police Reform Work*, 27.
6 Davis, *Police Discretion*, 145–49; *United States v. City of New Orleans*, Amended and Restated Consent Decree, 14–15.
7 *United States v. City of New Orleans*, Amended and Restated Consent Decree, 25.
8 Prior to the 2001 consent decree, the Los Angeles police department apparently had a policy of separating all officers involved in or witnesses to shooting inci-

dents, but it is not clear whether the policy was ever enforced. *United States v. City of Los Angeles*, Consent Decree, 25.

9 *United States v. City of New Orleans*, Amended and Restated Consent Decree, 24.

10 U.S. Civil Rights Division, *Investigation of the Cleveland Division of Police* (2014), 12–28, 31–33; U.S. Civil Rights Division, *Investigation of the Seattle Police Department*, 8–15, 17–19.

11 Walker, "The Justice Department's Pattern-or-Practice Police Reform Program," 27, 37.

12 Lee, Weitzer, and Martinez, "Recent Police Killings," 204 (table 2). See also the discussion of this issue in chapter 6.

13 New Orleans Police Department, *Special Report: Use of Force*, 9 ("Executive Summary").

14 Cleveland Police Monitor, *Eighth Semiannual Report*.

15 *United States v. City of New Orleans*, Amended and Restated Consent Decree, 25.

16 *United States v. City of New Orleans*, Amended and Restated Consent Decree, 78.

17 Engel, *How Police Supervisory Styles Influence Patrol Officer Behavior*, 1.

18 See the inspector general reports at the websites of the inspectors general for the NYPD (www1.nyc.gov), LAPD (https://lapdonline.org), and Chicago (https://igchicago.org). See also Walker and Archbold, *The New World of Police Accountability*, 219–29. Additional inspectors general have since been created in a number of other police departments.

19 Strote and Hutson, "Taser Use in Restraint-Related Deaths"; Smith et al., *A Multi-Method Evaluation*.

20 Terrill and Paoline, "Police Use of Less Lethal Force"; Police Executive Research Forum, *2011 Electronic Control Weapon Guidelines*, 17–24 ("Electronic Control Weapons Guidelines").

21 *United States v. City of New Orleans*, Amended and Restated Consent Decree, 17–20.

22 Bobb, *18th Semiannual Report*, 9.

23 Police Executive Research Forum, *An Integrated Approach to De-Escalation*; "21 States Still Do Not Require De-Escalation Training for Police," *APMReports*, June 24, 2021, https://apmreports.org.

24 *United States v. City of Pittsburgh*, Consent Decree, para. 35 ("The PBP shall train all officers in the use of verbal de-escalation techniques as an alternative to the use of force"); President's Task Force, *Final Report*, 21 (Action Item 2.2.1).

25 Seattle Police Department, *Policy Manual*, Policy 8.000 ("Use of Force Core Principles"); Policy 8.100 ("De-Escalation").

26 Seattle Police Monitor, *Ninth Systematic Assessment*, 1–11 ("Introduction and Executive Summary").

27 Police Executive Research Forum, *Guiding Principles on Use of Force*, 41; *United States v. Police Department of Baltimore City, et al.*, Consent Decree, 54.

28 Rahr and Rice, *From Warriors to Guardians*.

29 Police Executive Research Forum, *An Integrated Approach to De-Escalation*, 9, 26, 30, 59.

30 *Graham v. Connor*, 490 U.S. 386 (1989). See also Police Executive Research Forum website for its free online documents, www.policeforum.org.

31 Police Executive Research Forum, *Guiding Principles on Use of Force*. On the concept of "lawful but awful," see Police Executive Research Forum, *Re-Engineering Training*, iii.

32 A model duty to intervene law, with a discussion of the relevant issues, is in Kaufman, "Police Policing Police." A duty to intervene requirement was included in the Memorandum of Agreement involving the Washington, DC, police department in 2001 ("The MPD shall require officers to report to MPD without delay" any excessive use of force, false arrest, unlawful seizure, unlawful discrimination, and three other types of misdeeds). United States Department of Justice, *United States Department of Justice and the District of Columbia and the District of Columbia Metropolitan Police Department*, Memorandum of Agreement (2001), para 77, www.justice.gov.

33 The first major work on police officer subculture, which subsequent studies have modified considerably, is Westley, *Violence and the Police*, 109–52 (chap. 4, "The Morality of Secrecy and Violence").

34 New York City, Commission to Investigate Allegations of Police Corruption, *Commission Report*, 53 (hereinafter cited as Mollen Commission, *Commission Report*).

35 Westley, *Violence and the Police*, 111.

36 San Francisco District Attorney, *Report of the Blue Ribbon Panel*, 143; Hodges and Pugh, "Crossing the Thin Blue Line"; Walker, "The Justice Department's Pattern-or-Practice Police Reform Program," 33–34, 38; Police Executive Research Forum, *Guiding Principles on Use of Force*, 41–42.

37 Minneapolis Police Department, "Duty to Intervene"; Kerri Miller and Ariana Rosas, "What Duty to Intervene Means in Policing," *MPR News*, June 24, 2021, www.mprnews.org; Celina Tebor, "Three Former Minneapolis Officers Found Guilty on All Counts of Violating George Floyd's Civil Rights," *USA Today*, February 24, 2022, www.usatoday.com.

38 Minnesota Department of Human Rights, *Investigation*, 46. The Minnesota report is discussed in detail in chapter 6 of this book.

39 Westley, *Violence and the Police*, 109–52.

40 See the New Orleans police department website for *Ethical Policing Is Courageous*, http://epic.nola.gov.

41 New Orleans Police Department, *Ethical Policing Is Courageous*.

42 Hodges and Pugh, "Crossing the Thin Blue Line."

43 "Police Train to Step In When Police Step Too Far," *New York Times*, February 28, 2022, www.nytimes.com.

44 Thacher, "The Learning Model of Use-of-Force Reviews."

45 See the website of the Force Science Institute for articles and other materials, www.forcescience.org. See also Stoughton, "Principled Policing," 652. Stoughton persuasively argues that the "warrior" mentality did not emerge until the 1960s and that the Los Angeles police department's development of SWAT (Special Weapons and Tactics) teams played a major role in that development (641–43). On the "warrior" mentality, see Walker, "The Justice Department's Pattern-or-Practice Police Reform Program," 30, 33–34.

46 Rahr and Rice, *From Warriors to Guardians*.

47 Walker, "'Not Dead Yet,'" 1818–23.

48 Walker, "The Justice Department's Pattern-or-Practice Police Reform Program," 33–34.

49 U.S. Civil Rights Division, *The Civil Rights Division's Pattern or Practice Police Reform Work*, 2.

50 Harris, "Driving While Black."

51 *United States v. State of New Jersey*, Consent Decree; Walker, "The Justice Department's Pattern-or-Practice Police Reform Program," 27–29. Including the New Jersey state police and East Haven, Connecticut, police department, a total of thirteen consent decrees or MOAs had some provision related to "stops," although in many cases the term "stops" referred to both motor vehicle and pedestrian stops.

52 U.S. Civil Rights Division, *The Civil Rights Division's Pattern or Practice Police Reform Work*, 11 ("The Role of Data Analysis in Pattern-or-Practice Investigations").

53 White, Fradella, and Flippin, "How Can We Achieve Accountability," 420.

54 *United States v. State of New Jersey*, Consent Decree, 11–12.

55 *United States v. State of New Jersey*, Consent Decree, 9–18 ("Motor Vehicle Stops").

56 U.S. Civil Rights Division, *The Civil Rights Division's Pattern or Practice Police Reform Work*, 30–31 ("Reforming Accountability Systems").

57 *United States v. State of New Jersey*, Consent Decree, 14.

58 *United States v. State of New Jersey*, Consent Decree, 14–15.

59 U.S. Civil Rights Division, *The Civil Rights Division's Pattern or Practice Police Reform Work*, 31.

60 *United States v. State of New Jersey*, Consent Decree, 15–16.

61 *United States v. State of New Jersey*, Consent Decree, 17.

62 Fagan and Geller, "Profiling and Consent," 17, 53, 54, 56.

63 U.S. Civil Rights Division, *The Civil Rights Division's Pattern or Practice Police Reform Work*, 26 ("Promoting Bias-Free Policing"); Walker, "The Justice Department's Pattern-or-Practice Police Reform Program," 27–29, 37.

64 Police Executive Research Forum, *Racially Biased Policing*, 51–53.

65 *United States v. City of New Orleans*, Amended and Restated Consent Decree, 50; Lopez, *Disorderly (Mis)Conduct*; Mazerolle et al., *Procedural Justice and Legitimacy in Policing*; Weisburd et al., "Reforming the Police" (finding that procedural justice training resulted in "more procedurally just behavior in the field," fewer

arrests, and a "significant relative decline" in crime in the procedurally just hot spots); *United States v. Town of East Haven*, Settlement Agreement and [Proposed] Order.

66 *United States v. County of Los Angeles*, Settlement Agreement, 7; Lopez, *Disorderly (Mis)Conduct*.

67 Police Executive Research Forum, *Re-Engineering Training*, 21–22 ("culture trumps policy").

68 Fridell, *Producing Bias-Free Policing*, 7. See the Fair and Impartial Policing website for reports and other materials, https://fipolicing.org.

69 Eberhardt, *Biased*.

70 Alexander, *The New Jim Crow*.

71 Fridell, *Producing Bias-Free Policing*; *United States v. Police Department of Baltimore City, et al.*, Consent Decree, 91, 92.

72 Eberhardt, *Biased*, 50.

73 Eberhardt, *Biased*, 68.

74 U.S. Civil Rights Division, *Investigation of the East Haven Police Department*, 4.

75 U.S. Civil Rights Division, *Investigation of the East Haven Police Department*, 2–3; *United States v. Town of East Haven*, Settlement Agreement and [Proposed] Order, 13–15.

76 *United States v. Town of East Haven*, Settlement Agreement, 13–14.

77 *United States v. Town of East Haven*, Settlement Agreement, 14–15.

78 *United States v. Town of East Haven*, Settlement Agreement, 42.

79 U.S. Civil Rights Division, *Investigation of the New Orleans Police Department*, 43. The only two major investigations of gender bias by the pattern or practice program have been the New Orleans police department; three agencies in Missoula, Montana (the Missoula police department, the University of Montana Office of Public Safety, and the Missoula County Attorney's Office); and a relatively brief section of the Settlement Agreement involving the Puerto Rico police department. *United States v. City of Missoula*, Memorandum of Understanding; *United States v. Commonwealth of Puerto Rico*. The Justice Department's manual on preventing gender bias is *Improving Law Enforcement Response to Sexual Assault and Domestic Violence by Identifying and Preventing Gender Bias* (Washington, DC: Department of Justice, n.d.), www.justice.gov.

80 U.S. Civil Rights Division, *The Civil Rights Division's Pattern or Practice Police Reform Work*, 6. The New Orleans consent decree's attention to gender discrimination was clearly designed as a model that other police departments could embrace. Only one other consent decree, Baltimore, however, included reforms related to sexual assault cases, and no other pattern or practice consent decrees included domestic violence. See *United States v. City of Missoula*, Memorandum of Understanding.

81 *United State v. City of New Orleans*, Amended and Restated Consent Decree, 54–55.

82 *United State v. City of New Orleans*, Amended and Restated Consent Decree, 57–58, 60–63 (broader community engagement program); U.S. Civil Rights Division, *The Civil Rights Division's Pattern or Practice Police Reform Work*, 33–34.

83 New Orleans Police Monitor, *Report of the Consent Decree Monitor*, 42–46.

84 President's Crime Commission, *Task Force Report: The Police*; Kerner Commission, *Report*, 310–12. On the fight for independent public complaint procedures, see Walker, *Police Accountability*, 19–49.

85 U.S. Civil Rights Division, *The Civil Rights Division's Pattern or Practice Police Reform Work*, 29.

86 Walker, *Police Accountability*; Community Oriented Policing Services, *Standards and Guidelines*.

87 Hickman, *Citizen Complaints*.

88 ACLU of New Jersey, *The Crisis inside Police Internal Affairs*; Attorney General of New Jersey, *Internal Affairs Policy and Procedures*.

89 *United States v. City of Pittsburgh*, Consent Decree (multiple paragraphs); Walker, "The Justice Department's Pattern-or-Practice Police Reform Program," 29, 37.

90 See the Seattle police department's Office of Police Accountability website for materials on its work, www.seattle.gov/opa.

91 U.S. Civil Rights Division, *Investigation of the Seattle Police Department*, 24, appendix D, 1–8.

92 *United States v. City of Seattle*, Settlement Agreement, appendix D, 1–8.

93 *United States v. City of Seattle*, Settlement Agreement.

94 De Angelis, Rosenthal, and Buchner, *Civilian Oversight of Law Enforcement*; Walker, *Police Accountability*, 53–55 ("The Independent Review of Complaints").

95 See the Washington, DC, Office of Police Complaints at https://policecomplaints.dc.gov.

96 Walker, *Police Accountability*, 86–116 ("The Monitoring Role"); De Angelis, Rosenthal, and Buchner, *Civilian Oversight of Law Enforcement*.

97 Walker, *Police Accountability*, 123–25 ("The Reporting of Police Misconduct"); Phil Rogers and Shelby Bremer, "Chicago Police Misconduct Investigations Averaging 3.8 Years to Reach Board for Discipline," NBC, November 11, 2022; Ydav Gonen, "CCRB Police Misconduct Investigations Now Take, on Average, More Than 19 Months to Close, New Data Shows," *The City*, October 6, 2022, www.thecity.nyc; Hickman, *Citizen Complaints*, table 2, 3.

98 See the inspector general reports at the websites of the inspectors general for the NYPD (www1.nyc.gov), LAPD (https://lapdonline.org), and Chicago (https://igchicago.org). See also Walker and Archbold, *The New World of Police Accountability*, 215–29. In 2022, however, it was revealed that the New York City police department successfully blocked implementation of the majority of the inspector general's recommendations; the inspector general resigned and the future of the agency is uncertain.

99 Walker and Archbold, *The New World of Police Accountability*, 216–99, 220–23. See also the websites for the Denver independent monitor (www.denvergov.org) and the San Jose independent police auditor (www.sanjoseca.gov).

100 U.S. Civil Rights Division, *The Civil Rights Division's Pattern or Practice Police Reform Work*, 30–32; Walker, "The Justice Department's Pattern-or-Practice Police Reform Program," 29–30, 37 (calling for research on the subject).

101 *United States v. City of New Orleans*, Amended and Restated Consent Decree, 32.

102 *United States v. City of New Orleans*, Amended and Restated Consent Decree.

103 U.S. Civil Rights Division, *The Civil Rights Division's Pattern or Practice Police Reform Work*, 30–32.

104 Geller, "Suppose We Were Really Serious". See also White, Fradella, and Flippin, "How Can We Achieve Accountability," 418–19.

105 Informal survey by the author; Special Litigation Section website, sections "Cases and Matters," "Law Enforcement Agencies"; and also "Archives" (for closed cases).

106 *United States v. City of Newark*, Consent Decree, 51–52.

107 Walker, *Early Intervention Systems*; U.S. Civil Rights Division, *Investigation of the Seattle Police Department*, 22–23; U.S. Civil Rights Division, *Investigation of the Cleveland Division of Police* (2014), 47–48.

108 White, Fradella, and Flippin, "How Can We Achieve Accountability," 433.

109 Survey of Civil Rights Division findings letter and news reports of EIS problems by the author of this book. Walker, *Early Intervention Systems*.

110 U.S. Civil Rights Division, *Investigation of the Seattle Police Department*, 22–24; U.S. Civil Rights Division, *Investigation of the Cleveland Division of Police* (2014), 47–48.

111 *Brady v. Maryland*, 373 U.S. 83 (1963).

112 The single best discussion of Brady lists is in San Francisco District Attorney, *Report of the Blue Ribbon Panel*, 123–36. See Deena Winter, "Hennepin County Attorney: Police Misconduct Must Be Disclosed to Defense," *Minnesota Reformer*, November 2, 2022, https://minnesotareformer.com.

113 A valuable collection of useful articles is Marshall Project, *Brady List: A Curated Collection of Links*, n.d., www.themarshallproject.org.

114 U.S. Civil Rights Division, *The Civil Rights Division's Pattern or Practice Police Reform Work*, 29–30 ("Learning Curve"); Walker, "The Justice Department's Pattern-or-Practice Police Reform Program," 30, 38 (calling for research that assesses "meaningful community engagement").

115 U.S. Civil Rights Division, *The Civil Rights Division's Pattern or Practice Police Reform Work*, 29.

116 President's Crime Commission, *Task Force Report: The Police*, 156–59 (finding that the various advisory commissions established by police departments across the country "have been seriously deficient"). The common problem was that commissions were appointed by police chiefs and consisted of elite members of the community who were both poorly informed about policing and unwilling to seriously criticize their local police department.

117 Walker, "Governing the American Police."

118 Sklansky, *Democracy and the Police*; Friedman and Ponomarenko, "Democratic Policing."

119 Pittsburgh Working Group, *Report to the U.S. Attorney General*.

120 *In Re Cincinnati Policing, Collaborative Agreement*, para. 4.

121 Scott, *Problem-Oriented Policing*.
122 *United States v. City of Portland*, Amended Settlement Agreement, 26; U.S. Civil Rights Division, *The Civil Rights Division's Pattern or Practice Police Reform Work*, 34, 55, 57, 59.
123 President's Task Force, *Final Report*, 43 (Recommendation 4.1), 46 (Recommendation 4.5).
124 President's Task Force, *Final Report*, 14 (Recommendation 1.5.1, "law enforcement agencies should involve the community in the process of developing and evaluating policies and procedures") and other similar recommendations.
125 See the 2023 "Our Work" section of the Seattle Community Police Commission website, www.seattle.gov.
126 Cheng, "Input without Influence."
127 Cheng and Qu, "Regular Intermediaries," 63–65.
128 The original statement on problem-oriented policing was Goldstein, "Improving Policing." See Scott, *Problem-Oriented Policing*; Walker, "The Justice Department's Pattern-or-Practice Police Reform Program," 30.
129 Weisburd et al., "Is Problem-Oriented Policing Effective" (finding a modest but significant impact" on crime and disorder); Scott, *Problem-Oriented Policing*.
130 President's Task Force, *Final Report*, 46 (Recommendation 4.5).
131 Survey of existing current and past consent decrees conducted by author. See, for example, *United States v. Police Department of Baltimore City, et al.*, Consent Decree, 6–7.
132 Ridgeway et al., *Police-Community Relations in Cincinnati*, xvii.

CHAPTER 5. RESISTANCE, COSTS, AND SUSTAINABILITY

1 Several of these issues are discussed in Walker, "'Not Dead Yet,'" 1807–18.
2 Walker, "'Not Dead Yet,'" 179–82; Walker, "The Justice Department's Pattern-or-Practice Police Reform Program," 22, 32–33.
3 Rushin, *Federal Intervention in American Police Departments*, 71–102.
4 U.S. Civil Rights Division, *The Civil Rights Division's Pattern or Practice Police Reform Work*, 41–42.
5 Various chronologies of pattern or practice cases are in U.S. Civil Rights Division, *The Civil Rights Division's Pattern or Practice Police Reform Work*, 19, 36, 41–48. See also the discussion of the Trump administration and the pattern or practice program in Lopez, "The Civil Rights Division."
6 U.S. Civil Rights Division, *Investigation of the Cleveland Division of Police* (2002), findings letter; U.S. Civil Rights Division, *Investigation of the Miami Police Department*. See also the discussion in Walker, "The Justice Department's Pattern-or-Practice Police Reform Program," 25.
7 U.S. Civil Rights Division, *The Civil Rights Division's Pattern or Practice Police Reform Work*, 4, 20, 23; Walker, "'Not Dead Yet,'" 1807.
8 Walker, "'Not Dead Yet,'" 1779–82; Attorney General Jeff Sessions, *Memorandum for Heads of Department Components*.

9 The Justice Department issued its findings letter on the Louisville, Kentucky, police department on March 8, 2023. U.S. Civil Rights Division, *Investigation of the Louisville Metro Police Department.*

10 Attorney General Merrick Garland, *Memorandum for Heads of Civil Litigation Components*, 6, 8.

11 U.S. Civil Rights Division, *The Civil Rights Division's Pattern or Practice Police Reform Work*, 47 (Alamance County, North Carolina); Simone Weichselbaum, "A Rural Sheriff Stares Down the Justice Department," Marshall Project, updated October 6, 2015; *United States v. Alamance County Sheriff Terry Johnson*, Agreement.

12 U.S. Civil Rights Division, *The Civil Rights Division's Pattern or Practice Police Reform Work*, 42 (Columbus, Ohio).

13 U.S. Civil Rights Division, *The Civil Rights Division's Pattern or Practice Police Reform Work*, 42, 46, 47; *United States v. Maricopa County*, Settlement Agreement.

14 John Spangenthal-Lee, "SPD 20/20: A Vision for the Future," *SPD Blotter*, March 29, 2012, https://spdblotter.seattle.gov.

15 Kroll Associates, *Report of the Independent Monitor.*

16 Green and Jerome, *City of Cincinnati's Independent Monitor's Final Report.*

17 Public Management Resources, *Monitor's Thirteenth Report*, 2.

18 Public Management Resources, *Monitor's Thirteenth Report*, 2–6.

19 Elise Kaplan, "City Council Seeks to Renegotiate Police Reform Agreement," *Albuquerque Journal*, March 10, 2022.

20 Elise Kaplan, "Significant Gains Seen in APD Reforms," *Albuquerque Journal*, May 12, 2022; Public Management Resources, *Monitor's Fifteenth Report.*

21 Public Management Resources, *Monitor's Fifteenth Report*, 1–2.

22 Damali Ramirez, Taylor Bayly, and Kiersten Foote, "Push and Pull: Unions Play Multiple Roles in Police Reform Efforts," *Tucson Sentinel*, October 12, 2022, www.tucsonsentinel.com.

23 Walker, "The Neglect of Police Unions."

24 The most comprehensive assessment of the American police is Skogan and Frydl, *Fairness and Effectiveness in Policing.* See also President's Crime Commission, *Task Force Report: The Police*, 181–83 ("Physical Force). On the use of deadly force, see Fyfe, "Administrative Interventions."

25 Eli Hager, "Blue Shield: Did You Know Police Have Their Own Bill of Rights?," Marshall Project, April 27, 2015.

26 Bureau of Labor Statistics, *Collective Bargaining Agreements for Police and Firefighters.*

27 Keenan and Walker, "An Impediment to Police Accountability?"; Ovetta Wiggins and Erin Cox, "Maryland Enacts Landmark Police Overhaul, First State to Repeal Police Bill of Rights," *Washington Post*, April 10, 2021, www.washingtonpost.com.

28 Walker, *Popular Justice*, 150–51, 199–200.

29 Check the Police, *Police Union Contract Project*; Schwartz, "Police Indemnification" (finding in a national survey of forty-four of the largest police departments that officers are "virtually always" indemnified).

30 Rushin, "Police Arbitration," 1073–77 ("Alternative Appellate Procedures"); Rushin, "Police Disciplinary Appeals," 588–96 ("Reforming Police Disciplinary Appeals"); Rushin, "Police Union Contracts," 1239–52.

31 Rushin, "Police Union Contracts," 1220–39 (categories of union contract provisions).

32 Jake Pearson, "A Police Union Contract Puts Taxpayers on the Hook to Defend Officers When the City Won't," *ProPublica*, March 26, 2021, www.propublica.org.

33 Westley, *Violence and the Police*, 111–18; Mollen Commission, *Commission Report*, 53–58.

34 Slobogin, "Testilying."

35 Chevigny, *Police Power*, 141.

36 Leo, *Police Interrogation and American Justice*, 325. The book contains many references to police officer lying.

37 Maas, *Serpico*.

38 San Francisco District Attorney, *Report of the Blue Ribbon Panel*, 143–48.

39 Chicago Police Accountability Task Force, *Recommendations for Change*, 69–77, 70 (quote on police secrecy).

40 Walker, *Popular Justice*, 199–200.

41 Bies, "Let the Sunshine In," 124 ("Police Resistance to Civilian Review Boards"), 140–41 ("Playing the Public Safety Card"). For an account of the CCRB controversy by a key figure, see Algernon Black, *The Public and the Police*.

42 Stephanie Wykstra, "The Fight for Transparency in Police Misconduct, Explained," *Vox*, June 16, 2020 (New York State Law Section 50-A); "Certain Police Disciplinary Records No Longer Confidential," *BBLaw*, October 9, 2018; Bies, "Let the Sunshine In," 131–35.

43 Ramirez, Bayly, and Foote, "Push and Pull"; David Zahniser, "LA's Police Union Spending Big on City Elections, Seeking to Boost City Hall Influence," *Los Angeles Times*, June 1, 2022, www.latimes.com.

44 Ramirez, Bayly, and Foote, "Push and Pull."

45 The conservative Manhattan Institute in 2021 published a brief report on collective bargaining and police reform that had only one substantive recommendation: giving police chiefs more authority over arbitration of police disciplinary decisions, but with no details about how that would be accomplished. There is an erroneous statement regarding the public complaint process, claiming that union contracts interfere with it, when in fact Justice Department consent decrees have mandated significant reforms in several cases. Finally, there is a vague suggestion that police chiefs should seek "buy-in" regarding accountability. DiSalvo, *Enhancing Accountability*.

46 Rushin, "Police Union Contracts," 1244.

47 A New York State Supreme Court judge invalidated the forty-eight-hour rule in the New York police department (NYPD) holding that the rule was "improper" and could not be negotiated into police union contracts. "Judge Axes '48-Hour Rule': Says the PBA Can't Use It," *NYPD Confidential*, September 17, 2003. The PBA is the rank-and-file officers' union.

48 Huq and McAdams, "Litigating the Blue Wall of Silence."

49 Rushin, "Police Arbitration," 1023–78.

50 U.S. Civil Rights Division, *The Civil Rights Division's Pattern or Practice Police Reform Work*, 23 (costs); Kimbrell Kelly, Sarah Childress, and Steven Rich, "Forced Reforms, Mixed Results," *Washington Post*, November 13, 2015, www.washingtonpost.com; Powell and Worrall, "Willingness to Pay for Police Reform" (arguing unpersuasively in support of a "publicly-supported police reform fund" that would encourage more police departments to not resist intervention by the DOJ pattern or practice program).

51 Walker, "The Justice Department's Pattern-or-Practice Police Reform Program," 36.

52 Rushin, *Federal Intervention in American Police Departments*, 208–30.

53 Rushin, *Federal Intervention in American Police Departments*, 209–12.

54 Goodwin, Shepard, and Sloan, *Police Brutality Bonds*.

55 U.S. Civil Rights Division, *Investigation of the Cleveland Division of Police* (2014), 55; U.S. Civil Rights Division, *Investigation of the Baltimore City Police Department, et al.*, 10–11; Rushin, *Federal Intervention in American Police Departments*, 211.

56 Rushin, *Federal Intervention in American Police Departments*, 211; Walker, "'Not Dead Yet,'" 1806–7.

57 Keith Alexander, Steven Rich, and Hannah Thacker, "The Hidden Billion-Dollar Cost of Repeated Police Misconduct," *Washington Post*, March 9, 2022, www.washingtonpost.com.

58 U.S. Civil Rights Division, *The Civil Rights Division's Pattern or Practice Police Reform Work*, 23.

59 Discussed in Walker, "'Not Dead Yet,'" 1801–7. See also Walker, "The Justice Department's Pattern-or-Practice Police Reform Program," 34–36.

60 U.S. Civil Rights Division, *The Civil Rights Division's Pattern or Practice Police Reform Work*.

61 Walker, "The Justice Department's Pattern-or-Practice Police Reform Program."

62 Davis, Henderson, and Ortiz, *Can Federal Intervention Bring Lasting Improvement*. On the earlier evaluation, see Davis et al., *Turning Necessity into Virtue*.

63 Rushin and Edwards, "De-Policing" (finding an "uptick in crime rates" following the end of consent decrees and a decline in later years). See also Shjarback et al., "De-Policing and Crime in the Wake of Ferguson" (finding that Missouri police officers made sixty-seven thousand fewer vehicle stops in 2015 compared with 2014, but that stops were of higher quality than before and that searches yielded contraband more consistently, indicating that officers were better trained and/or supervised than before or simply avoided stops and searches where they felt they did not have proper legal authority).

64 Davis, Henderson, and Ortiz, *Can Federal Intervention Bring Lasting Improvement*, 8, 9, 40.

65 Stone, Fogelsong, and Cole, *Policing Los Angeles*, ii, 46, 48–49.

66 Stone, Fogelsong, and Cole, *Policing Los Angeles*, ii (Executive Summary), 46, 48–49.

67 Stone, Fogelsong, and Cole, *Policing Los Angeles*, 19–32.

68 Stone, Fogelsong, and Cole, *Policing Los Angeles*, 54–58; Los Angeles Police Commission, Office of the Inspector General, *Comparative Review of Selected Agency Policies*; Walker and Archbold, *The New World of Police Accountability*, 223–26.

69 Rushin, *Federal Intervention in American Police Departments*, 160–243, quote on 239. See the International Law Enforcement Auditors Association website for its activities, https://ileaa.org. On the LAPD Audit Unit, see Jiao, "Federal Consent Decrees," 799–800.

70 Chanin, "Examining the Sustainability," 170, 173–75, 177, 179–82.

71 Green et al., *Progress Report*.

72 42 U.S.C. 1983 gives any individual the right to sue if deprived of his or her rights by a person or official "acting under color of law."

73 Powell, Meitel, and Worrall, "Police Consent Decrees."

74 Bromwich Group, *The Durability of Police Reform*, i, iv, 107–14 (summary of recommendations). See the International Law Enforcement Auditors Association website, https://ileaa.org.

75 Police Executive Research Forum, *Civil Rights Investigations of Local Police*, 34–35; Walker, "'Not Dead Yet,'" 1806–7.

76 See the discussion in the evaluation section of the impact of the Los Angeles consent decree on officer law enforcement patterns and the resulting impact on crime: Stone, Fogelsong, and Cole, *Policing Los Angeles*, 6–10, 19–32.

77 Davis, Henderson and Ortiz, *Can Federal Intervention Bring Lasting Improvement*, 41 (concluding, "We heard no indications from civic leaders that any backsliding had occurred since many of the decree's requirements had been lifted"). Yet a subsequent evaluation did find evidence of "backsliding" soon after the end of the consent decree. Chanin, "Examining the Sustainability," 8–13.

78 *United States v. City of Detroit*, Consent Judgment; Tresa Baldas, "Detroit Sues to Get Back Millions It Spent on Federal Monitor for Kilpatrick," *Detroit Free Press*, May 14, 2011.

79 Walker, "'Not Dead Yet,'" 1833–37. On collateral consequences, see White and Fradella, *Stop and Frisk*, 81–115 ("Crime Control Benefits and Collateral Consequences"). See also Walker, "The Justice Department's Pattern-or-Practice Police Reform Program," 33–34, 38 (calling for more research on the subject).

80 U.S. Civil Rights Division, *Investigation of the Cleveland Division of Police* (2014), 17–23.

81 Stone, Fogelsong, and Cole, *Policing Los Angeles*, 19–32.

82 *United States v. City of New Orleans*, Amended and Restated Consent Decree, 50.

83 New Orleans Police Department, Office of the Consent Decree Monitor, *Comprehensive Reassessment*.

84 New Orleans Police Department, Office of the Consent Decree Monitor, *Comprehensive Reassessment*.

85 White, Weisburd, and Wire, "Examining the Impact of the Freddie Gray Unrest."

86 Nix et al., "Demeanor, Race, and Police Perceptions."

87 Scott Thomson quoted in Police Executive Research Forum, *Re-Engineering Training*, 22, 23.

88 New Orleans Police Department, Office of the Consent Decree Monitor, *Comprehensive Reassessment*, 14.

89 "With No Police Shootings in 2020, Newark Makes Case for Consent Decrees," *Newsy*, May 6, 2021, www.ksby.com.

90 White, Fradella, and Flippin, "How Can We Achieve Accountability," 435; Walker, "Institutionalizing Police Accountability Reforms"; Walker, "The Justice Department's Pattern-or-Practice Police Reform Program," 37 (recommending research that identifies factors that contribute to or impede sustainability).

91 Skogan, "Why Reforms Fail."

92 *Knapp Commission Report on Police Corruption*; Sherman, *Scandal and Reform*.

93 Murphy and Plate, *Commissioner*.

94 Walker, "Institutionalizing Police Accountability Reforms," 60–61; Mollen Commission, *Commission Report*, 45 ("The Link between Brutality and Acts of Corruption").

95 Following the 1994 Mollen Commission report, New York City created a Commission to Combat Police Corruption, with the authority to review "all corruption allegations," monitor the handling of corruption cases by the NYPD's internal affairs bureau, and issue annual reports of its work. To date, however, there has been no independent assessment of the commission's work.

96 Sherman, Milton, and Kelly, *Team Policing*; Walker, "Does Anyone Remember Team Policing?"; Walker, "Institutionalizing Police Accountability Reforms," 61.

97 Sherman, Milton, and Kelly, *Team Policing*, 91, 93–96, 107–8.

98 Skogan, "Prospects for Reform?"; Skogan and Hartnett, *Community Policing, Chicago Style*, 38–69 ("Crafting a Program"), 110–60 ("Citizen Involvement").

99 U.S. Civil Rights Division, *The Civil Rights Division's Pattern or Practice Police Reform Work*, 37.

100 Green et al., *Progress Report*.

101 *United States v. City of Newark*, Consent Decree, 37–38.

102 See the website of the Seattle inspector general, www.seattle.gov.

103 See the website of the inspector general for the NYPD, "Reports" section, www.nyc.gov.

104 *United States v. City of Seattle*, City of Seattle's Memorandum.

CHAPTER 6. THE FUTURE OF POLICE REFORM

1 Sam Levin, "'It Never Stops': Killings by U.S. Police Reach Record High in 2022," *Guardian*, January 6, 2023, https://theguardian.com. The most comprehensive analysis of police shootings is Zimring, *When Police Kill*.

2 Jamiles Larty, "Biden Struck Out on Police Reform. Is Trump's Remaining Policy Enough?," Marshall Project, March 30, 2022, https://themarshallproject.org; Isaiah Poritz, "Breakdown of Police Reform Talks Highlights Power of Police Union Lobby," *Open Secrets*, September 23, 2021; Anastasia Valeeva, Weihua Li, and Susie

Cagle, "Rifles, Tasers and Jails: How Cities and States Spent Billions of COVID-19 Relief, " Marshall Project, September 7, 2022, https://themarshallproject.org.

3 White, Fradella, and Flippin, "How Can We Achieve Accountability," 406, 410–24, 424–35, 439–41.

4 New Orleans Police Department, Office of the Consent Decree Monitor, *Comprehensive Reassessment.*

5 Seattle Police Monitor, *Comprehensive Assessment.*

6 Department of Justice, "Justice Department and Baltimore Police Provide Progress Report Five Years after Consent Decree," media release, April 21, 2022, www.justice.gov.

7 The U.S. Civil Rights Division issued its findings letter on the Louisville, Kentucky, police department on March 8, 2023. U.S. Civil Rights Division, *Investigation of the Louisville Metro Police Department.* See the Special Litigation Section website for Minneapolis, MN, Phoenix, AZ, Columbus, OH, and other police departments for the findings letters and consent decrees as those cases progress.

8 Lopez, "DOJ Police Pattern-or-Practice Investigations," 38–42.

9 Department of Justice, Office of Community Oriented Policing, Collaborative Reform Initiative website, https://cops.usdoj.gov.

10 Department of Justice, Office of Community Oriented Policing, Collaborative Reform Initiative, https://cops.usdoj.gov.

11 U.S. Department of Justice, "Department of Justice Announces Next Steps in the Critical Incident Review of the Law Enforcement Response to the Mass Shooting in Uvalde, Texas," press release, June 8, 2022, www.justice.gov.

12 Fachner and Carter, *Six-Month Assessment Report*, 3–5, 52, 54; Fachner and Carter, *Final Assessment Report.*

13 U.S. Department of Justice, Collaborative Reform Initiative, *An Assessment of the San Francisco Police Department.*

14 Cole et al., *The Collaborative Reform Initiative Process*, vii–ix.

15 The ACLU of Nevada strongly objected to the CRI process because of the lack of judicial oversight. ACLU of Nevada, *Collaborative Reform Process or Abdication of Responsibility?* Copy in possession of this author.

16 "How George Floyd Died and What Happened Next," *New York Times*, November 1, 2021, www.nytimes.com; Lowery, *They Can't Kill Us All*; President's Task Force, *Final Report.*

17 Lowery, *They Can't Kill Us All.*

18 Jay Caspian Kang, "Bring the Fight to the Streets," *New York Times*, May 8, 2022, www.nytimes.com.

19 "ABC-NORC Poll: Police Violence Remains High Concern in U.S.," *AP News*, May 21, 2021, https://abcnews.go.com.

20 "New Low See Progress for Black Civil Rights," Gallup, September 9, 2020, https://news.gallup.com; "Heightened Racial Concern a Clear Legacy of Floyd's Death," Gallup, May 21, 2021, https://news.gallup.com.

21 Lee, Weitzer, and Martinez, "Recent Police Killings," 204 (table 2), 210, 217; Weitzer, "American Policing under Fire," 477; Weitzer, "Theorizing Racial Discord," 1147.

22 Hassan Kanu, "Major Police Reform Remains Elusive under Biden's Executive Order," *Reuters*, June 8, 2022, www.reuters.com.

23 Attorney General of California, *Memorandum of Understanding*.

24 Walker and Macdonald, "An Alternative Remedy for Police Misconduct," 536–51 (model statute discussed). See, for example, Attorney General of California, *People of the State of California ex. Rel. Bill Lockyer*.

25 U.S. Civil Rights Division, *The Civil Rights Division's Pattern or Practice Police Reform Work*, 3.

26 Hathaway, "A Necessary Expansion of State Power" (making a strong case for expanding the role of state attorneys general but also making unsubstantiated criticisms of the U.S. Justice Department's pattern or practice program).

27 For a critique of the use of the *parens patriae* doctrine by state attorneys general, see Mazzone and Rushin, "State Attorneys General as Agents of Police Reform"; and Walker and Macdonald, "An Alternative Remedy for Police Misconduct," 536–51. The Nevada attorney general sought enabling legislation in 2021. Michelle Rindels, "Attorney General Bill Seeks Investigations of Police Practices That Look beyond Individual 'Bad Apples,'" *Nevada Independent*, March 17, 2021, https://the-nevadaindependent.com.

28 White, Fradella, and Flippin, "How Can We Achieve Accountability," 455; Center for American Progress, *Expanding the Authority of State Attorneys General*. See also Mazzone and Rushin, "State Attorneys General as Agents of Police Reform."

29 Attorney General Xavier Becerra, *Letter to the Honorable Nancy Pelosi, et al.*

30 Becerra, *Letter to the Honorable Nancy Pelosi, et al.*; Attorney General Xavier Becerra, "Attorney General Becerra Calls for Broad Police Reforms," press release, June 15, 2020, https://oag.ca.gov.

31 Attorney General of California, *Sacramento Police Department*.

32 Jack Moore, "MD New AG Anthony Brown Seeks More Authority to Investigate Civil Rights Violations, Police Misconduct," *WTOP News*, January 3, 2023, https://wtop.com.

33 Madigan, Hendrickson, and Ehler, "Stepping into the Shoes of the Department of Justice," 138. Madigan's first-person account of the case as the Illinois attorney general is extremely valuable in terms of the details about issues that arose.

34 U.S. Department of Justice, *Agreement in Principle between the United States Department of Justice and the City of Chicago*.

35 Attorney General of Illinois, *State of Illinois v. City of Chicago*, Consent Decree; Attorney General of Illinois, *Memorandum of Agreement*.

36 Madigan, Hendrickson, and Ehler, "Stepping into the Shoes of the Department of Justice," 142, 143, 147, 153–54, 157, 160–63.

37 Attorney General of Illinois, *Memorandum of Agreement*.

38 Colorado, Office of the Attorney General, *Investigation of the Aurora Police Department*; Wilson Beese and Kelly Reinke, "Independent Monitor Releases First Report on Aurora Consent Decree," *9News*, July 25, 2022, www.9news.com. On the public demand for investigations, see John Frank, "Colorado Police Misconduct Investigations Are Limited by Money," *Axios Denver*, April 1, 2022; *State of Colorado v. City of Aurora, Colorado*, Joint Motion.

39 Colorado, Office of the Attorney General, *Investigation of the Aurora Police Department*, 18; U.S. Civil Rights Division, *The Civil Rights Division's Pattern or Practice Police Reform Work*, 20.

40 Attorney General of New Jersey, Matthew J. Platkin, *Excellence in Policing Initiative*.

41 Vera Institute of Justice, *To Protect and Serve*.

42 Vera Institute of Justice, *To Protect and Serve*, 21–31.

43 Vera Institute of Justice, *To Protect and Serve*, 14–17.

44 Vera Institute of Justice, *To Protect and Serve*, 17–19.

45 Vera Institute of Justice, *To Protect and Serve*, 36–40.

46 President's Task Force, *Final Report*.

47 Steven Eder, Michael H. Keller, and Blacki Migliozzi, "As New Police Reform Laws Sweep across the U.S., Some Ask: Are They Enough?," *New York Times*, updated, October 10, 2021, www.nytimes.com; White, Fradella, and Flippin, "How Can We Achieve Accountability."

48 National Conference of State Legislatures, *Investigation and Prosecution of Use of Force*; *Criminal Justice Database and Bill Tracking* (June 19, 2020), www.ncsl.org.

49 Texas Legislature, H.B. 1036, *An Act Relating to Reporting Requirements for Certain Injuries or Deaths Caused by Peace Officers and for Certain Injuries or Deaths of Peace Officers* (effective September 1, 2015), https://capitol.texas.gov.

50 "Gov. Jerry Brown Signs Landmark Laws That Unwind Decades of Secrecy Surrounding Police Misconduct, Use of Force," *Los Angeles Times*, September 30, 2018, https://latimes.com; Slobogin, "Testilying"; Openstates, SB16, "Peace Officers: Release of Records" (n.d.).

51 Joseph Geha, "San Jose Launches Portal of Police Misconduct Records," *San Jose Spotlight*, December 2, 2022, https://sanjosespotlight.com.

52 "In a Historic Victory, NY Governor Cuomo Signs Repeal of 50-A into Law," Innocence Project, June 9, 2020, https://innocenceproject.org; C. J. Ciaramella, "New York Repealed Its Police Secrecy Law Two Years Ago. Departments Are Still Trying to Hide Misconduct Files," *Reason*, December 5, 2022, https://reason.com.

53 Hassan Kanu, "A Novel Pathway in NJ to Police Misconduct Records: Will Other States Follow?," *Reuters*, March 22, 2022, https://reuters.com; Regalia, "The Common Law Right to Information"; Zansberg and Campos, "Sunshine on the Thin Blue Line" (arguing that there is a "public interest" in being able to review certain police files).

54 Erin Rhoda and Callie Ferguson, "Maine State Police Must Reveal Officer Misconduct, Judge Rules in Newspaper Lawsuit," *Bangor Daily News*, May 31, 2022.

55 Editorial Board, "Bad Cops Deserve to Be Exposed. Police Must Stop Dodging Information Requests," *USA Today*, July 20, 2022, www.usatoday.com; Kallie Cox and William Freivogel (Pulitzer Center), "Analysis of Police Misconduct Record Laws in All 50 States," *AP News*, May 12, 2021, https://apnews.com.

56 Kate Heston, Brooke Newman, and Krya O'Connor, "Increasing Police Transparency Is 'Messy,' but Efforts Come from Many Directions," *Cronkite News*, October 18, 2022, https://cronkitenews.azpbs.org; Jonathan Abel, "Police Misconduct Records Should Be Public: Policies and Practices," Justice Collaborative Initiative, July 2020, www.dataforprogress.org.

57 City of Houston, Houston Police Department, Police Transparency Hub, https://policetransparency-mycity.hub.arcgis.com.

58 See the websites of the Chicago inspector general (https://igchicago.org) and the Invisible Institute (https://invisible.institute).

59 Invisible Institute, Citizens Police Data Project; Chicago, Office of the Inspector General, Public Safety Dashboard; Heston, Newman, and O'Connor, "Increasing Police Transparency Is 'Messy.'"

60 Minnesota Department of Human Rights, *Investigation*, 9, 10–11, 20–31, 38, 40, 44, 61–63 (criticism of the department's early intervention system). See the website of the Twenty-First Century Policing Solutions, www.21cpsolutions.com. Also see the discussion of the Christopher Commission report and its impact on the pattern or practice program in chapter 3.

61 Minnesota Department of Human Rights, *Investigation*, 71–72.

62 Guy Oron, "Advocates and Legislators Announce New Police Accountability Package for 2023," Real Change, December 7, 2022, https://realchangenews.org. See also the Seattle Community Police Commission website for its active work on state police reform legislation, www.seattle.gov.

63 New York State, Police Reform and Reinvention Collaboration, *Police Reform and Reinvention Collaborative*.

64 See, for example, Town of Greenburgh [NY], *New York State Police Reform and Reinvention Collaborative Initiative Report* (February 2021), https://greenburghny.com.

65 Samuel Walker, personal notes, June–Labor Day, 2020.

66 Samuel Walker, personal notes, June–Labor Day, 2020.

67 See the 8CantWait website, https://8cantwait.org; Jelani Cobb, "The Matter of Black Lives," *New Yorker*, March 14, 2016, www.newyorker.com.

68 Fairley, "Survey Says: U.S. Cities Double Down on Civilian Oversight," 50 ("mainstream" quote); "Philadelphia's Police Oversight Agency to Start Work Soon," Governing, March 29, 2022, www.governing.com.

69 "Scott Signs Bill Establishing Baltimore City Police Accountability Board," *CBS News*, June 30, 2022, www.cbsnews.com.

70 Brennon Dixson, "Pasadena's Community Police Oversight Commission Must 'Restart' with New Independent Police Auditor," *Pasadena Star-News*, June 3, 2022, www.pasadenastarnews.com; "Phoenix Police Oversight Office to Move Forward," *AZCentral*, July 13, 2022, https://azcentral.com.

71 See the National Association for Civilian Oversight of Law Enforcement website, www.nacole.org.

72 Grassroots Alliance for Police Accountability, *Leadership, Partnership, and Trust*; Heather Cherone, "City Council Approves Elected Board to Oversee Chicago Police with 36–13 Vote," *WTTW*, July 21, 2021, https://news.wttw.com.

73 John Byrne, Bill Ruthhart, Alice Yin, and Annie Sweeney, "Civilian Oversight for Chicago Police Wins Final Approval after Yearslong Fight," *Chicago Tribune*, July 21, 2021, https://chicagotribune.com.

74 Heather Cherone, "Long-Delayed Push to Create Police Oversight Board Stalls without Lightfoot's Interim Picks," *WTTW*, July 25, 2022, https://news.wttw.com; Gregory Pratt and Alice Yin, "In Four Years Lori Lightfoot Went from Breakout Political Star to Divisive Mayor of a City Beset by Pandemic and Crime," *Chicago Tribune*, February 28, 2023, www.chicagotribune.com.

75 Walker and Archbold, *The New World of Police Accountability*, 215–26.

76 Walker and Archbold, *The New World of Police Accountability*, 215–26.

77 "Police Misconduct Investigations in Louisville Could Speed Up with New Inspector General's Office," *LEO Weekly*, July 13, 2022, www.leoweekly.com; City of Columbus, Department of the Inspector General, *The Department of Inspector General Will Start Accepting Complaints*; Andy Grimm and Fran Spielman, "New Inspector General Gives Sharp Critique of Chicago Watchdog Agencies," *Chicago Sun-Times*, June 16, 2022, https://chicago.suntimes.com.

78 White, Fradella, and Flippin, "How Can We Achieve Accountability," 451.

79 The Police Executive Research Forum reports are free and available online at the PERF website, www.policeforum.org.

80 Police Executive Research Forum, *Constitutional Policing as a Cornerstone of Community Policing*, 2, 3.

81 Police Executive Research Forum, *Re-Engineering Training*.

82 Police Executive Research Forum, *Guiding Principles on Use of Force*, 5, 15.

83 Police Executive Research Forum, *Guiding Principles on Use of Force*.

84 Police Executive Research Forum, *Guiding Principles on Use of Force*, 16, 33–71 ("30 Guiding Principles").

85 See the discussion of three policies for reducing officer use of force in chapter 4.

86 International Association of Chiefs of Police, *Policy Framework for Improved Community-Police Engagement*; International Association of Chiefs of Police, *National Consensus Policy and Discussion* (October 2017), www.theiacp.org.

87 International Association of Chiefs of Police, *Policy Framework for Improved Community-Police Engagement*.

88 "Misconduct Settlements Have Led Insurers to Force Police Reform," *Washington Post*, September 14, 2022, www.washingtonpost.com; Rashawn Ray, "Why Police Departments Are the Key to Progress on Police Reform," Brookings Institution, June 26, 2020, www.brookings.edu; "The Hidden Hand That Uses Money to Reform Troubled Police Departments," *NBC News*, July 19, 2020, www.nbcnews.com.

89 Epp, *Making Rights Real*, 95–130.

90 Grace Manthey, Frank Esposito, and Amanda Hernandez, "Despite 'Defunding' Claims, Police Funding Has Increased in Many U.S. Cities," *ABC News*, October 16, 2022, https://abcnews.go.com.

91 Vera Institute of Justice, *Investing in Evidence-Based Alternatives to Policing*. See also Vera Institute of Justice, *Understanding Police Enforcement*; Dholakia and Gilbert, *What Happens When We Send Mental Health Providers instead of Police*. On the pattern or practice program's response to gender discrimination by the New Orleans police department, see *United States v. City of New Orleans*, Amended and Restated Consent Decree, 54–60.

92 U.S. Department of Justice, "Justice Department Awards $34 Million to Support Community Crisis Response," December 23, 2021, www.justice.gov.

93 Friedman, "Disaggregating the Police Function," 997; Policing Project, *Reimagining Public Safety*.

94 See the illuminating discussion of the different local legal "ecosystems" across the country in Schwartz, "Civil Rights Ecosystems."

95 Walker, "The Community Voice in Policing"; Seattle Community Police Commission, "Our Work," November 23, 2022 (Seattle Police Contracts, State Legislative Activity, Recommendations Tracker, and four other issues), www.seattle.gov.

REFERENCES

Abraham, Henry J. *Justices, Presidents, and Senators: A History of the U.S. Supreme Court Appointments from Washington to Bush II.* 5th ed. Lanham, MD: Rowman and Littlefield, 2007.

ACLU of Nevada. *Collaborative Reform Process or Abdication of Responsibility?* Las Vegas: ACLU of Nevada, n.d.

ACLU of New Jersey. *The Crisis inside Police Internal Affairs: A Report of the American Civil Liberties Union of New Jersey.* Newark: ACLU of New Jersey, 2009. www.aclu-nj.org.

Alexander, Michelle. *The New Jim Crow: Mass Incarceration in the Age of Colorblindness.* Rev. ed. New York: New Press, 2018.

Allen, Marshall. "How Many Die from Medical Mistakes in U.S. Hospitals?" *ProPublica*, September 19, 2013.

Alpert, Geoffrey P., and Cynthia Lum. *Police Pursuit Driving: Policy and Research.* New York: Springer, 2014.

Amsterdam, Anthony M. "Perspectives on the Fourth Amendment." *Minnesota Law Review* 58 (1973–1974): 349–477.

Armacost, Barbara. "Organizational Culture and Police Misconduct." *George Washington Law Review* 72, no. 3 (2004): 453–546.

Arsenault, Raymond. *Freedom Riders: 1961 and the Struggle for Racial Justice.* New York: Oxford University Press, 2006.

Attorney General of California. *Memorandum of Understanding.* February 5, 2018. https://oag.ca.gov.

———. *People of the State of California ex. Rel. Bill Lockyer, Attorney General of the State of California v. City of Riverside, and Docs 1 through 200, Inclusive.* March 5, 2001.

———. *Sacramento Police Department: Report and Recommendations.* Sacramento: Office of the Attorney General, 2019.

Attorney General of California, Xavier Becerra. *Letter to the Honorable Nancy Pelosi, et al., Request to Expand the Violent Crime Control and Law Enforcement Act to Give State Attorneys General "Pattern-or-Practice" Authority.* June 5, 2020. https://oag.ca.gov.

Attorney General of Illinois. *Memorandum of Agreement between the Office of the Illinois Attorney General and the City of Chicago and Campbell v. City of Chicago Plaintiffs and Communities United v. City of Chicago Plaintiffs.* Springfield: Office of the Attorney General, 2018. http://chicagopoliceconsentdecree.org.

———. *State of Illinois v. City of Chicago*, Consent Decree. Springfield: Office of the Attorney General, 2019.

Attorney General of New Jersey, Matthew J. Platkin. *Excellence in Policing Initiative.* Trenton: Office of the Attorney General, n.d. www.njoag.gov.

———. *Internal Affairs Policy and Procedures.* Trenton: Office of the Attorney General, 2019. www.njoag.gov.

Attorney General of the United States, Merrick Garland. *Memorandum for Heads of Civil Litigation Components, United States Attorneys, Review of the Use of Monitors in Civil Settlement Agreements and Consent Decrees Involving State and Local Government Entities.* Washington, DC: Office of the Attorney General, September 13, 2021. https://justice.gov.

Attorney General of the United States, Jeff Sessions. *Memorandum for Heads of Department Components and United States Attorneys: Supporting Federal, State, Local and Tribal Law Enforcement.* Washington, DC: Office of the Attorney General, March 31, 2017. https://justice.gov.

Baker, Liva. *Miranda: Crime, Law and Politics.* New York: Atheneum, 1983.

Baldwin, James. *The Fire Next Time.* New York: Dial Press, 1963.

Baltimore Police Department Monitoring Team. *First Semiannual Report.* Baltimore: Baltimore Police Monitoring Team, 2018.

Bies, Katherine J. "Let the Sunshine In: Illuminating the Powerful Role Police Unions Play in Shielding Officer Misconduct." *Stanford Law and Policy Review* 28, no. 1 (2017): 109–49.

Black, Algernon. *The Public and the Police.* New York: McGraw-Hill, 1968.

Black, Donald J. *The Manners and Customs of the Police.* New York: Academic Press, 1980.

Bobb, Merrick, Special Counsel. *18th Semiannual Report.* Los Angeles: Police Assessment Resource Center, 2004.

Brady v. Maryland, 373 U.S. 83 (1963).

Bromwich Group. *The Durability of Police Reform: The Metropolitan Police Department and Use of Force: 2008–2015.* Washington, DC: Office of the District of Columbia Auditor, January 28, 2016. https://dcauditor.org.

———. *Special Report of the Independent Monitor for the Metropolitan Police Department.* Washington, DC: Office of the District of Columbia Auditor, 2002.

Brophy, Alfred L. *Reconstructing the Dreamland: The Tulsa Riot of 1921: Race, Reparations and Reconciliation.* New York: Oxford University Press, 2002.

Bryant, Nick. *The Bystander: John F. Kennedy and the Struggle for Black Equality.* New York: Basic Books, 2006.

Bureau of Labor Statistics. *Collective Bargaining Agreements for Police and Firefighters.* Bulletin 1885. Washington, DC: Bureau of Labor Statistics, 1976. https://fraser.stlouisfed.org.

Cannon, Lou. *Official Negligence: How Rodney King and the Riots Changed Los Angeles and the LAPD.* New York: Basic Books, 1999.

Center for American Progress. *Expanding the Authority of State Attorneys General to Combat Police Misconduct.* Washington, DC: Center for American Progress, 2018.

Chanin, Joshua M. "Examining the Sustainability of Pattern or Practice Police Misconduct Reform." *Police Quarterly* 18, no. 2 (2015): 163–92. https://doi. org/10.1177/1098611114561305.

Check the Police. *Police Union Contract Review*. N.d. https://communityresourcehub. org.

Chemerinsky, Erwin. *Presumed Guilty: How the Supreme Court Empowered the Police and Subverted Civil Rights*. New York: Liveright, 2021.

Cheng, Tony. "Input without Influence: The Silence and Scripts of Police Community Relations." *Social Problems* 67, no. 1 (2020): 171–89. https://doi.org/10.1093/socpro/ spz007.

Cheng, Tony, and Jennifer Qu. "Regular Intermediaries and the Challenge of Democratic Policing." *Criminology and Public Policy* 21 (February 2022): 59–81. https:// doi.org/10.1111/1745-9133.12573.

Chevigny, Paul. *Police Power: Police Abuses in New York City*. New York: Vintage, 1969.

Chicago Commission on Race Relations. *The Negro in Chicago*. Chicago: University of Chicago Press, 1922.

Chicago Police Accountability Task Force. *Recommendations for Change: Report*. Chicago: Chicago Police Accountability Task Force, 2016. https://chicagopatf.org.

Christopher Commission. *Report of the Independent Commission on the Los Angeles Police Department*. Los Angeles: Christopher Commission, 1991.

City of Chicago, Office of the Inspector General. Website. https://igchicago.org.

City of Columbus [Ohio], Department of the Inspector General. *The Department of Inspector General Will Start Accepting Complaints on July 11, 2022*. Columbus: Department of the Inspector General, 2022.

City of Los Angeles v. Lyons, 461 U.S. 95 (1983).

Clark, Kenneth. Testimony. In National Advisory Commission on Civil Disorders, *Report*, 483. New York: Bantam, 1968.

Cleveland Police Monitor. *Eighth Semiannual Report*. Cleveland: Police Monitor, July 2020.

Clinton, Bill. State of the Union address. February 17, 1993.

Cole, Christine, Megan Collins, Julie Finn, and Sarah Lawrence. *The Collaborative Reform Initiative Process: Experiences of Selected Sites*. Washington, DC: Office of Community Oriented Policing Services, 2017. https://cri.org.

Colorado, Office of the Attorney General. *Investigation of the Aurora Police Department and Aurora Fire Rescue*. Denver: Office of the Attorney General, 2021. https://coag. gov.

Colorado v. City of Aurora, Colorado. Joint Motion to Enter Judgment of Stipulated Consent Decree and Judgment under C.R.S. #24-31-113. Denver: Office of the Attorney General, 2021.

Community Oriented Policing Services. *Standards and Guidelines for Internal Affairs: Recommendations from a Community of Practice*. Washington, DC: Department of Justice, n.d. https://cops.usdoj.gov.

Davis, Kenneth Culp. *Police Discretion*. St. Paul: West Publishing, 1975.

Davis, Robert C., Nicole J. Henderson, and Christopher Ortiz. *Can Federal Intervention Bring Lasting Improvement in Local Policing? The Pittsburgh Consent Decree.* New York: Vera Institute of Justice, 2005. https://vra.org.

Davis, Robert C., Christopher W. Ortiz, Nicole J. Henderson, and Joel Miller. *Turning Necessity into Virtue: Pittsburgh's Experience with a Federal Consent Decree.* New York: Vera Institute of Justice, 2002. www.vera.org.

De Angelis, Joseph, Richard Rosenthal, and Brian Buchner. *Civilian Oversight of Law Enforcement: A Review of the Strengths and Weaknesses.* Tucson, AZ: National Association for Citizen Oversight of Law Enforcement, 2016.

Dholakia, Nazish, and Daniela Gilbert. *What Happens When We Send Mental Health Providers instead of Police?* New York: Vera Institute of Justice, 2021.

DiSalvo, Daniel. *Enhancing Accountability: Collective Bargaining and Police Reform.* New York: Manhattan Institute, 2021. https:/manhattan.institute.org.

Domanick, Joe. *To Protect and Serve: The LAPD's Century of War in the City of Dreams.* New York: Pocket Books, 1994.

Drinan, Robert J. 1964. "The Pre-Election Moratorium on Demonstrations and the Future of the Civil Rights Movement." Speech, November 29, 1964. Boston College Law School Digital Commons. https://nicic.gov.

Eagly, Ingrid, and Joanna C. Schwartz. "Lexipol: The Privatization of Police Policymaking." *Texas Law Review* 96 (April 2018): 891–973.

———. "Lexipol's Fight against Police Reform." *Indiana Law Journal* 97 (Winter 2022): 1–57.

Eberhardt, Jennifer L. *Biased: Uncovering the Hidden Prejudice That Shapes What We See, Think, and Do.* New York: Viking, 2019.

Engel, Robin Shepard. *How Police Supervisory Styles Influence Patrol Officer Behavior.* Washington, DC: Department of Justice, 2003. www.ojp.gov.

Epp, Charles. *Making Rights Real: Activists, Bureaucrats, and the Creation of the Legalistic State.* Chicago: University of Chicago Press, 2009.

Epp, Charles R., Steven Maynard-Moody, and Donald P. Haider-Markel. *Pulled Over: How Police Stops Define Race and Citizenship.* Chicago: University of Chicago Press, 2014.

Fachner, George, and Steven Carter. *Final Assessment Report of the Las Vegas Metropolitan Police Department.* Washington, DC: CNA, 2014. https://cops.usdoj.gov.

———. *Six-Month Assessment Report of the Las Vegas Metropolitan Police Department.* Washington, DC: CNA, 2013. https://cops.usdoj.gov.

Fagan, Jeffrey, and Amanda Geller. "Profiling and Consent: Stops, Searches, and Seizures after Soto." *Virginia Journal of Social Policy and the Law* 27, no. 1 (2020): 16–58.

Fairley, Sharon R. "Survey Says: U.S. Cities Double Down on Civilian Oversight of Police despite Challenges and Controversy." *Cardozo Law Review de*novo* (2020): 1–54.

Fine, Sidney. *Violence in the Model City: The Cavanaugh Administration, Race Relations, and the Detroit Riot of 1967.* Reprint, East Lansing: Michigan State University Press, 2007.

Flamm, Michael W. "Law and Order at Large: The New York Civilian Review Board Referendum of 1966 and the Crisis of Liberalism." *Historian* 64 (Spring–Summer 2020): 643–65.

Fogelson, Robert M. *Big-City Police*. Cambridge: Harvard University Press, 1977.

Fridell, Lorie. *Producing Bias-Free Policing: A Science-Based Approach*. New York: Springer, 2017.

Friedman, Barry. "Disaggregating the Police Function." *University of Pennsylvania Law Review* 169 (March 2021): 925–99.

Friedman, Barry, and Maria Ponomarenko. "Democratic Policing." *New York University Law Review* 90 (December 2015): 1827–1907.

Fyfe, James J. "Administrative Interventions on Police Shooting Discretion: An Empirical Examination." *Journal of Criminal Justice* 7, no. 4 (1979): 309–24. https://doi.org/10.1016/0047-2352(79)90065-5.

Geller, William A., ed. *Police Leadership in America: Crisis and Opportunity*. New York: Praeger, 1985.

———. "Suppose We Were Really Serious about Police Departments Becoming 'Learning Organizations'?" *National Institute of Justice Journal*, December 1997: 2–8. www.ojp.gov.

Geller, William A., and Michael S. Scott. *Deadly Force: What We Know*. Washington, DC: Police Executive Research Forum, 1992.

Gillon, Steven. *Separate and Unequal: The Kerner Commission and the Unravelling of American Liberalism*. New York: Basic Books, 2018.

Goldstein, Herman. "Improving Policing: A Problem-Oriented Approach." *Crime and Delinquency* 25, no. 2 (1979): 236–58. https://doi.org/10.1177/001112877902500207.

———. "Police Policy Formulation: A Proposal for Improving Police Performance." *Michigan Law Review* 65, no. 6 (1967): 1123–46.

———. *Policing a Free Society*. Cambridge: Ballinger Press, 1977.

Goodwin, Alexandra, Whitney Shepard, and Carrie Sloan. *Police Brutality Bonds: How Wall Street Profits from Police Violence*. N.p.: Acre Action Center, n.d. https://acre-campaigns.org.

Gould, Jon B., and Stephen D. Mastrofski. "Suspect Searches: Assessing Police Behavior." *Criminology and Public Policy* 3 (July 2004): 315–62. https://doi.org/10.1111/j.1745-9133.2004.tb00046.x.

Governor's Commission on the Los Angeles Riots. *Violence in the City: An End or a Beginning?* Sacramento: Office of the Governor, 1965.

Grassroots Alliance for Police Accountability. *Leadership, Partnership, and Trust: A Community Plan for a Safer Chicago*. Chicago: Grassroots Alliance for Police Accountability, 2018.

Green, Saul A., Joseph E. Brann, Jeffrey A. Fagan, and John E. Eck. *Progress Report: City of Cincinnati Collaborative Agreement. The Status of Community Problem Oriented Policing*. Cincinnati, January 4, 2018. https://cincinnati-oh.gov.

Green, Saul A., and Richard B. Jerome. *City of Cincinnati's Independent Monitor's Final Report*. Cincinnati, 2008. www.cincinnati-oh.gov.

Greene, Jack R. "Community Policing: Changing the Nature, Structure, and Function of the Police." In *Criminal Justice 2000: Policies, Processes, and Decisions of the Criminal Justice System*. Washington, DC: Department of Justice, 2000.

Hannah-Jones, Nikole. *The 1619 Project: A New Origin Story*. New York: One World, 2021.

Harmon, Rachel A. "Limited Leverage: Federal Remedies and Police Reform." *St. Louis University Public Law Review* 32, no. 1 (2012): 33–56.

———. "The Problem of Policing." *Michigan Law Review* 110 (March 2012): 761–817.

Harris, David A. "Driving While Black and All Other Traffic Offenses: The Supreme Court and Pretextual Traffic Stops." *Journal of Criminal Law and Criminology* 87, no. 2 (1997): 544–82. https://doi.org/10.2307/1143954.

———. "How Accountability-Based Policing Can Reinforce—or Replace—the Fourth Amendment Exclusionary Rule." *Ohio State Journal of Criminal Law* 7 (Fall 2009): 149–213.

Hathaway, Brianna. "A Necessary Expansion of State Power: A 'Pattern or Practice' of Failed Accountability." *New York University Review of Law and Social Change* 44, no. 1 (2019): 61–95.

Hayde, Michael J. *My Name's Friday: The Unauthorized but True Story of "Dragnet" and the Films of Jack Webb*. Los Angeles: Cumberland House, 2001.

Hickman, Matthew J. *Citizen Complaints about Police Use of Force*. Washington, DC: Bureau of Justice Statistics, 2006. https://bjs.ojp.gov.

Hodges, Ann C., and Justin Pugh. "Crossing the Thin Blue Line: Protecting Law Enforcement Officers Who Blow the Whistle." *University of California Law Review Online* 52 (June 2018): 1–39.

Huq, Aziz Z., and Richard H. McAdams. "Litigating the Blue Wall of Silence: How to Challenge the Police Privilege to Delay Investigations." *University of Chicago Legal Forum*, 2016: 213–53.

Hyland, Shelley S., and Elizabeth Davis. *Local Police Departments, 2016: Personnel*. Rev. ed. Washington, DC: Bureau of Justice Statistics, 2021. https://bjs.gov.

Inbau, Fred. *Criminal Investigation and Confessions*. 2nd ed. Philadelphia: Williams and Wilkins, 1967.

In Re Cincinnati, Collaborative Agreement, Order, Case No. 99–3170. October 19, 2002.

Institute of Medicine. *To Err Is Human: Building a Safer Health System*. Washington, DC: National Academies Press, 2000.

International Association of Chiefs of Police. *Policy Framework for Improved Community-Police Engagement*. Alexandria, VA: International Association of Chiefs of Police, n.d. www.theiacp.org.

Jiao, Allan. "Federal Consent Decrees: A Review of Policies, Procedures, Processes, and Outcomes." *Police Practice and Research* 22, no. 1 (2021): 793–804. https://doi.org/10.1080/15614263.2020.1722664.

Kaufman, Zachary. "Police Policing Police." *George Washington Law Review* 91, no. 2 (2023): 353–445.

Keenan, Kevin, and Samuel Walker. "An Impediment to Police Accountability? An Analysis of Statutory Law Enforcement Officers' Bills of Rights." *Boston University Public Interest Law Review* 14 (2005): 185–243.

Kennedy, David M. *Don't Shoot: One Man, a Street Fellowship, and the End of Violence in Inner-City America*. New York: Bloomsbury, 2012.

Klinger, David. "Organizational Accidents and Deadly Police-Involved Violence: Some Thoughts on Extending Theory, Expanding Research, and Improving Police Practice." *Annals of the American Academy* 687 (January 2020): 28–48. https://doi.org/10.1177/0002716219892913.

Knapp Commission Report on Police Corruption. New York: Braziller, 1973.

Kroll Associates, Office of the Independent Monitor. *Report of the Independent Monitor for the Los Angeles Police Department. Third Quarterly Report*. Los Angeles: Kroll Associates, May 15, 2002.

LaFave, Wayne R. *Arrest: The Decision to Take a Suspect into Custody*. Boston: Little Brown, 1965.

Lee, Angela S., Ronald Weitzer, and Daniel Martinez. "Recent Police Killings in the United States: A Three-City Comparison." *Police Quarterly* 21, no. 2 (2017): 196–222. https://doi.org/10.1177/1098611117744508.

Leo, Richard A. *Police Interrogation and American Justice*. Cambridge: Harvard University Press, 2008.

Long, Carolyn. *Mapp v. Ohio: Guarding against Unreasonable Searches and Seizures*. Lawrence: University Press of Kansas, 2006.

Lopez, Christy E. "The Civil Rights Division: The Crown Jewel of the Justice Department." *Yale Law Journal Forum* 130 (January 2021): 465–72.

———. *Disorderly (Mis)Conduct: The Problem with "Contempt of Cop" Arrests*. Issue Brief. Washington, DC: American Constitution Society, 2010. https://cdn.ca9.uscourts.gov.

———. "DOJ Police Pattern-or-Practice Investigations." *Criminal Justice* 37 (Spring 2022): 34–41.

Los Angeles Police Commission, Office of the Inspector General. *Comparative Review of Selected Agency Policies, Interrogations and Training of the Use of Force: OIG Final Report*. Los Angeles: Police Commission, 2016. www.oig.lacity.org.

Loving, Nancy. *Responding to Spouse Abuse and Wife Beating: A Guide for Police*. Washington, DC: Police Foundation, 1980.

Lowery, Wesley. *They Can't Kill Us All: Ferguson, Baltimore, and a New Era in America's Racial Justice Movement*. Boston: Little, Brown, 2016.

Maas, Peter. *Serpico*. New York: Bantam, 1974.

MacNamara, Donal E. J. *New Jersey Municipal Police Survey*. Trenton: New Jersey Law Enforcement Council, 1958.

Madigan, Lisa, Cara Hendrickson, and Karyn L. Bass Ehler. "Stepping into the Shoes of the Department of Justice: The Unusual, Necessary, and Hopeful Path the Illinois Attorney General Took to Require Police Reform in Chicago." *Northwestern Journal of Law and Social Policy* 15 (Winter 2020): 121–71.

Mapp v. Ohio, 367 U.S. 643 (1961).

Mazerolle, Lorraine, et al. *Procedural Justice and Legitimacy in Policing*. New York: Springer, 2014.

Mazzone, Jason, and Stephen Rushin. "State Attorneys General as Agents of Police Reform." *Duke Law Journal* 69 (February 2020): 999–1073.

McWhorter, Diane. *Carry Me Home: Birmingham, Alabama, the Climactic Battle of the Civil Rights Revolution*. New York: Simon and Schuster, 2001.

Miller, Wilbur R. *Cops and Bobbies: Police Authority in New York and London*. Rev. ed. Columbus: Ohio State University Press, 1999.

Milton, Catherine, Jeanne Wahl Hallbeck, James Lardner, and Gary L. Albrecht. *Police Use of Deadly Force*. Washington, DC: Police Foundation, 1977.

Minneapolis Police Department. "Duty to Intervene." In *Policy Manual*, Policy 5-303.01. July 28, 2016. www.minneapolismn.gov.

Minnesota Department of Human Rights. *Investigation of the City of Minneapolis and the Minneapolis Police Department*. Minneapolis: Minnesota Department of Human Rights, 2022. https://mn.gov.mdhr.

Miranda v. Arizona, 384 U.S. 436 (1966).

Monell v. Department of Social Services, 436 U.S. 658 (1978).

Murphy, Patrick V., and Thomas Plate. *Commissioner: A View from the Top of American Law Enforcement*. New York: Simon and Schuster, 1978.

National Academies of Science, Engineering, Medicine. *Proactive Policing: Effects on Crime and Communities*. Washington, DC: National Academies Press, 2018.

National Advisory Commission on Civil Disorders [Kerner Commission]. *Report*. New York: Bantam, 1968.

National Association for Citizen Oversight of Law Enforcement. Website. www.nacole.org.

National Conference of State Legislatures. *Investigation and Prosecution of Use of Force*. Washington, DC: National Conference of State Legislatures, June 30, 2022. www.ncsl.org.

New Orleans Police Department. *Ethical Policing Is Courageous*. N.d. http://epic.nola.gov/.

———. *Operations Manual*. N.d.

New Orleans Police Department, Office of the Consent Decree Monitor. *Comprehensive Reassessment of the Consent Decree Pursuant to Paragraph 456 of the NOPD Consent Decree*. New Orleans: New Orleans Police Monitor, January 24, 2019.

———. *Special Report: Use of Force*. New Orleans: New Orleans Police Monitor, May 5, 2017.

New Orleans Police Monitor. *Report of the Consent Decree Monitor for the Third and Fourth Quarters of 2015*. New Orleans: New Orleans Police Monitor, 2016. https://nola.gov.

New York City, Commission to Investigate Allegations of Police Corruption and the Anti-Corruption Procedures of the Police Department. *Commission Report*. New York: City of New York, 1994.

New York City Police Department. *Use of Force Report*. New York: New York City Police Department, Annual. ww1.nyc.gov.

New York State, Police Reform and Reinvention Collaboration. *Police Reform and Reinvention Collaborative: Resources and Guide for Public Officials and Citizens*. Albany: Office of the Governor, 2020. https://policereform.ny.gov.

Nix, Justin T., Justin T. Pickett, Scott E. Wolf, and Bradley A. Campbell. "Demeanor, Race, and Police Perceptions of Procedural Justice: Evidence from Two Randomized Experiments." *Justice Quarterly* 34, no. 7 (2017): 1154–83.

Orfield, Myron, Jr. "The Exclusionary Rule and Deterrence: An Empirical Study of Chicago Narcotics Officers." *University of Chicago Law Review* 54 (Summer 1987): 1016–69.

Packer, Herbert L. *The Limits of the Criminal Sanction*. Stanford, CA: Stanford University Press, 1968.

———. "Two Models and the Criminal Process." *University of Pennsylvania Law Review* 113 (November 1964): 11–68.

Peffley, Mark, and Jon Hurwitz. *Justice in America: The Separate Realities of Blacks and Whites*. New York: Cambridge University Press, 2010.

People v. Cahan, 44 Cal.2d 434, 282 P.2d 905 (1955).

Perrow, Charles. *Normal Accidents: Living with High-Risk Technologies*. New York: Basic Books, 1984.

Pittsburgh Working Group. *Report to the U.S. Attorney General on Pattern or Practice Litigation*. 2009. Copy in possession of author.

Platt, Anthony M. *The Politics of Riot Commissions, 1917–1970: A Collection of Official Reports and Critical Essays*. New York: Collier, 1971.

Police Executive Research Forum. *Civil Rights Investigations of Local Police: Lessons Learned*. Washington, DC: Police Executive Research Forum, 2013. www.policeforum.org.

———. *Constitutional Policing as a Cornerstone of Community Policing*. Washington, DC: Police Executive Research Forum, 2015. www.policeforum.org.

———. *Guiding Principles on Use of Force*. Washington, DC: Police Executive Research Forum, 2016. www.policeforum.org.

———. *An Integrated Approach to De-Escalation and Minimizing Use of Force*. Washington, DC: Police Executive Research Forum, 2012. www.policeforum.org.

———. *Racially Biased Policing: A Principled Response*. Washington, DC: Police Executive Research Forum, 2001. www.policeforum.org.

———. *Re-Engineering Training on Police Use of Force*. Washington, DC: Police Executive Research Forum, 2015. www.policeforum.org.

———. *2011 Electronic Control Weapon Guidelines*. Washington, DC: Police Executive Research Forum, 2011. www.policeforum.org.

Policing Project. *Reimagining Public Safety*. New York: New York University Law School, n.d. https://policingproject.org.

Ponomarenko, Maria. "Rethinking Police Rulemaking." *Northwestern University Law Review* 114, no. 1 (2019): 1–64.

Powell, Zachary A., Michele Bisaccia Meitel, and John L. Worrall. "Police Consent Decrees and Section 1983 Civil Rights Litigation." *Crime and Public Policy* 16 (May 2017): 575–605.

Powell, Zachary A., and John L. Worrall. "Willingness to Pay for Police Reform." *Criminal Justice Policy Review* 32, no. 6 (2021): 567–90. https://doi.org/10.1177/0887403420988310.

President's Commission on Law Enforcement and Administration of Justice. *The Challenge of Crime in a Free Society*. New York: Avon Books, 1968.

———. *Task Force Report: The Police*. Washington, DC: Government Printing Office, 1967.

President's Task Force on 21st Century Policing. *Final Report*. Washington, DC: Department of Justice, 2015. https://cops.usdoj.gov.

Public Management Resources. *Monitor's Fifteenth Report*. Albuquerque: Public Management Resources, 2022. www.cabq.gov.

———. *Monitor's Thirteenth Report*. Albuquerque: Public Management Resources, 2020. www.abqmonitor.org.

Purdum, Todd. *An Idea Whose Time Has Come: Two Presidents, Two Parties, and the Battle for the Civil Rights Act of 1964*. New York: Henry Holt, 2014.

Rahr, Sue, and Stephen K. Rice. *From Warriors to Guardians: Recommitting American Police Culture to Democratic Ideals*. Cambridge: Harvard Kennedy School of Government, 2015. www.ojp.gov.

Regalia, Joe. "The Common Law Right to Information." *Richmond Journal of Law and Public Policy* 18 (2015): 89–132.

Reiss, Albert J. *The Police and the Public*. New Haven: Yale University Press, 1971.

Ridgeway, Greg, Terry L. Schell, Brian Gifford, Jessica Saunders, Susan Turner, Jack Riley, and Travis Dixon. *Police-Community Relations in Cincinnati*. Santa Monica, CA: Rand Corporation, 2009. www.rand.org.

Rizzo v. Goode, 423 U.S. 362 (1976).

Rushin, Stephen. *Federal Intervention in American Police Departments*. New York: Cambridge University Press, 2017.

———. "Police Arbitration." *Vanderbilt Law Review* 74, no. 4 (2021): 1023–78.

———. "Police Disciplinary Appeals." *University of Pennsylvania Law Review* 167 (February 2019): 545–610.

———. "Police Union Contracts." *Duke Law Journal* 66 (March 2017): 1191–1266.

Rushin, Stephen, and Griffin Edwards. "De-Policing." *Cornell Law Review* 102 (March 2017): 721–81.

San Francisco District Attorney. *Report of the Blue Ribbon Panel on Transparency, Accountability, and Fairness in Law Enforcement*. San Francisco: Office of the District Attorney, 2016. https://sfblueribbonpanel.com.

Schmidt, Christopher W. *The Sit-Ins: Protest and Change in the Civil Rights Era*. Chicago: University of Chicago Press, 2018.

Schwartz, Joanna C. "Civil Rights Ecosystems." *Michigan Law Review* 118 (June 2020): 1539–1602.

———. "Police Indemnification." *New York University Law Review* 89 (June 2014): 885–1005.

———. "Systems Failures in Policing." *Suffolk University Law Review* 51, no. 4 (2018): 535–63.

Scott, Michael S. *Problem-Oriented Policing: Reflections on the First 20 Years*. Washington, DC: Department of Justice, 2000.

Seattle, Community Police Commission. Website. https://seattle.gov.

Seattle Police Department. *Policy Manual*. https://seattle.gov.

Seattle Police Monitor. *Comprehensive Assessment of the Seattle Police Department*. Seattle: Seattle Police Monitor, May 2022.

———. *Ninth Systematic Assessment: Use of Force*. Seattle: Seattle Police Monitor, April 2017.

Sherman, Lawrence W. "Evidence-Based Policing and Fatal Police Shootings: Promise, Problems, and Prospects." *Annals of the American Academy* 687 (January 2020): 8–26. https://doi.org/10.1177/0002716220902073.

———. "Reducing Fatal Police Shootings as System Crashes: Research, Theory, and Practice." *Annual Review of Criminology* 1 (2018): 421–49. https://doi.org/10.1146/annurev-criminol-032317-092409.

———. *Scandal and Reform: Controlling Police Corruption*. Berkeley: University of California Press, 1978.

Sherman, Lawrence W., Catherine H. Milton, and Thomas V. Kelly. *Team Policing: Seven Case Studies*. Washington, DC: Police Foundation, 1973. https://ojp.gov.

Shjarback, John A., David C. Pyroz, Scott E. Wolfe, and Scott H. Decker. "De-Policing and Crime in the Wake of Ferguson: Racialized Changes in the Quantity and Quality of Policing among Missouri Police Departments." *Journal of Criminal Justice* 50 (May 2017): 42–52. https://doi.org/10.1016/j.jcrimjus.2017.04.003.

Simmons, Kami Chavis. "The Politics of Policing: Ensuring Stakeholder Collaboration in the Federal Reform of Local Law Enforcement Agencies." *Journal of Criminal Law and Criminology* 98 (Winter 2008): 489–546.

Sklansky, David. *Democracy and the Police*. Stanford, CA: Stanford University Press, 2007.

Skogan, Wesley G. "Prospects for Reform? The Collapse of Community Policing in Chicago." *University of Chicago Law Review* 89 (March 2022): 383–404.

———. "Why Reforms Fail." *Policing and Society* 18 (March 2008): 23–34. https://doi.org/10.1080/10439460701718534.

Skogan, Wesley, and Kathleen Frydl, eds. *Fairness and Effectiveness in Policing: The Evidence*. Washington, DC: National Academies Press, 2015. https://doi.org/10.17226/10419.

Skogan, Wesley G., and Susan M. Hartnett. *Community Policing, Chicago Style*. New York: Oxford University Press, 1997.

Slobogin, Christopher. "Testilying: Police Perjury and What to Do about It." *University of Colorado Law Review* 67 (Fall 1996): 1037–60.

Smith, Michael R., Robert J. Kaminski, Geoffrey Alpert, Lorie A. Fridell, John MacDonald, and Bruce Kubu. *A Multi-Method Evaluation of Police Use of Force*

Outcomes: Final Report to the National Institute of Justice. Washington, DC: Department of Justice, 2010. https://ojp.gov.

State of Illinois v. City of Chicago, Case No 17-cv-6260. January 31, 2019.

Steffens, Lincoln. *The Shame of the Cities.* 1904; New York: Hill and Wang, 1992.

Stone, Christopher, Todd Fogelsong, and Christine M Cole. *Policing Los Angeles under a Consent Decree: The Dynamics of Change at the LAPD.* Cambridge: Harvard Kennedy School of Government, 2009.

Stoughton, Seth W. "Principled Policing: Warrior Cops and Guardian Officers." *Wake Forest Law Review* 51 (2016): 611–76.

Strote, Jared, and H. Range Hutson. "Taser Use in Restraint-Related Deaths." PubMed. gov, December 2006.

Stuntz, William J. "The Political Constitution of Criminal Justice." *Harvard Law Review* 119 (January 2006): 750–851.

Tennessee v. Garner, 471 U.S. 1 (1985).

Terrill, William, and Eugene A. Paoline III. "Police Use of Less Lethal Force: Does Administrative Policy Matter?" *Justice Quarterly* 34, no. 2 (2017): 193–216. https://doi.org/10.1080/07418825.2016.1147593.

Terry v. Ohio, 392 U.S. 1 (1968).

Thacher, David. "The Learning Model of Use-of-Force Reviews." *Law and Social Inquiry* 45 (2020): 755–86. https://doi.org/10.1017/lsi.2019.80.

United States Civil Rights Division. *The Civil Rights Division's Pattern or Practice Police Reform Work: 1994–Present.* Washington, DC: Department of Justice, 2017. www.justice.gov/crt/file/922421/download.

———. *Investigation of the Baltimore City Police Department.* 2016.

———. *Investigation of the Cleveland Division of Police.* 2002.

———. *Investigation of the Cleveland Division of Police.* 2014.

———. *Investigation of the East Haven Police Department.* 2011.

———. *Investigation of the Ferguson Police Department.* 2015.

———. *Investigation of the Louisville Metro Police Department and Louisville Metro Government.* 2023.

———. *Investigation of the Miami Police Department.* 2003.

———. *Investigation of the Newark Police Department.* 2014.

———. *Investigation of the New Orleans Police Department.* 2011.

———. *Investigation of the Portland Police Bureau.* 2012.

———. *Investigation of the Seattle Police Department.* 2011.

———. *Letter to Hon. Mayor Regalado, RE: Investigation of the Miami Police Department.* 2013.

———. *Letter to the Honorable Anthony Williams, and Charles Ramsey, Chief of Police, Findings Letter, RE Use of Force by the Metropolitan Police Department.* 2001.

United States Department of Justice. *Agreement in Principle between the United States Department of Justice and the City of Chicago Regarding the Chicago Police Department.* January 13, 2017.

———. *Identifying and Preventing Gender Bias in Law Enforcement Responding to Sexual Assault and Domestic Violence.* 2022.

———. *Memorandum of Agreement between the United States Department of Justice and the City of Cincinnati, Ohio, and the Cincinnati Police Department.* 2002.

United States Department of Justice, Office of Community Oriented Policing, Collaborative Reform Initiative. https://cops.usdoj.gov.

United States Department of Justice Collaborative Reform Initiative. *An Assessment of the San Francisco Police Department.* Washington, DC: Department of Justice, October 2016. https://cops.usdoj.gov.

United States v. Alamance County Sheriff Terry Johnson. Agreement between the United States and Alamance County Sheriff Terry Johnson. 2016.

United States v. City of Albuquerque. Settlement Agreement. 2014.

United States v. City of Cleveland. Settlement Agreement. 2015.

United States v. City of Detroit, Michigan, and Detroit Police Department. Consent Judgment. Use of Force and Arrest and Witness Detention. June 12, 2003.

United States v. City of Los Angeles, Board of Commissioners of the City of Los Angeles, and the Los Angeles Police Department. Consent Decree. 2001.

United States v. City of Missoula. Memorandum of Understanding between the United States Department of Justice and the City of Missoula Regarding the Missoula Police Department's Response to Sexual Assault. 2013.

United States v. City of Newark. Supplementary Motion for Entry of Consent Decree. 2016.

United States v. City of New Orleans. Amended and Restated NOPD Consent Decree. 2018.

United States v. City of Pittsburgh, Pittsburgh Bureau of Police, and Department of Public Safety. Consent Decree. 1997.

United States v. City of Portland. Amended Settlement Agreement. 2018.

United States v. City of Seattle. City of Seattle's Memorandum RE: Agreed Phase II Sustainment Period Plan. March 2, 2018.

United States v. City of Seattle. Settlement Agreement. 2012.

United States v. Commonwealth of Puerto Rico and the Puerto Rico Police Department. Settlement Agreement. 2013.

United States v. County of Los Angeles and the Los Angeles County Sheriff's Department. Settlement Agreement. 2015.

United States v. Maricopa County, Arizona and Joseph M. Arpaio, in His Official Capacity as Sheriff of Maricopa County, Arizona. Settlement Agreement. 2015.

United States v. Police Department of Baltimore City, et al. Consent Decree. 2017.

United States v. State of New Jersey and Division of State Police of the New Jersey Department of Law and Public Safety. Consent Decree. 1999.

United States v. The Territory of the Virgin Islands and The Virgin Islands Police Department. Consent Decree. 2009.

United States v. Town of East Haven and East Haven Board of Police Commissioners. Settlement Agreement and (Proposed) Order. 2012.

United States v. Town of East Haven and East Haven Commissioners. Settlement Agreement and [Proposed] Order. 2012.

Vera Institute of Justice. *Investing in Evidence-Based Alternatives to Policing.* New York: Vera Institute of Justice, 2021. www.vera.org.

———. *To Protect and Serve: New Trends in State-Level Policing Reform, 2015–2016.* New York: Vera Institute of Justice, 2017. www.vera.org.

———. *Understanding Police Enforcement: A Multicity Analysis.* New York: Vera Institute of Justice, 2020. www.vera.org.

Walker, Samuel. "The Community Voice in Policing: Old Issues, New Evidence." *Criminal Justice Policy Review* 27, no. 5 (2016): 537–52. https://doi.org/10.1177/0887403415598556.

———. *A Critical History of Police Reform.* Lexington: Lexington Books, 1977.

———. "Does Anyone Remember Team Policing? Lessons from the Team Policing Experience for Community Policing." *American Journal of Police* 12, no. 1 (1993): 33–55.

———. *Early Intervention Systems for Law Enforcement Agencies: A Planning and Management Guide.* Washington, DC: Department of Justice, 2003. https://cops.usdoj.gov.

———. "Governing the American Police: Wrestling with the Problems of Democracy." *University of Chicago Legal Forum,* 2016: 615–60.

———. "Institutionalizing Police Accountability Reforms: The Problem of Making Police Reforms Endure." *St. Louis University Public Law Review* 32, no. 1 (2012): 57–92.

———. "The Justice Department's Pattern-or-Practice Police Reform Program, 1994–2017: Goals, Achievements, and Issues." *Annual Review of Criminology* 5 (January 2022): 21–42. https://doi.org/10.1146/annurev-criminol-030920-102432.

———. "The Neglect of Police Unions: Exploring One of the Most Important Areas of American Policing." *Police Practice and Research* 9 (May 2008): 95–112. https://doi.org/10.1080/15614260802081253.

———. "'Not Dead Yet': The National Police Crisis, a New Conversation about Policing, and the Prospects for Accountability-Related Reform." *University of Illinois Law Review* 2018, no. 5: 1777–1839.

———. "Origins of the Contemporary Criminal Justice Paradigm: The American Bar Foundation Survey, 1953–1969." *Justice Quarterly* 9, no. 1 (1992): 47–76. https://doi.org/10.1080/07418829200091251.

———. *Police Accountability: The Role of Citizen Oversight.* Belmont, CA: Wadsworth, 2001.

———. *The Police in America: An Introduction.* 2nd ed. New York: McGraw-Hill, 1992.

———. *Popular Justice: A History of American Criminal Justice.* 2nd rev. ed. New York: Oxford University Press, 1997.

———. "Setting the Standards: The Impact of 'Blue-Ribbon' Commissions on the Police." In *Police Leadership in America: Crisis and Opportunity,* edited by William A. Geller, 354–70. New York: Praeger, 1985.

Walker, Samuel, and Carol A. Archbold. *The New World of Police Accountability.* 3rd ed. Thousand Oaks, CA: Sage, 2020.

Walker, Samuel, and Morgan Macdonald. "An Alternative Remedy for Police Misconduct: A Model State 'Pattern or Practice' Statute." *George Mason University Civil Rights Law Journal* 19 (Summer 2009): 479–552.

Waskow, Arthur. *From Race Riot to Sit-In, 1919 and the 1960s: A Study of the Connections between Conflict and Violence*. New York: Doubleday, 1966.

Weeks v. United States, 232 U.S. 383 (1914).

Weisburd, David, Cody W. Telep, Joshua Hinkle, and John E. Eck. "Is Problem-Oriented Policing Effective in Reducing Crime and Disorder? Findings from a Campbell Systematic Review." *Criminology and Public Policy* 9 (June 2010): 139–72. https://doi.org/10.1111/j.1745-9133.2010.00617.x.

Weisburd, David, Cody W. Telep, Heather Vovak, and Brandon Turchan. "Reforming the Police through Procedural Justice Training: A Multicity Randomized Trial at Crime Hot Spots." *PNAS* 119 (March 28, 2022): 1–6. https://doi.org/10.1073/pnas.2118780119.

Weitzer, Ronald. "American Policing under Fire: Misconduct and Reform." *Social Science and Public Policy* 52 (October 2015): 475–80.

———. "Theorizing Racial Discord over Policing before and after Ferguson." *Justice Quarterly* 34, no. 7 (2017): 1129–53. https://doi.org/10.1080/07418825.2017.1362461.

Westley, William A. *Violence and the Police: A Sociological Study of Law, Custom and Morality*. Cambridge: MIT Press, 1970.

White, Claire, David Weisburd, and Sean Wire. "Examining the Impact of the Freddie Gray Unrest on Perceptions of the Police." *Criminology and Public Policy* 17, no. 4 (2018): 829–57. https://doi.org/10.1111/1745-9133.12404.

White, Michael D., and Henry F. Fradella. *Stop and Frisk: The Use and Abuse of a Controversial Policing Tactic*. New York: New York University Press, 2016.

White, Michael D., Henry F. Fradella, and Michaela Flippin. "How Can We Achieve Accountability in Policing? The (Not So Secret) Ingredients to Effective Police Reform." *Lewis and Clark Law Review* 25, no. 2 (2021): 405–52.

Wilson, O. W., and Roy C. McLaren. *Police Administration*. 4th ed. New York: McGraw-Hill, 1977.

Zachs, Richard. *Island of Vice: Theodore Roosevelt's Doomed Quest to Clean Up Sin-Loving New York*. New York: Doubleday, 2012.

Zansberg, Steven Z., and Pamela Campos. "Sunshine on the Thin Blue Line: Public Access to Police Internal Affairs Files." *Communications Lawyer* 22 (Fall 2004): 34–40.

Zeidman, Steven. "From Dropsy to Testilying: Prosecutorial Apathy, Ennui, or Complicity?" *Ohio State Journal of Criminal Law* 16 (Spring 2019): 423–39.

Zimring, Franklin E. *When Police Kill*. Cambridge: Harvard University Press, 2017.

INDEX

ABLE program. *See* Active Bystander in Law Enforcement program
academic police experts, 75–77, 118, 129
accidental shootings, 47
accidents, 70–71
accountability, 21; administrative rulemaking and, 44–45; building web of, 9–10; city councils and, 178–81; consent decree and, 9–10, 45, 88–90; deficiency in, 9, 89, 165; EIS and, 115–16; GAPA and, 179–80; in Justice Department, 6–7; obstacles to, 136; OPA and, 111–12, 156; Police Accountability Act and, 55, 130; police management and, 114–17; police reform and, 6, 9–11; state-level legislation and, 171; use of force and, 88–90, 99–100; WCPA and, 176–77; web of, 9–10, 59
ACLU. *See* American Civil Liberties Union
ACRE Action Center, 138
Active Bystander in Law Enforcement (ABLE) program, 97
Administrative Procedure Act (APA), 4, 42, 44
administrative rulemaking, 4, 31, 41–45, 87; accountability and, 44–45; civil rights and, 48–50; deadly force policy and, 45–48, 50–52; firearm discharges and, 46–47; framework for, 44–45; implementing, 44–45; Lexipol and, 51–52; on police discretion, 41–45, 50–51; police management and, 43–44, 50–51; police misconduct and, 42–44, 48–50;

police reform and, 41–52; policy guidelines and officer discretion, 36; push for, 48–52; Supreme Court and, 49; use of force and, 42–44, 45–48, 50–52
AELE. *See* Americans for Effective Law Enforcement
African Americans. *See* civil rights; race; racial discrimination; racial divide
Albuquerque police department, 127–29
Alexander, Michelle, 105
alternative oversight agencies, 112–13; inspectors general, 155; Seattle Memorandum of Agreement, 156
alternative reform remedies, 82
American Bar Foundation Survey, research by, 42
American Civil Liberties Union (ACLU), 26, 52, 110, 225n15
American Rescue Plan Act (ARPA), 159
Americans for Effective Law Enforcement (AELE), 49–50
annual firearms discharges reports (NYPD), 47
APA. *See* Administrative Procedure Act
arbitration, 136
Archbold, Carole, 113
Armacost, Barbara, 75
ARPA. *See* American Rescue Plan Act
Arpaio, Joe, 126
Arrest (LaFave), 42
attorneys general. *See* state attorneys general
Aurora, Colorado, 169
Avery, Michael, 49

ABOUT THE AUTHOR

SAMUEL WALKER is Professor Emeritus of Criminal Justice at the University of Nebraska at Omaha. He is the author of fourteen books, including *The New World of Police Accountability*, *The Color of Justice: Race and Ethnicity in American Criminal Justice*, and *The Police in America: An Introduction*. In 2018 he received the Lifetime Achievement Award from the Police Division of the American Society of Criminology.

www.ingramcontent.com/pod-product-compliance
Lightning Source LLC
Chambersburg PA
CBHW031535260326
41914CB00032B/1817/J